Praise for
Oola for Christians

"With advice that will ignite your spirit and inspire you about the future, the OolaGuys' latest book hands over the keys for growing in every area of your life. Jump on the OolaBus with Dave and Troy, step on the gas, and let God take you on an amazing journey to the life He's planned for you!"

—**Danny Gokey**, Grammy-nominated recording artist and Dove Award recipient

"Dave Braun and Troy Amdahl have done it again! With life-changing, paradigm-shifting, crazy good advice, you'll discover how to create a life that's balanced, growing and focused on living and loving like Jesus. Plus the stories will make you feel like you're not alone on your journey toward greater faith and more joy. I loved it."

—**Jack Canfield**, co-creator of the *Chicken Soup for the Soul*® book series

"Instead of seeking work-life balance...strive for work-life fulfill-ment. *Oola for Christians* shares how to achieve true work-life fulfillment, what roadblocks you may face and how to blast through them, as well as ways to accelerate your success. It is entertaining, informative, and will drive you to take action."

—**Sharon Lechter**, CPA, CGMA, author of *Think and Grow Rich for Women*, coauthor of *Success and Something Greater, Outwitting the Devil, Three Feet from Gold, New York Times* bestseller *Rich Dad Poor Dad*, and 14 other Rich Dad books

"A must-read for anyone looking for ultimate balance, both natural and spiritual, in all areas of life. Personally, we love that there is a book about not only making Jesus the centrality of your life, but challenging us to prepare our minds, souls, bodies, and finances for what God wants to do in our lives."

—**Aaron** and **Becky Lucas**, Citipointe Church Northern Colorado

FOR **CHRISTIANS**

FOR **CHRISTIANS**

FIND BALANCE AND GROW
in the seven key areas of life to LIVE the LIFE OF YOUR DREAMS

DAVE BRAUN and TROY AMDAHL
and 21 Incredibly Inspiring Christians

Health Communications, Inc.
Deerfield Beach, Florida

www.hcibooks.com
www.oolalife.com

Library of Congress Cataloging-in-Publication Data
is available through the Library of Congress

© 2019 Oola LLC

ISBN-13: 978-07573-2037-8 (Paperback)
ISBN-10: 07573-2037-6 (Paperback)
ISBN-13: 978-07573-2038-5 (ePub)
ISBN-10: 07573-2038-4 (ePub)

Publisher: Health Communications, Inc.
      3201 S.W. 15th Street
      Deerfield Beach, FL 33442–8190

Cover design by Svetlana Uscumlic
Cover graphics and author photo by Max Amdahl
Cover photo by Ryan Longnecker
Interior design and formatting by Lawna Patterson Oldfield

This book is dedicated to my parents,
who have supported me through
all things and taught me
life's greatest lessons.

—Dave Braun

This book is dedicated to my dad,
my biggest supporter while on earth, and
now my biggest supporter in heaven.
I miss you.

—Troy Amdahl

CONTENTS

Living Fit the Oola Way
Garbage In, Garbage Out
Jesus Played Full Out, but Was Intentional in His Focus, Too
Is Your Body and Mind Ready for What God Has in Store for You?
The Daniel Fast
Time with Him by Tony Ochoa
Jesus, the Original Ironman

Section Three:
OOLABLOCKERS

Why Do We Keep Ourselves from Moving Forward?
Silencing "You Are" with "I Am"
"I Am Designed by God for Greatness"
Voices by Hannah Crews
Living Water
Listen to the Voice That Created You
Stop Sabotaging Your Health
Consider How Self-Sabotage Keeps You from Living Your Life for Christ

Section Four:
OOLAACCELERATORS

Section Five:
3 **SIMPLE** STEPS TO THE **OOLA**LIFE
Your daily action plan for living the life of your dreams.

"Some want to live within the sound of a church or chapel bell.

I want to run a rescue shop within a yard of Hell."

—C.T. STUDD

19th century British writer, pioneering missionary in China and Africa, and seriously good cricket player

W*e'll probably never see her again,* we thought as we handed over 10,000 Oola dream stickers to an energetic young woman with a bright purple hat and faux-fur jacket.

For the past four years, we'd spent months on the road—driving our 1970 VW Surf Bus (the one on the cover of this book) from city to city, state to state—meeting people and teaching strategies for getting from where you are to where you want to be. We'd written a book series that talked about taking this often-overwhelming journey called "life," and applying a simple road map to finding more balance and tapping into our untapped potential. We'd written about creating a life where everything's solid: money, health, family, career—a balanced and growing life in 7 key areas.

The OolaLife.

And in every town, once we were finished sharing, we'd ask the small group of people who had graciously gathered to commit to a dream that would change the course of their lives—a single positive change that could be the spark that would ignite a complete transformation.

To anchor their commitment, we handed out Sharpies and colorful round stickers, asking them to write down their dream and then slap it on the OolaBus. It's powerful: that simple gesture of thinking about the change you want in life and then taking the time to write it down and slap it on the bus. We call it a "healthy-level-of-disgust" moment—that instant where you declare, *Life doesn't have to be this way. It can be so much better.*

Countless small towns, big cities, and layers of colorful vinyl dreams later, Heather Thomas—a pastor's daughter—emerged from the crowd at Florida Atlantic University and told us she'd just gotten out of her abusive marriage. She'd been raised in the church and was a walking Bible concordance, but during a rough patch, she'd connected with a guy who was bad on every level. She'd stayed long enough to have three kids with him, but every day the abuse, anxiety, and depression had gotten worse. She'd divorced and then hit rock bottom.

This is simply where you are, not who you are, we told her. *You are designed by God for greatness and a purpose. If you could dream again, what would that dream be?*

Go on another missions trip, she wrote on her sticker, desperate to reclaim the happiness and sense of purpose she'd had years earlier.

While we were supportive of her dream, we were even more intrigued by her story. If she—like thousands of other Christians we'd met at Oola events over the years—was struggling to get past life's hardships and create the ultimate life, maybe a book that accessed the wisdom of Jesus in a whole new way should be Oola's next defining project.

In fact, the more we thought about it, the more a book that would reveal Jesus's actions—and interactions—with people, money, fitness, family (plus how He and others overcame roadblocks) got us excited about getting off the road and back to our laptops. By the time Heather re-surfaced three months later at another book signing—*Oola for Christians* had morphed from an idea to a working manuscript.

"I'm headed to Nicaragua on a missions trip," she told us. "Give me 10,000 stickers, and I'll bring back some dreams."

Oola had changed Heather. Now Heather was going to change the world!

WHY **OOLA** FOR CHRISTIANS?

When we wrote our first *Oola* book, then sent it to potential publishers for consideration, a well-known publisher reviewed it and said, *Love the book and the concept. In fact, I think it will sell. But, you need to remove faith.* In that moment, we grabbed our manuscript and decided to self-publish. Why? Because we feel it's impossible to have a full and complete life without faith.

As Christians, faith is what got Dave, the OolaSeeker, through the most challenging season of his life—a time when he lost it all: bankrupt, divorced, with a failed business, and living in a motel.

Faith is also something that Troy, the OolaGuru, has been working on improving in his life for over three decades—recognizing that achieving excellence in all 7 key areas is amazing and worth the pursuit, but also understanding that, without God at the core, everything else loses meaning, importance, and purpose.

WHY NOW?

Numbers don't lie. Our culture is adrift. Our society is focused more on "them" and less on Him. Debt is out of control, 41 percent of first marriages* end in divorce, more than 60 percent of us and those we love† are overweight, 70 percent of people hate their jobs‡—and toxicity, judgment, and negativity fill social-media feeds.

While the Bible has a lot to say about how to live, people are drifting away from it. We thought that, by lining up the simple, modern-day principles of Oola with what Scripture has to say about living an exceptional life, we could inspire readers to step back and consider their own Christian life—and simultaneously challenge them to ask, *"Can I do more?"*

REVISITING
THE 7 F'S OF OOLA

Ooh la la! That's the only way to describe how amazing it feels when the key areas of your life—Fitness, Finance, Family, Field (career), Faith, Friends, and Fun—are balanced and growing. It's when you've reached the point where you're happy, growing, and looking forward to the future. It's the kind of life where everything *just works.* Like a circus performer spinning seven plates in front of a cheering crowd, you manage to get through your entire performance without a single plate crashing to the floor. That's Oola. But the amazing thing is, the Bible has a lot to say about these key areas. And it's no surprise that Jesus, the ultimate teacher and mentor, shows us how.

Like that ongoing battle with your teenager? Done. That job you hate? Gone for something better. And that extra weight or unhealthy lifestyle you've been dealing with? Over it. The stress of seemingly insurmountable debt and bills? Lifted.

---

* According to *www.divorcestatistics.org.*

† According to a study by The Institute for Health Metrics and Evaluation, and reported in *The Lancet* magazine.

‡ Gallup, www.gallup.com/poll/180404/gallup-daily-employee-engagement.aspx, January 15, 2017.

By the time you've read *Section Two: The 7 F's of Oola*, you'll have dialed in this overwhelming thing called *life*—and simplified it to the seven areas that really matter. You'll be on track to prioritize your new-found goals, focus on the steps that will get you there, and meet milestones on your new path.

Throughout your journey (and throughout the chapters of this book), Jesus has your back—just as He said He would. He'll be showing up with new ideas, bringing on unexpected resources, and helping you take the scary steps. He'll be the voice in your head. And the guiding force in your life.

And because Jesus himself obeyed the Word of God, we repeatedly turn to the Bible, too, in every page of this book, helping you see Jesus as the ultimate life coach—an ally who understands your struggles, dreams, and roadblocks. During His ministry in Galilee, Jesus was tuned into the human condition like no one else. It's these stories of His understanding, new thinking, and right action that we've brought forth—as told by the people who encountered Him, knew Him, and were transformed by Him.

Jesus was the original Oola expert.

But more than that: how He lived, what He thought, and what He prioritized gives us a pretty awesome picture of how we can live the OolaLife on this earth.

JESUS UNDERSTANDS YOUR **BLOCKERS** AND **ACCELERATORS**, TOO

Fear, guilt, love, and gratitude are just some of the *blockers* and *accelerators* that will either stop you from getting what you want, or springboard you to the next step in your plan. Jesus knew that if you can overcome the blockers and master the accelerators, your ultimate life happens much more quickly.

In *Section Three: OolaBlockers,* you'll discover stopping points that will not only keep you stuck in your current life situation, but keep you disconnected from an awesome relationship with the Lord. We'll dive into the top seven: fear, guilt, anger, self-sabotage, laziness, envy, and focus issues (whether lack of focus or misdirected focus). Blockers are the negative habits and behaviors that will defeat your ability to grow in abundance, happiness, and success. We will not only discuss them, but teach you real-life strategies to break through the things that are holding you back.

Section Four: OolaAccelerators, on the other hand, introduces you to seven *positive habits and behaviors* that will ignite your journey instantly. Want to get to the life of your dreams faster? Check out how Jesus incorporated gratitude, love, discipline, integrity, passion, humility, and wisdom accelerators into his ministry, relationships, and life.

3 SIMPLE STEPS TO A LIFE OF MORE BALANCE: A WHEEL, A PLAN, AND A PATH

Of course, it's not enough to just read about the 7 F's, Blockers, and Accelerators—you have to have a plan. So in *Section Five: 3 Simple Steps to the OolaLife,* we help you assess where you are today, create a plan for where you want to be tomorrow—then identify concrete daily action steps that will get you to your goal.

MODERN-DAY SEEKERS JOIN JESUS, THE ULTIMATE GURU

Along the way—in every chapter—you'll meet some pretty amazing people delivering extraordinary messages. They're everyday people, many of whom we've met on the Oola Dream Tour, who are searching for an extraordinary life. They're working their plan. And their stories reveal some profound insights we can learn from as they travel their journey.

Jesus of Nazareth, on the other hand, was a living example of Oola, as you'll discover through the unique and compelling stories featured in each chapter. What Jesus taught, who He chose as friends, and—most importantly—how He interacted with people during His life and ministry gives us a great example of what it's like to live the OolaLife.

It's why Jesus is the ultimate Guru. And it's why we chose stories directly from the Bible to help you discover His wisdom. Through these rich and vibrant accounts, you'll meet biblical characters experiencing modern-day problems (and using modern-day thinking) before learning something entirely new from Jesus of Nazareth. While the original account may have been just a few verses of Scripture, we've made these familiar stories larger than life—placing *you* in the Gospel with Jesus to experience the sights, sounds, and everyday people of Judea.

OOLA MEETS YOU WHERE YOU ARE

Ultimately, *Oola for Christians* is written to reconnect you with a caring and proactive Jesus who—more than ever in our modern times—brings balance to an unbalanced world. If it feels like the world is going sideways and the wheels have come off your runaway train, there's a way to get back to center. We've seen transformation in the lives of thousands of Oola readers over the years, who created a workable plan and began living again but with more balance, less stress, and greater purpose.

But more than that, as you get to know many of these readers—through their stories in the book—you'll come to realize how profoundly loyal Jesus can be. He's on your side. And He's ready to bring a steadying hand to your journey, even if your days seem unhinged. While your life might seem like it's beyond fixing, rest assured you're not the only one we've met in crazy dire circumstances.

A few pages ago, we started this Introduction with a quote that inspires us and explains better than anything why in the world we took this on. It's from Charles Thomas Studd, one of the earliest British missionaries to China, and founder—in 1913—of the Heart of Africa Mission.

> "Some want to live within the sound of a church or chapel
> bell. I want to run a rescue shop within a yard of Hell."
>
> —*C.T. Studd*

He was born into a wealthy family, went to Cambridge University, and inherited the modern-day equivalent of $4.8 million, but he gave it all away to focus on his calling: bringing unreached and unheard people to Christ.

While Studd traveled to exotic lands in those days to reach those who others wouldn't, Oola's journey has been at 55 mph on the back roads of America. We're meeting people wherever they are—in forty-three states and counting at this point—all in our little VW Bus. And all too often, many of those we meet are on the one-yard line—Studd's "one yard from Hell"—living with fear, remorse, anxiety, depression, and even contemplating suicide.

Sometimes they're mad at God or have been burned by organized religion. Others have become so busy over the years that they've slowly pushed Christ out of their lives. Many have settled for a blah existence and called that a life. Still others are *devout Christians,* but are so reliant on God's provision that the other six areas of Oola—finances, fitness, careers, and more—need reviving.

With over a million followers at our events, on social media, and at our annual event called OolaPalooza, we've met people in virtually every situation and from every type of background. Now it's time to ensure that their lives are balanced, growing, and amazing in every way. It's also time to give past believers a reason—and a path—to reconnect with a loving and supportive life mentor: Jesus.

We want *you* to become the next Oola success story by dreaming again, including Jesus in your vision, and creating a plan for achieving an amazing new future.

A COUPLE OF **CONSIDERATIONS** AS YOU BEGIN READING

First, we respect and understand the passion and polarity of all this as a topic. But instead of running away from its controversy (as that initial publisher recommended), we decided to face it head on. In reading this book, we encourage you not to focus on where we *differ* as Christians, but instead on where we overlap—at a place of unfailing love and belief that Jesus is our Lord and Savior.

Second, as you read *Oola for Christians*, you'll discover we've chosen Scriptures from various versions of the Bible—both modern and historic. This was by design. We understand that everyone has their favorite version, and we wanted this book to be inclusive for everyone. In the same way, if you and other readers were guests riding in the OolaBus with us, out of respect for you as our guests, we'd include songs from all your favorite playlists. The same concept applies here. Our readers range from newbie Christians to devout believers to every type in between. The goal of this book is to challenge us all to live fully and become better Christians.

WHEREVER YOU FIND YOURSELF, IT'S EASY TO GET STARTED ON YOUR **OOLA**LIFE

Turn the page and start the process of becoming who God intended you to be. By the time you've read just the first few chapters of *Oola for Christians*, you'll meet Jesus in a whole new way—and see your faith walk in a whole new light.

WHAT IS **OOLA**?

"I pray that God, the source of hope,
will fill you completely with joy and peace
because you trust in him."

—ROMANS 15:13a NLT[*]

Oo´•la \ *n. adj.* \ **1 a** : *derived from the expression ooh la la!* **b** : *a state of awesomeness* **c** : *a life that is balanced and growing in the key areas of health, finances, career, relationships and well-being* **d** : *a destination (i.e., getting to Oola)* **2 a** : *describing actions, insights, and goals that lead to a balanced life (ex: That's so Oola.)* **3 a** : *the ultimate plan for achieving balance in an unbalanced world.*

O ola is the ultimate Christ-centered life. It's a life where you're happy and growing, taking action on your goals, and bringing balance into your life. It's a life where you're focused on those things that truly matter: good

---

[*] New Living Translation.

relationships, healthy finances, an engaging and meaningful career, fitness and wholesome eating, and plenty of downtime when you can rest, reflect, and simply have fun again.

It's the life that our Lord wants for you.

But most importantly, it's a life that includes *faith*—a daily walk where you're checking in with Him, sharing high-fives when you win, bringing Him the tough stuff, and getting closer if you aren't already. It's the kind of life that isn't just handed to you or without challenges, but an amazing life that you're prepared to handle because you've done the work of getting ready for the good to show up. It's an awesome life, filled with achievement and the wonder and joy of heartfelt moments. It's a life of less stress, more balance, and greater purpose.

In this first section, we'll introduce you to Oola and show you that, regardless of where you are right now—with your career, finances, relationships, health, and faith—the ultimate life can be yours, even if it means (as you'll discover in our first story) climbing from the depths of despair.

ARE YOU FOCUSED, HAPPY, AND GROWING?

"I alone know the plans I have for you,
plans to bring you prosperity and not disaster,
plans to bring about the future you hope for."

—JEREMIAH 29:11 GNT*

---

* Good News Translation.

A s he slowly approached the corner and turned onto the highway, headed for his youngest son's football game across town, Matt Logan reflected on his workday and how blessed he truly was. He had a great family, a loving wife, and four awesome kids. But more than that, God had brought Matt to a close relationship with Him—and to a passionate and growing community church with a children's ministry his family loved.

As a dad, Matt recognized the impact that knowing Jesus could bring to a kid. Hadn't his own children—two sons and two daughters—grown in confidence and maturity and patience and benevolence? His daughter D.J., especially. Short for Deianerah, she had a sunny disposition and an infectious smile. She was level-headed, a deep thinker, with tremendous love for her family and friends. Steady and sensible, she was passionate about life.

And now, today, D.J. had started the first day back at high school—a senior on campus for her very last year. Excited for her and enthusiastic about her future, Matt was eager to hear all about it. She was on her way home by now, but after the game, Matt knew he'd get a lively and exuberant earful of the latest and greatest on campus.

Well, this is odd, he thought, as he rounded the final turn and encountered traffic on the small-town road he'd driven a thousand times before. It led past the high school, but as the afternoon sun dipped slowly to the horizon, Matt realized it was far too late for typical after-school congestion.

Something must have happened, he assumed as he saw they were turning traffic around and sending cars back down the highway. A vague feeling of unease prompted Matt to pull to the side of the road. When he did, a traffic cop approached his car.

"Can I see some ID, sir?" the policeman asked respectfully. "We're diverting anyone who's not a resident."

Handing over his driver's license, a sense of foreboding began to flood Matt's agile brain. Like a jolt to the senses, his heart raced slightly, and his mind began to panic. Eyeing Matt's name on the license, the officer hesitated.

"Come with me, sir," he said, taking Matt to a closer vantage point.

There, in the distance, was D.J.'s car—wedged into the back of a school bus with Matt's precious daughter trapped inside. She'd been texting a note about her first day of school, unaware that the school bus had stopped in front of her. Now, hours later, as the first responders and paramedics still worked feverishly to free her shattered body, Matt prayed as he'd never prayed before.

Let her live. Keep her safe. Don't let her die, Matt begged the Lord.

But it was no use. Injured beyond saving, D.J. died later that night at Mayo Clinic in Rochester surrounded by her parents and siblings. Soon, her classmates and friends poured into the hospital, grief-stricken at the unthinkable and desperate to process their pain.

In one brief moment of distracted driving—something D.J. knew was dangerous and illegal—she had made a choice that ended her life.

How do Christians deal with it when unexplainable things like this happen? thought Matt. *How can I make sure that no other family has to bear the pain that we are suffering now?*

As news of the accident began to circulate, local reporters called to interview Matt. Seeing the news, an insurance company called to ask him to speak at their upcoming young drivers' training day. Soon, another invitation came in. Then another.

As Matt continued to grapple with the overwhelming loss of his daughter, God began to develop a new purpose for his life—to educate teens about distracted driving. Instead of focusing on his own loss, Matt—like so many Christians we'd met—had taken up the role that God had placed on his heart.

We fell silent for a time as we ourselves began to process the sheer heartbreak of Matt's story, wondering how, as a Christian, he would make sense of such a senseless tragedy. His story made things real for us. It reminded us that *it is possible* to slow the hectic pace of modern-day reality long enough to get closer to God and discover His unique calling on your life.

Not only were we challenged to examine our own mission with Oola, but we also recalled the hundreds of stories of God's infinite grace we'd heard from fellow Christians who were faithful, but—like Matt—still needed a game plan to regain a sense of purpose and refocus their shattered or simply exhausted lives.

WHAT IS **OOLA**?

For you, Matt, and for the hundreds of thousands of Christians we've met who are already walking in faith but want to grow in other areas, Oola is a state of awesomeness. It's derived from the term *Ooh la la!*—that feeling you get when your life is balanced and growing in the 7 key areas of life: fitness, finance, family, field (career), faith, friends, and fun.

It's living the amazing life that God intended for you.

It's you, completely focused on the bigger picture, with your daily activities firing on all cylinders, free of missteps and with a lot less stress about your current circumstances.

It's a life guided by faith in God—living the unique calling that He's placed on your life—whether you belong to a church right now, are considering a faith walk for the first time, or whether you're getting reconnected to Jesus after being hurt or dispirited by organized religion or loved ones in the past.

Forget about what the world says you should be, do, own, or want. You and Jesus are in sync about *what matters most to you.* He's got this.

And it's this authenticity that will make you a Christian whom others want to know, support, and get close to. Don't be like anyone else on Earth. With Jesus on your side and you working your Oola plan, you'll finally be true to yourself, as well as be acting in the highest good.

WHAT GOT YOU HERE
WON'T GET YOU THERE

Realize, too, that if you've been focused on excelling in your career, growing your finances, creating a beautiful home, or building a network of business relationships and industry achievement, you've probably created an amazing life for you and your family. If your kids have been focused on sports, academic achievement, or extracurricular activities, they've probably got a great start on their future.

But while many people think this kind of success equates to "having it all," the reality is that you really don't have it all *without faith*.

In fact, we hear story after story from high achievers—people at optimum levels in every other area of their lives—who say either they couldn't have gotten there without a close relationship with God, or that the level of success they now enjoy has inspired them to become more faithful.

How important is this real-world evidence that *faith* is the key element? We mentioned in the Introduction that, when the first *Oola* book—which we self-published—began to gain traction in the marketplace, we approached publishers in New York about bringing out a revised edition for the broader trade channel. While they were excited about its success so far, one of them said we'd have to delete the *Faith* chapter in order to make it acceptable to mainstream buyers. While we hadn't really emphasized faith in our Oola talks and events previously, his comment gave us pause.

What did we really believe? we thought. *What were our own experiences (and those of our readers) with asking God to help bring balance, purpose, and success into our lives?* Although we realized that it might negatively affect book sales, in an instant we knew our answer: the only way to have a complete life—one that is deep and rich—is to include faith.

From that point forward, we boldly began to introduce more and more stories about God's purpose and intent in our posts, speeches, and book signings. We surveyed our audiences, kept track of what we heard, and interviewed more and more people. Eventually, we came to the overwhelming conclusion that virtually *every one of our readers* believed that *faith in God* is still an elemental factor in achieving the life you want.

The truth is, today, far too many people are successful but not happy. They've put their faith in things that fail. Only God is unfailing. And only God will repeatedly show up for you as you work your way toward creating your OolaLife.

IS SOMETHING **NEW** CALLING YOU?

To further the point, many people—perhaps you—have already arrived at the ideal life. You've got a wonderful family, great relationships, a comfortable home, and a terrific lifestyle, all because of hard work, determination, and divine influence in your life.

But have you ever considered if something new is calling you?

Stories abound of super-successful entrepreneurs, church leaders, and corporate executives, as well as artists, athletes, and retired people who branched out into humanitarian work, teaching, or advocacy.

Whatever inspires you, this book will give you a road map to maintain balance as you grow in a new direction and pursue God's new calling on your life.

Perhaps your OolaLife is missions work or bringing sense to our political climate or caring for a family member or sharing what you know with peers in your industry. Whatever new thing is calling you, *Oola for Christians* can help you grow in passion, enthusiasm, and discernment—all while making sure things are solid on the home front, too. Plus, imagine the impact of the *Oola* message on those who'll support you as you branch out. Get your family members on board and watch them grow to enjoy the OolaLife, too.

FAST-TRACK YOUR FUTURE IN JUST 21 DAYS

If we could recommend just one self-help book that would get you to the next level, we already know which one we'd choose: *the Bible.* As the world's first book about balance, achievement, relationships, and healthy living, it's still the best, and not surprisingly, it's also the most published self-help book of all time.

To help you dive deep into its teachings and learn from the life of Jesus as recorded in Scripture, we've populated the chapters of *Oola for Christians* with instructive verses. But we've also gone one step further and created a 21-day Oola for Christians challenge to encourage you to read God's Word and implement it in your life.

To register—it's free—go to *oolalife.com/christians-challenge.*

GOING THROUGH A SEASON ON THE WAY TO **OOLA**

"We know that God is always at work for
the good of everyone who loves him. They are the
ones God has chosen for his purpose."

—ROMANS 8:28 CEV*

* Contemporary English Version.

W hile Jesus tells us, "I am the way, the truth, and the life," He also knows that everyone has free will and follows their own path in creating the ideal life. Sometimes, that path means going through a season of struggle. Whether it's a health crisis, exploding debt, a troubled marriage, being out of work, or simply someone in your life—teenager, spouse, or controlling ex—causing you grief, this is your season to survive, emerging on the other side of it more prepared to tackle your future.

For others, it's your season of opportunity, where the world has opened its riches of possibility to you. If you're already doing well, tapping into a close relationship with God means there is so much more you can do. You'll take your life to the next level in a season of opportunity.

Heather Thomas—the pastor's daughter whom you met in the Introduction—lived through a season before returning to missions work (and taking 10,000 Oola dream stickers with her to Nicaragua). In fact, living through years of anguish and consequences is what gave her the motivation to return to fulfilling her God-given purpose.

IF THERE'S A BREATH LEFT IN ME

by Heather Thomas

ighteen, nineteen, twenty, I counted as I swallowed the last handful of prescription pills from the bottle. After an afternoon of binge drinking, shame, and misery, I'd decided to end my own life. A few days earlier, my three small children and I had celebrated Mother's Day alone, but my thoughts were far from maternal. By ending it all, I actually believed my kids would be better off with their grandparents. Without me, they'd be free to grow up solid, right?

The crazy thing is, I'd grown up in the church—a pastor's daughter, no less. I knew Jesus. But somehow, I'd lost my purpose, and with it, my will to live.

Eight years earlier, I'd met a man at church who I thought was the love of my life. Soon after, we were married in Panama on a missions trip and then welcoming our first child back home in Boca Raton, Florida. Though becoming a wife and mother had interrupted my original plan of traveling the world, planting churches, and winning souls for Jesus, there was a certain appeal in having a helpmate join me in my vision.

Little did I know the wreck my life was to become.

Married to a man who was secretly using OxyContin, I struggled to protect my parents (and now my kids) from the harm and reputational damage of my husband's drug-induced lies and volatile habit. *If my dad's congregation really knew the truth,* I thought, *my parents would look bad.* And with more and more people disbelieving my fake marital bliss and sketchy explanations for his absences, I knew things already looked bad enough.

Too prideful to confide in anyone, I coped with the anguish in secret—always covering for my husband—my life alternating between emotionally abusive episodes and uneasy silence.

Finally, stretched to my limit, I filed for divorce. As a pastor's daughter who was now single and financially broken, depression soon followed. As part of my coping mechanism, I occasionally turned to sleeping pills. It wasn't the best solution or even a good one, but at least for a few hours, I could dull the pain and deaden the shame— checked out, numbed out, passed out.

By the time that fateful Mother's Day came and went, I was beyond making rational decisions. As the pills and alcohol slowly combined and sent me toward oblivion, a friend stopped by unexpectedly and found me on the floor. Level-headed enough to help me purge what I'd swallowed, my rescuer stayed with me while I slowly came to.

As the taste of alcohol and bile lingered on my lips, I lay there feeling miserable and degraded and ashamed. *What was I doing?* I'd nearly thrown away the life I'd been given, the beautiful children I'd brought into the world, and the magnificent future that other people had empowered in me.

Truly waking up to my reality for the first time in years, oddly I couldn't help remembering what I knew about the creation story in Genesis. When God breathed life into man, my dad had taught me, He also instilled in man His purpose.

I can do something with my life, I thought. *As long as I have God's breath in me, I have a purpose.*

Vulnerable now, with the truth about me exposed, I committed to doing the hard work of getting my life back on track—hoping that God would show up for me.

I knew that I needed help: emotionally, physically, and spiritually. But I also needed an outlet for what I knew I could do for other Christians. I'd been raised with the expectation that I would accomplish awesome things for the world—giving, helping, and mobilizing people for some greater good. Leadership and ministry were qualities my parents had instilled in me. But I'd lost my compass. Shepherding was something I knew I needed to do.

This legacy was in the back of my mind as I thought of my own recent past. *How many Christians are hurting, as I had been? How many need to reconnect with their purpose, passion, and God-given talents?*

Within days, a friend recommended that I attend an event at Florida Atlantic University. Two Christian guys—Dave Braun and Troy Amdahl—spoke about something called Oola.

Where you are is simply where you are. It's not who you are, they said. *You are designed by God for greatness and a purpose. Why settle for ordinary when extraordinary is within you?*

In that moment, I knew what I had to do. They'd given me permission to dream again. As I grabbed a Sharpie and wrote out an Oola dream sticker, I told myself that the words I'd inscribed were just the beginning.

Go on another missions trip, I wrote. When I slapped the colorful round shape onto the side of the old VW Bus, I felt something change in me. It was the defining moment of my life. It would reset my life to the point in time when my dream had been interrupted and would allow me to move on with God's original purpose for my life—more prepared, more focused, and more passionate.

While it's been work to take back control over my life, the Oola formula has shown me that you can't do great things in the world if your life is secretly a train wreck. Thriving and growing and firing on all cylinders is *necessary* to fulfill God's purpose for your life.

Within months, I'd scheduled a missions trip to Nicaragua, arranged to leave my kids with my parents, and found myself back in front of the OolaGuys at a book signing. I was excited to share that I'd soon be achieving my goal of returning to missions work.

But the thing is, I was nervous for what came next.

Written on a sticker I was holding in my hand was a goal: *Collect 10,000 dream stickers in Nicaragua*. I needed to ask for those 10,000 stickers from two guys who didn't even know me, so I could distribute them to the local men, women, and children I would meet. In a moment of courage, I asked, and enthusiastically they said, "Yes."

When my team and I met up with Dave and Troy once again—this time while they were on tour in Delray Beach, Florida—we carried in bag after bag of Oola dreams—8,800 stickers in all. But the biggest dream stayed with me: The Heather Project, which provides free Oola dream stickers* to readers who want to share the message and challenge others to pursue their God-given greatness.

Yeah, sometimes, you just have to go through a season.

JUST LIKE HEATHER, YOU MAY BE GOING THROUGH A **SEASON** OF STRUGGLE, TOO

If life has you down at the moment and yearning for a brighter future, realize that *where you are* is not *who you are*. Your struggles aren't a life sentence. Our Lord hasn't abandoned you. It's just a season you're going through.

Like Heather, your focus now should be on recovering, facing forward, and planning for a better future with Jesus's help.

You can do this. God has a plan for you. It's time to go get it.

---

* Read more about it at *www.oolalife.com/heatherproject*.

THE 7 F'S OF
OOLA

"The door will be opened to

those who knock."

—MATTHEW 7:8b GNT

G et ready to master the basics of an inspired and exceptional Christ-centered life. Over the next seven chapters, you'll learn the fundamentals of Oola—those areas where you need to focus in order to achieve more balance, have less stress, and begin following your life purpose.

As you roll through the chapters covering fitness, finance, family, field (career), faith, friends, and fun, you'll be learning new skills, gaining new insights from Jesus's ministry, and thinking about goals for what you want to be, do, and have.

These seven areas are where your major life goals will live. These are the areas you *must master* in order to lead a complete life.

To begin each chapter, we've got a few words of wisdom. To finish each chapter, we've delivered some tips based on what Scripture
teaches us to do. And in between, you'll meet some of the most inspiring people on this planet. Some are professed Christians who are *seeking* Oola, working on their lives—in specific F areas—and learning
some profound insights along the way. Other seekers are less strong
in their faith but are meeting Christ in unexpected ways as they build
(or rebuild) lives of meaning and mastery with Him as their coach.

Finally, through modern-day interpretations of familiar Bible
stories, you'll meet the ultimate *Oola guru:* Jesus. A guiding mentor
and loving advisor who can help you get it right—a major player in
your future who wants you to live your OolaLife and enjoy the benefits of His wisdom.

To live and love like Jesus should be a principal goal of any Christian. So, travel back in time through these stories to discover how He
mastered it in Galilee two thousand years ago and how we can apply
his example in our modern-day world.

Of course, as you study the *7 F's of Oola,* take a look at your own
life. Are you good with where you're at? Are you stronger in some
areas than others? By taking mental notes (or even writing them
down), you'll be ultra-prepared for the conclusion of this book: creating a life plan to balance and grow your life and keep you solid in
the future. Are you ready?

Let's get started on the 7 F's with the first area: OolaFitness.

OOLAFITNESS

"Dear friend I pray that you may enjoy
good health and that all may go well with you,
even as your soul is getting along well."

—JOHN 1:2 NIV

Your body and mind are amazing feats of engineering. They're designed to work hard, reboot overnight, and be active team players in your quest for the optimum life. When needed, they can also heal rapidly, and (even better) they can present a pretty impressive statement to the world when you're at the top of your game.

If you've ever jumped out of bed in the morning after a great night's sleep—energetic, with a positive attitude, and ready to take on the world and make progress on your goals—you already know what it's like to be living OolaFitness. If you're eating nutritious foods, working out a few times a week, happy, upbeat, and confident about the future—you're not only physically healthy, you're in a great mental and emotional state, too.

But if you haven't felt that way in years—eating on the run, sitting too much, perpetually unhappy, overwhelmed, exhausted, and worrying a lot—well, you've got some work to do.

GARBAGE **IN**, GARBAGE **OUT**

Whether you're a hot mess right now or an elite athlete with years of training, the key to OolaFitness is to continually challenge yourself, work out more consistently, cut the sugar and simple carbs, and choose more nutrient-rich foods. If you take garbage into your body—via bad fats, sugars, toxins, chemicals, or recreational drugs—you're going to get garbage out in terms of your stamina, productivity, on-the-job performance, and vitality.

You've got to call out the fad foods, too. On the road for a month driving the OolaBus from town to town, Dave began to object to Troy's energy drink addiction. "They're garbage," Dave complained.

Soon after, the guys founded the OolaTea Company to produce healthy alternatives to sugary, caffeinated drinks and help put a stop to the garbage-in, garbage-out lifestyle.

Of course, the same kind of toxic input goes for your mind, too.

So much of the social media, television, and news we consume in Western culture is like the food we eat: toxic, deficient in nutrients, and lacking in substance. The key is to reclaim your life, your energy, and your time—then spend it on pursuing your goals.

One popular method for unplugging and rebooting is the 30-day "information diet" popularized by Tim Ferriss, author of *The Four-Hour Workweek*. Go cold turkey. Turn off the television, your smartphone (except for important calls and necessary business), the radio, and especially social media. You'd be surprised not only by how much more time you have to work on your own goals, but you'll be amazed at how freeing it can feel to live your own life—and with a lot less stress—rather than mindlessly watching other people live theirs.

JESUS PLAYED FULL OUT, BUT WAS **INTENTIONAL** IN HIS FOCUS, TOO

Of course, the Judea of Jesus's time didn't have juice bars, twenty-four-hour gyms, or Spin bikes, but we can still learn a lot from the way He managed His own health and fitness. For one thing, we know that Jesus did everything 100 percent—no slacking, no warming the bench. He was committed. Scholars say He likely walked twenty-five miles *a day* during His ministry, while still being fully present, teaching, and ministering to the crowds.

But He also rested when necessary and judiciously protected His private time for prayer and downtime with friends.

IS YOUR BODY AND MIND **READY** FOR WHAT GOD HAS IN STORE FOR YOU?

Jesus was here to do His Father's work. And there's no question that God has placed a unique calling on your life, too—one that *only you* can pursue. Whether it's to raise amazing kids, crush it as a company executive, start a charity, write books, take a missions trip, build a business, or simply bring people joy through your compassionate listening skills, there is some *one thing* that only you can do.

Unfortunately, you can't show up for the job if you're tired, sick, or emotionally depleted. Getting healthy means getting ready for the purpose you've been given. So how can you get ready?

THE DANIEL **FAST**

Avoiding meat at certain times, fasting from all foods, or submitting to the Spartan diet of pilgrimage were all a thing in the time of Jesus. But one regimen prescribed in the Bible that's still popular today (Chris Pratt even follows it) is The Daniel Fast: a twenty-one-day, plant-based diet that's devoid of added sweeteners, dairy, meat, caffeine, alcohol, and food additives and preservatives.*

By fasting, you're pushing the pause button on the hectic pace and mindless consumption of your life. When you fast, God gets more of you, your time, and your focus. And a nice by-product is mental clarity—as Jesus found when he fasted for forty days in the desert. Fasting has been a tradition of many religions throughout history. *How you fast* is really different for everyone.

Isn't it time for *you* to spend more time with God and less time on the busyness of life?

---

* Read about it in Daniel 1:8-16. Check with a licensed physician before starting any new eating program.

TIME WITH HIM

by Tony Ochoa

Thirty-two years old; it must be something else. There is no way this feeling in my chest is anything but an anomaly, a remnant of the fast food they handed me through a window on the way home from work last night. With the food digested, however, the chest pain remained. And when I awoke the next morning with pain in my jaw, it was enough to make me jump on the phone to my doctor. I was sure that this was all in my head and not my body. But I set up an appointment anyway, if only to ease my mind.

Poking and prodding ensued, and the test results soon came in. My cholesterol was high, my triglycerides were off the chart, and I had high blood pressure. All were signs my heart was unhappy with how I'd been treating it and how unhealthy it had become.

Somewhere between twenty-two and thirty-two years old something had happened. I spent less time outside and more time behind a desk. I was less aware of the quality of food I put in my body, and more concerned with convenience and cost. Even when I needed bigger clothes, I barely thought about it. For fun, I calculated it. Just eight and a half pounds a year is just seven-tenths of a pound per month. I hadn't even noticed it—but my heart did.

And when my cousin, also in his early thirties, died from a heart attack, I realized that it could have been me. I could have been the one leaving my children fatherless and my wife alone to raise and provide for our family.

This was real. No one was going to do it for me. I needed to lose the weight I had found over the past ten years. The weight that slowly and magically appeared, the weight my heart didn't like was the weight that was putting me on a path I did not want to be on.

I began running with the sole purpose of losing the weight to take the pressure off my heart. Diligently, I put my shoes on, kept my head down, and kept my feet moving forward.

I started my runs on a rural road near my house in upstate New York. It's the other New York that most people don't think about. Most of the time, I'm running alongside corn fields. The air is fresh with the scent of cut grass, farmers' fields, and the rainfall from the night before. You can hear the sound of the wind pushing through the stalks, crows cawing in the distance, and dogs barking. I pass by local dairy farms as I traverse the countryside and hear the sound of the cows in the field, mooing as if to show their support as I pass by. On my early runs, I hear the roosters crowing. On my late runs, I hear crickets chirping. I feel like a kid again, seeing, hearing, and smelling things for the very first time. And above all of nature's beautiful background noises, I hear the sound of the gravel beneath my feet as my running shoes push into the ground beneath me.

To stay accountable, I began to run for causes like TAPS (Tragedy Assistance Program for Survivors), an organization that offers care, support, and resources to those who have lost a loved one serving in our Armed Forces. Each year I paired up with a fallen soldier, running with that soldier's photo pinned to the back of my shirt all year long. While I ran, I thought about that soldier and their sacrifice—realizing that the pain they suffered was more than I would ever endure while on my runs. Feeling the sacrifice of their families, I wanted to do more, so I began to pray for these loved ones when I ran.

Then something happened.

As I prayed, I found special time with God. Instead of looking at a countdown on my wristwatch I began to lose track of time in awe of God's creation around me: His animals, the mountains, the streams, and the sunrise and sunset. My wife likes to tell me that I might get more running done if I would stop taking pictures on my route. However, I am mesmerized by what He has made for us to enjoy and can't help but thank Him in prayer. My prayers always start by thanking God for the beauty that He has set before me each day. It then leads to me being thankful for all that He has done for me and provided for my family. Then it comes to those I haven't met that I feel would benefit by knowing Him.

It's weird. I grew up thinking that time with God was in a place, like a church, at the dinner table, or on my knees by my bed at night. I discovered that my most precious and sacred time with Him is often on a rural road in upstate New York with the sound of gravel under my feet and the cool breeze providing a distraction from the heat and my fatigue.

I ran to have a healthier heart. The weight came off, but my heart changed in an unexpected, life-changing way. I found time to pray and become closer to Him.

As Tony tells us in his story above, getting healthy often leads to a better relationship with God. Pursuing OolaFitness provides a closeness and focus that keeps you on track to living a vibrant and robust life—pursuing God's purpose. Of course, you don't have to compete in the next Ironman competition to fulfill His purpose. Or do you?

◎ ◎ ◎ ◎

JESUS, THE ORIGINAL IRONMAN

"The man himself kept insisting, 'I am the one!'"

—JOHN 9:9 NET[*]

'd heard about Him, this man whom some called a prophet and others a rabbi. They said He traveled the hills of Galilee, healing the sick and teaching new ideas to the masses—sometimes walking twenty-five miles a day and even braving rough seas.

What would it be like to be that strong? I thought, as I sat on the street, begging for my living and comparing what I'd heard to my own miserable existence. Every now and again, above the din of carts and travelers, I could hear a baby cry. And I could always recognize the pungent scent of frankincense and resin mixed with the sharp tang of donkeys as people hurried by with their pack animals.

Faintly, too, I could hear some merchants haggling at a distant produce stand over a basket of figs.

What did a fig even look like? I wondered—just as I'd pictured a thousand times in my mind how life would really look if I could see it.

You see, I'd been blind since birth. And for some reason, all of society thought that it was because either my parents or I had committed a sin. It felt harsh, this life sentence. But the worst part was the whispers of the local gossips that hung in the air.

---

[*] New English Translation.

Though I couldn't see what was right in front of me, I could hear them talking. It was soul-wrenching.

They believed that God had punished me because of some awful thing my family had done. Sadly, some of those talking were even Pharisees. Imagine being blamed for something I couldn't control by those who considered themselves the most spiritual!

Worse yet, it was thought "customary" for people to shout hurtful names at me as I made my way through town. They would throw objects and often spit on me. It was like a cloak I had to wear day after day. With no filter or protection, I had no advance warning of the jabs people would throw until it was too late.

Sadly, I was used to it. But being accustomed to something and being okay with it were two totally different things.

On the day the Man from Galilee found me, I was completely caught off guard at being addressed by this vibrant and energetic young teacher. Of course, there had been talk of Him throughout the town. He was the guy who fasted for forty days and nights, swam in the Sea of Galilee, and stood all day in the heat, teaching and feeding thousands of people.

I found myself face-to-face with Ironman Jesus.

Though I don't know for certain, I could sense that He looked at me differently from the others. And when His disciples questioned Him about me, I heard Him respond differently than anyone ever had. His words carried weight, I knew, and His kindness brought miracles for countless others I'd heard about.

In fact, one word from Him and lives were transformed.

What would my word *be,* I wondered, as I could feel His presence next to me. Would He speak a word to heal me and help me to finally see? Or would He ridicule and spit upon me as others had done?

Then, as a sound I'd heard a thousand times before reached my ears, my heart sank: He had spit—validating the actions of the cruel townspeople whose malice I endured every day.

He's just like everyone else, I thought. *Or was He?*

As I felt the sensation of cold wet mud spread across my shuttered eyes, I realized He had made a vulgar paste from the spittle and mud. *Why?* I cried inwardly. *Why me!?*

An observer who was there later wrote in John 9:5–9:

> *"As long as I am in the world, I am the light of the world," said Jesus. Having said this, he spat on the ground and made some mud with the saliva. He smeared the mud on the blind man's eyes and said to him, "Go wash in the pool of Siloam."*

As neighbors who'd seen me previously began to gather, they asked, "Hey, isn't that the blind guy who used to sit and beg?"

"Yes!" some said. "This is the man!" while others contradicted that, saying, "No, he only looks like him."

But I know the truth: Jesus had touched me, and now I could see. With others, Jesus had used a mere word to bring about healing. But with me, He'd used the same hideous saliva that so many others had used to taunt me. He used the instrument that had heretofore wounded my spirit to bring about total healing in me.

And when He commanded me to go and wash, I realized that washing the spit and mud off my face healed more than my eyes. It washed away every negative word ever spoken over me. I was blind, but with Jesus, now I could see.

If Jesus was the world's first Ironman, what can we learn from the way He lived and the work He did? The days were long and the demands constant. Imagine trying to do His Father's work in the hill towns and seaside villages of Galilee—walking everywhere in the heat and dust. Would you have survived it?

But more than just being physically fit, Jesus was *mentally* fit to do His Father's work, too. What do you need to do (both physically and mentally) to pursue your unique calling? These tips can help.

IMPROVE YOUR MENTAL CLARITY

"After fasting for forty days and forty nights,
He was hungry."

—MATTHEW 4:2

Today's food manufacturers have loaded processed foods with preservatives, artificial flavors, and fillers to the point where these additives can create "foggy brain": that feeling that you just can't focus, aren't motivated, and lack energy for days at a time. If you're also addicted to sugar, smoking, caffeine, or recreational drugs, you're probably experiencing an even greater lack of attention.

Clearing your mind will help you focus on your priorities again and face the world with some seriously improved brainpower. Even Jesus tackled his most important speaking gig—the Sermon on the Mount—after "fasting for forty days and forty nights" (Matthew 4:2).

While not everyone can handle fasting as He did, one thing that does improve mental clarity is an "elimination diet" where you eat clean for three to six weeks. Originally designed to identify foods that may be causing allergic and digestive reactions, the diet recommends consuming only healthy vegetables, fruits, and protein at first, and then reintroducing "problem foods," such as gluten, dairy, soy, refined sugar, and alcohol, one at a time to see which are causing you problems like indigestion, skin flare-ups, insomnia, migraines, lack of focus, and more. A pretty cool byproduct of this diet is the mental clarity and boost in energy the body delivers as it clears out the toxins and heals past inflammation.

GET **PHYSICAL**

"She girds herself with strength;
she exerts her arms with vigor."

—PROVERBS 31:17

Greek and Roman societies before the time of Christ had a long tradition of physical training for sports and overall health. And even Proverbs 31:17 tells us that "She girds herself with strength; she exerts her arms with vigor." A regular workout regimen that includes resistance training, cardio, and regular movement like walking, swimming, or yoga will help you maintain a body that's ready for anything (and one that looks terrific, too).

But don't just join a gym in January and forget your commitment by March. Figure out *what works best for you,* so you'll stick with it over the long term. Physical fitness is a lifestyle.

LET GOD **MANAGE** YOUR EMOTIONAL HEALTH

"The fruit of the Spirit is love, joy, peace, patience, kindness,
generosity, faithfulness, gentleness, and self-control."

—GALATIANS 5:22–23

Despite the presence of Jesus and the Word in our lives, Christians experience emotional setbacks, too. Eating disorders, substance abuse, trauma, rape, bullying, and other abuse and emotional disorders are real—even for believers. Add to that the daily stressors and worry that the world heaps on us, and our emotional health takes a hit almost every day. Even our own bad habit of negative thinking can rewire the brain, causing health issues and loss of brain function over time.* And, of course, the growing occurrence of depression, anxiety, and suicide—the perception that life will never get better, even with the presence of God in our lives—is heartbreaking.

Luckily, "the fruit of the Spirit is love, joy, peace, patience, kindness, generosity, faithfulness, gentleness, and self-control" (Galatians 5:22–23). Let God handle this tough stuff by going to Him in prayer and meditation. To get you started, one book we like is *Prayers That Avail Much* by Germaine Copeland; it is filled with effective prayers for renewal, recovery, and emotional healing.

If you can't get past this challenge using prayer alone, don't be afraid to ask for help from a Christian counselor, a trusted pastor, a lay minister, or another professional trained in emotional health. Asking for help isn't a sign of weakness; it's actually a sign of strength. It's you knowing that you're designed by God for something greater, but understanding that you just need some help to overcome this season and move on with your life.

---

* According to neuroscientist Dr. Daniel Amen in his book, *Change Your Brain, Change Your Life.*

OOLAFINANCE

"Lazy hands make poverty,
but diligent hands bring wealth."

—PROVERBS 10:4 NIV

Sit in church on any given Sunday, and you'll hear Christians who are stressed about their finances. As the modern-day world takes up more and more of our focus, it's also taking up more and more of our money.

Overspending, the crushing burden of debt, getting locked into financial commitments for things that don't matter are all symptoms of the heavy and worrisome weight of our finances.

It's a barrier that can keep you from living a Christ-centered life. It puts your focus on making payments, not pursuing your purpose. Plus, you don't need that kind of stress as you're working toward your OolaLife.

What's the worst part of money stress?

It changes your relationship with God—especially when you go to Him in prayer. In the back of your mind are the poor choices you've made. When you go into debt, you're testing God and His promise to provide for you (Philippians 4:19). And when you take the easy way out of a jam by using your credit cards, you've circumvented an occasion that would otherwise force you to grow in faith.

What else does the Bible say about money?

TAKE **CARE** OF YOUR FAMILY'S BASIC NEEDS

The Apostle Paul writes in 1 Timothy 5:8 (GWT),* "If anyone doesn't take care of his own relatives, especially his immediate family, he has denied the Christian faith and is worse than an unbeliever."

Think about your own life: have you ever been unable to pay basic expenses at home because of a selfish and pointless impulse purchase?

---

* God's Word Translation.

Are you so strapped for cash before each paycheck that you live on credit cards the rest of the month or take money out of your savings or investments?

Here's where a monthly budget and some serious self-discipline will keep you on track. After tithing and investing, pay your most important household bills in full, even if it means you have to cook at home, cut back on streaming, or plan a staycation instead of heading out of town.

But don't worry that Paul's stern warning about family requires you to take care of your drug-addicted, repeat-offender uncle. Or, your frequently overdrawn sister-in-law. Or, even your kids when they've spent their allowance and no longer have mad money.

Provision is covering basic needs—not funding bad habits, bailing someone out of debt, paying their fines, or solving financial disasters of their own making.

THE GREEN GAP: GET OUT OF **DEBT**, STAY OUT OF DEBT

While Romans 13:8 (WEB)* advises us, "Owe no one anything, except to love one another," the Bible doesn't specifically say it's a sin to borrow money. It does, however, contain many dire warnings against going into debt because of bad judgment or lack of discipline, and it also admonishes that any debt we undertake *must be paid back*.

One of our favorite books on getting out of debt and moving forward with stress-free finances is *The Total Money Makeover* by Dave Ramsey. We love Dave. In fact, Dave even has a dream sticker on the OolaBus. Along with Dave, we share a common disdain of debt—except for one allowable kind: a fifteen-year, fixed-rate home

---

* World English Bible.

mortgage where the payment is no more than 25 percent of your take-home pay. After that, all consumer debt, student loans, car loans, and other financed "stuff" needs to be paid off.

To fast-track your way to being debt-free, we recommend something we call "The Green Gap." This is how the OolaGuru got out of debt. In fact, by the time Troy had reached his mid-thirties, an avalanche of student loans, business startup loans, and a sizable mortgage had snowballed into more than $750,000. Feeling the stress of the debt and having a strong desire to pay it off, he was conflicted because he also realized he was in the prime of his life. He and his wife Kris wanted to enjoy their best years instead of living like paupers struggling to pay down loans. Not only that, but they also wanted to invest for their future so the decade ahead would compound any investments they could make. The Green Gap was the perfect fit.

If your debt load feels insurmountable or if you can't get your spouse onboard, The Green Gap makes the process of becoming debt-free more enjoyable than the scorched earth, no-fun-until-forever plans. It builds your investments while you're simultaneously paying down debt and becoming less consumptive. Here's how it works:

STEP 1: BUDGET FOR THE COMING MONTH, MAKING TWO SEPARATE LISTS. Detail what income you'll be earning and which expenses will be due. Total everything on the two lists.

STEP 2: IDENTIFY THE GAP. Subtract the money going *out* from the money coming *in*. This equals the gap. (Hopefully, you've got more income than expenses, which creates "The Green Gap." If you have more expenses than income, it's a "Red Gap" and signals a financial emergency.)

STEP 3: MAXIMIZE THE GREEN GAP. Maximize The Green Gap, that is make the gap bigger, by first identifying ways to bring in more money—whether it's garage sales, selling unused sports equipment, or taking on extra work. Next, cut down your expenses by cancelling anything that's not needed.

STEP 4: APPORTION THE GREEN GAP. Commit 45 percent of the gap to debt reduction, 45 percent to investments, and 10 percent to fun, such as weekend trips, eating out, hobbies, or good times with the kids. You'll experience the joy of the journey and see your investments grow, too, which keeps you focused on the long-term goal of getting out of debt. This Green Gap 45-45-10 formula provides a financial feel-good way to become debt-free and increase wealth. By following this plan, you will see your debt going down, while your investment portfolio is going up, all while having a little fun along the way. The only exception to this rule, is extremely high interest rate loans (i.e., payday loans, etc.) or if the IRS is knocking on your door. In this case, apportion 100 percent to the financial crisis in front of you until it's taken care of.

STEP 5: REPEAT THE ABOVE STEPS EVERY MONTH. Carve out an hour, go on a date night, put on a movie—but on the last week of *every month*, calculate your next month's budget, identifying The Green Gap and deciding where you can both cut costs *and* increase your income. Strive for a bigger gap each month so the 45-45-10 formula works in your favor.

This must be done monthly because every month is different. If you get paid every two weeks, there are a couple of months when you'll get three checks. If you have a garage sale every spring, that is more income in May. Also, Christmas comes every December, so plan for it in November.

INVEST FOR YOUR FUTURE

When you drive a car, you probably buckle your seatbelt. And before you head to bed for the night, you probably lock your doors.

So why do some Christians question whether God allows prudent investing to secure their future?

Investing doesn't mean you don't trust God. It's only when *the pursuit of riches* becomes your focus that God questions your motives.

Setting aside 15 percent to 30 percent* of your paycheck after tithing to invest in conservative and well-managed retirement funds, a college fund, saving for a house, and other planned expenses is just good stewardship of the money God gives us. Not only does investing help defer instant gratification-type expenses, it also helps us become better long-term givers—instead of the reverse: having to ask for aid later in life.

If you are seeking financial advice on where and how to invest, be cautious not to take advice from your broke neighbor or the guy you sit next to at church who offers "the perfect plan." Do your research and find someone who is highly recommended. You have worked hard for your money. God trusts you with His money. Manage it well.

STOP TALKING NEGATIVELY ABOUT YOUR FINANCES

Proverbs 4:23 (GNT) tells us, "Be careful how you think; your life is shaped by your thoughts." God doesn't want you to put yourself down all the time. This is especially true if your finances are troubled.

Neuroscientists now know that the brain is designed to be goal-seeking; it responds to and acts upon the thoughts you think and the words you say.

Complaining about money, telling yourself you don't have enough, talking constantly about your financial stress—or thinking that money

---

* If you're following The Green Gap plan above, try to maximize the gap so that the 45 percent you invest matches 15 percent or more of your take-home pay. That's serious Oola investing.

is the root of all evil—could transform your life into the dire picture you're already painting for yourself.

And, by the way? Money is *not* evil, hard to manage, divisive, or any of the other myths we've heard since childhood. It's *the love of money* that is. Money is simply neutral. It's an amplifier. If you're kind, responsible, and generous, you will be more of that when you have more money. If you're selfish, indulgent, and greedy, guess what? You'll become more of that, too. Money simply makes you more of who you truly are.

ROUGH MATH

by Andy and Andrea Lahman

The room felt hollow and cold. The words, "It's not looking good," echoed off the walls and inside my head. I had heard him say these words many times before; this time the words felt distant, but the meaning of the words felt close and personal.

Tears welled up. I tried to blink them away. These monthly money talks have taught me to be good at that. But this time, I couldn't stop them. I felt them roll down my face and drip onto the floor of our cramped office. I looked down and away, avoiding eye contact, hoping he wouldn't notice. The pressure built in my chest, like an elephant was making itself comfortable there. It was a familiar pressure because this wasn't a new scenario.

It had become a cycle.

Month after month, my husband, Andy, would look over an Everest-like pile of bills and would report how we were doing. Most months, it felt hopeless. This month, it was completely overwhelming.

We were both schoolteachers. We had recently given birth to our first child, and we were instantly in love. We couldn't think of leaving him and dreamed of being home with him to raise him and be there for all the precious firsts.

We had done the rough math, and although we knew it would be tight and we would need to make sacrifices, we were confident

50

we could get it to work. Although we loved the dual income, travel, giving, five-dollar coffees, and trips to Target, these are easy sacrifices to make for the time we can't get back with our new baby.

Andy worked mornings, and I worked afternoons, and we traded parenting duties in the middle. Time with our new baby was totally a trade we were willing to make. This was perfect, at least in the beginning.

As time went on, we realized our math was wrong. Our optimism faded, and tension built. On my best days, I was discouraged about our situation and on my worst days, I was a stressed-out crying mess, balled up on the office floor. The choice was a risk, and we knew that.

Tonight, in the office, with tears rolling and almost unbearable financial stress, we could no longer see the gratitude in the precious time with our baby. All we could see were the bills piling up, and all we could feel was the tension building in our marriage.

The truth is, I am surprised we didn't hit this point sooner in our relationship. We are two people from distinct backgrounds and different upbringings when it comes to money. Andy grew up as a saver, and I grew up as a spender. Financially, he grew up planning for tomorrow, and I grew up living for today. So as the money tension built, he saw the need to tighten the strings, and I saw this idea as stifling, suffocating, and unbearable. My financial plan was "God will provide and it will all work out." But it didn't.

The reason I couldn't hold back the tears any longer is because although these monthly money meetings were usually stressful and full of tension, this one was different. We didn't fight. We were simply sad. We felt hopeless and defeated.

In this moment, we turned to Him. We were reminded of the biblical concept that those who are faithful with the small will become rulers of much. It was time to confront the problem, not simply acknowledge it monthly.

It was time for a plan. Our plan was to see what the Bible said about money. This is what we discovered:

1. Have a vision when it comes to your family's money. We were financial thermometers, and we needed to become thermostats. Thermometers simply report the temperature, whereas thermostats set the temperature. Instead of meeting monthly and checking how much money we had (or didn't have), we needed to devise a plan and direct our money toward what is best for our family. The Bible says that, "The noble make noble plans, and by noble deeds they stand." (Isaiah 32:8).

2. Then with big vision, spend an hour weekly looking over finances, making sure we aren't overspending in certain areas and continuing to flesh out our goals. "The plans of the diligent lead to profit as surely as haste leads to poverty." (Proverbs 21:5).

3. Be faithful with the small things. This means focusing on paying down debt, being sure to give even when we don't have much, and using restraint when it comes to frivolous spending. "His master said to him, 'Well done, good and faithful servant. You have been faithful over a little; I will set you over much.'" (Matthew 25:21).

4. Give! Even when we didn't have the rest of this figured out, my husband and I always tithed—and the LORD always provided for us. "Bring the whole tithe into the storehouse, that there may be food in my house. Test me in this," says the LORD Almighty, "and see if I will not throw open the floodgates of heaven and pour out so much blessing that there will not be enough to store it." (Malachi 3:10).

5. Focus! There *will* be things that try to throw us off our financial path, but we needed to stay focused on the bigger goal. We needed to be willing to sacrifice today to win tomorrow. "Let your eyes look directly forward, and your gaze be straight before you." (Proverbs 4:25).

6. Look at extra ways to make money. We are teachers, yes, but what else can we do to produce income for our family? I got started right away on a side hustle, and we are still blown away by what has transpired in six years. "Invest in seven ventures, yes, in eight; you do not know what disaster may come upon the land." (Ecclesiastes 11:2).

7. Ask for God's blessings. The Lord really does desire to bless His children. We know that all good gifts come from Him and that this money is really His anyway. We are thankful for the blessings He has given since we have been faithful these last few years. "And whatever you ask in prayer, you will receive, if you have faith." (Matthew 21:22).

For years, we worked our plan. We didn't work it perfectly, but we worked it diligently. Now, six years later, we are 100 percent debt-free including our home. *What!?* Didn't see that one coming. We both work flexible hours, and the initial dream of being available for our kids is a dream we can enjoy, without the weight of debt and financial stress on our family.

Was it easy? No. Was it worth it? Absolutely. Money isn't important, but the freedom it buys is. These days we think about money rarely, argue about it even less, and are free to live our life according to what we believe He has planned for us.

Have you ever wondered what God has planned for *you*—once your finances, debts, and cash flow are no longer a major stress in your life? With smart money decisions and CEO-like advice from Jesus—conserving, stewarding, and growing your wealth as He did with God's help—your calling could be something extraordinary and positive for the world.

◎ ◎ ◎ ◎

JESUS, CEO

"To those who use well what they are given,
even more will be given."

—MATTHEW 25:29 NLT

Jesus didn't know me personally; I was just one of the many in the crowd that would gather whenever we had the opportunity to learn from Him. On this particular day, as He was leaving the Temple grounds with His disciples, He stopped to share His insights. I had listened to Jesus speak many times before, and while I knew that He was teaching all of us, sometimes it felt like He was talking directly to me.

Shoulder to shoulder with the others, I leaned in and listened closely, knowing that just one word or one thought could change my life. Like I said, He didn't know me, but somehow it all felt very personal. On this day, Jesus began telling a story about three servants. What I heard challenged everything I had ever been taught.

Again, the Kingdom of Heaven can be illustrated by the story of a man going on a long trip. He called together his servants and entrusted his money to them while he was gone. He gave five bags of silver to one, two bags of silver to another, and one bag of silver to the last—dividing it in proportion to their abilities. He then left on his trip. (Matthew 25:14–15)

I marveled at how much the man in the story must have trusted his servants and wondered if anyone might ever trust me this much or in this way. Imagining myself in this scenario, I listened as Jesus went on to explain:

> *The servant who received the five bags of silver began to invest the money and earned five more. The servant with two bags of silver also went to work and earned two more. But the servant who received the one bag of silver dug a hole in the ground and hid the master's money. (Matthew 25:16–18)*

At first, I thought, *Wow! This master is kind and obviously wealthy.* But then I began thinking of the choices of the servants and tried to imagine the rationale behind their decisions. The choices made by the three servants intrigued me, and I wondered what I would do if I were given the money. Would I invest it and try and gain more? Or would I bury the money out of fear of losing what I had?

Jesus explained:

> *After a long time, their master returned from his trip and called them to give an account of how they had used his money. The servant to whom he had entrusted the five bags of silver came forward with five more and said, "Master, you gave me five bags of silver to invest, and I have earned five more."*
>
> *The master was full of praise. "Well done, my good and faithful servant. You have been faithful in handling this small amount, so now I will give you many more responsibilities. Let's celebrate together!"*
>
> *The servant who had received the two bags of silver came forward and said, "Master, you gave me two bags of silver to invest, and I have earned two more."*
>
> *The master said, "Well done, my good and faithful servant. You have been faithful in handling this small amount, so now I will give you many more responsibilities. Let's celebrate together!"*

Then the servant with the one bag of silver came and said, "Master, I knew you were a harsh man, harvesting crops you didn't plant and gathering crops you didn't cultivate. I was afraid I would lose your money, so I hid it in the earth. Look, here is your money back."

But the master replied, "You wicked and lazy servant! If you knew I harvested crops I didn't plant and gathered crops I didn't cultivate, why didn't you deposit my money in the bank? At least I could have gotten some interest on it."

Then he ordered, "Take the money from this servant, and give it to the one with the ten bags of silver. To those who use well what they are given, even more will be given, and they will have an abundance. But from those who do nothing, even what little they have will be taken away. Now throw this useless servant into outer darkness, where there will be weeping and gnashing of teeth." (Matthew 25:19–30)

At first, I was overwhelmed by this parable. And when Jesus finished and walked away continuing to talk with His disciples, I felt that I had so much to sort through. Finding a quiet place, I sat down alone and tried to figure it all out. *What was He saying? What did these outcomes mean? Was Jesus talking to me? Of course, He was! But how did it all relate it to my life?*

Is the story about money, talents, or both? If the master is God and God gives us talents and money, how can I use these talents and His money in a favorable way? Was I hiding the talents He has given me, burying them in the ground for no one to see, out of fear that I would fail? Was I making good decisions with my money, which belonged to Him and His Kingdom anyway?

Relieved, I realized that the answer to all of these questions floating around inside my head was—yes!

I was glad that I was unable to get this story out of my head as I walked the familiar streets on my way home because I wanted to take

His wisdom and further apply it in my own life. What clearly came to me was that I have talents and money, and both are gifts from God. And I need to use these talents and the money that God gave me to further His Kingdom and not my own selfish indulgences. I need to be a good steward of all I am trusted with. Also, I can't be lazy and live in fear; success in life is a product of our work and our action. I can't even begin to add up how many times I thought I wasn't good enough to be successful and make an impact on this world. My heart says go for it, and my mind says stop. Through this story, Jesus clearly taught me that God always gives us everything we need to do what He has placed in our hearts.

As I laid down to sleep on my mat that night, I stared up into the darkness and continued to ponder this story. I looked deeper into my life and started to think of the changes I could make from this point forward. As I thought about turning these ideas into actions, the deepest part of the story was revealed to me; I am going to be held accountable. I will be a good steward for my Master.

I closed my eyes and prayed that when the day comes that I meet my Creator, He will say to me, "Well done, My good and faithful servant."

What are you doing with the money that God has given to you? Is it in the right hands? When Jesus told the story above, He created an example for all of us to carefully steward our money—but most importantly, to bring God into the equation when we make financial decisions.

There's no option (or need) to take anything with us to Heaven. We enter this world with zero dollars—and we'll leave that way, too. It's up to us during our lifetime to prayerfully consider our financial decisions and recognize God as our source of plenty.

TITHE A PORTION OF YOUR
EARNINGS AND TIME

"Each one must give as he has decided in his heart, not
reluctantly or under compulsion, for God loves a cheerful giver."

—2 CORINTHIANS 9:7

The Bible is very clear that God wants us to tithe 10 percent (the word actually means "a tenth") of our income. It's God's money anyway. It flows to us through God's grace. So giving a portion to your local church recognizes not only the gift you've been given, but also the lock-step relationship God has with you in creating healthy finances in the first place. It puts God first in our lives. Plus, giving freely and joyfully releases money's control over us.

Tithing also allows His work to continue for others, helps you form a closer bond with those who receive the benefits of your tithes, and brings joy into your life. In fact, countless studies—including research from the National Institutes of Health—have shown that giving and self-sacrificing behavior activates that part of the brain associated with pleasure and social connection, creating a "warm glow" effect. It also releases endorphins, resulting in what's widely known as the "helper's high."*

In addition to money, you can also give of your time. Going on a missions trip, volunteering at a food bank, or helping an elderly neighbor with home repair are random acts of kindness that contribute to the well-being of God's people.

---

* According to UC Berkeley's online *Greater Good Magazine,* published February 1, 2010.

PAY OFF YOUR HOME MORTGAGE AS **QUICKLY** AS POSSIBLE

"The borrower is slave to the lender."

—PROVERBS 22:7b

If you've ever been debt-free—even for a few months—you know the feeling of lightness it can bring. If you haven't, imagine how liberating it would feel to have no payments of any kind. Perhaps that's why people describe debt as a crushing weight that's depressing, disheartening, and stressful.

God doesn't want this miserable existence for you.

If debt is a thing in your life—especially if it's compounding faster than you can pay it off—the time to act is now. Don't just make the minimum payments. Instead, find the extra money to knock out the smallest debts first, then roll that same extra money into making bigger payments on larger debts—*including paying off your home mortgage.*

While many financial advisors scoff at paying down a mortgage, the so-called "tax write-off" or "cheap money" benefits you get simply aren't worth the stress if something unexpected should happen. Once you're completely debt-free, you can put those mortgage payments toward building a secure retirement, sending your kids to college free of student loan debt, funding a special cause that God puts on your heart—or simply enjoying the life you've earned.

BUILD UP YOUR **SAVINGS** AND INVESTMENTS

"Be sensible and store up precious treasures;
don't waste them like a fool."

—Proverbs 21:20 CEV

One of the biggest stressors for Christians—and a ready source of conflict in marriages—is living paycheck to paycheck, spending everything you bring in, without an emergency fund or a savings account to carry you through a crisis.

If your savings are sketchy or nonexistent, take steps to build them up—with the initial goal of having at least three (and up to seven) months of living expenses put aside. For most people, that's $15,000 to $25,000.

After that, use the "pay yourself first" principle: after tithing, but before paying your bills, invest a fixed percentage of your pay-check into a Roth IRA, Traditional IRA, 401(k), or other investment vehicle—whether or not your employer offers a retirement plan and especially if you're self-employed. If your employer offers a match-ing retirement plan, so much the better; max out your contribution to take full advantage of the matching funds they'll put in for you. Experts recommend investing at least 15 percent of your net paycheck (more if you're over age fifty).

Once your emergency fund and retirement investments are han-dled for the month, consider saving even more for a large, upcoming purchase you're expecting to make, such as a home improvement, automobile, exotic vacation, or something else.

Saving and investing is your way of being a good steward of the money God has given you. It keeps you out of debt by allowing you to pay cash for major purchases. Plus, managing on what's left keeps your household expenses from expanding and becoming more important than God's presence in your life.

OOLA**FAMILY**

"As for me and my family, we will
worship the Lord."

—JOSHUA 24:15 CSB[*]

---

[*] Christian Standard Bible.

ociety seems to provide never-ending advice on how to manage a family. But while a white picket fence, two kids, and the annual vacation at Disney World might be society's prescription for the ideal family, for many Christians, this modern-day standard comes with a lot of disconnects.

GOD HAS A **GREATER** PURPOSE FOR YOUR FAMILY

Have you ever wondered what life would be like if you stopped pursuing the overscheduled, superficial, and pointless Instagram version of life—and *instead* asked God to reveal His purpose for your family?

Perhaps you're supposed to clean up a local river, fund a school in Africa, build a unique business, show kindness to an elderly neighbor, or help non-churched kids find Jesus. Lots of families have paved the way for new ways of thinking, acting, living, and appreciating just by the way they care about others and think outside the box. Plus it's a lot more enriching than playing *Fortnite* or spending hours on Facebook.

As a family unit, your crew is poised to play a key role in His Kingdom. Why not pray about it and ask for it to be revealed to you?

MAKE YOUR FAMILY A **PRIORITY**

While your family's relationship with God should be your top priority, your "inner circle" family relationships also deserve your highest commitment. This includes your spouse, if you're married, followed by your kids. And if you're single, it might be your ex-stepkids and siblings. If you have a grandparent, aunt, or "second mom" you grew up with, you might include them in this core group.

The key is to love unconditionally and be there for your core family. Codependency and enabling family members, however, is not cool. For instance, it's not your job to provide a permanent crash pad for your destitute uncle who needs somewhere to live but has no plan to get back on his feet. It's not your job to take in the niece who's addicted to meth simply because her mom "can't handle her." Give grace where it's needed, but find a middle ground: help from a distance, set boundaries, and put time limits on your assistance. Love these toxic relatives with two hands: one to hug them and one to figuratively smack them into a new way of moving forward in their lives.

IF YOU'RE NOT **WORKING** ON YOUR MARRIAGE, YOU'RE **WORKING** ON YOUR DIVORCE

When Dave was growing up, family meant everything. Yet at the height of his early success, he became the first of his family to go through a divorce. He discovered that, instead of working on his marriage, he'd been working on *everything but*.

If you're married, your highest priority in OolaFamily is your spouse. No exceptions. Invest in your marriage. Whether it's date nights, an evening walk, or frequent affectionate texts, be sure to focus quality time and energy on each other.

While your kids need attention, too, *more importantly*, they need to see what healthy love looks like in a marriage.

BLENDED, ADOPTED, UNCOUPLED: **IT'S COMPLICATED**

Today's Christian families are often as complicated as non-churched households. Between "step-this" and "co-that," managing how you interact with family members can get confusing. We've met virtually every combination, and our advice is this: be supportive, be kind, and be empathetic.

Love your core family members the same way Jesus does: recognize their strengths and weaknesses. Help them grow in maturity and wisdom. Appreciate their background and focus on the good they bring to the party. Help them flourish in their God-given talents.

If you need to work on your family dynamic—such as coping with a rebellious teenager, putting your marriage back on solid ground, dealing with addiction, or making decisions about aging parents—remember that prayer, faith-based programs, Bible wisdom, and even Christian counseling are great options. Pray together as a family, and keep God present in your household as you work through it.

But what if you're a Christian who's lost everyone, including parents, siblings, or kids? We've met many people in your shoes, whose family members passed away, abandoned them, or were so toxic that leaving was the only safe alternative. Our "family" advice for you is to develop family-like friendships in your community, church, and social circle. As the Baby Boomer generation ages and Millennials are waiting until later to marry and have kids, there are now millions of people who would like to be in close, loving, protective relationships that aren't necessarily bound by traditional family ties. Find them, welcome them, and invest in these valuable relationships.

SUIT UP AND **PROTECT** YOUR KIDS FROM **TOXIC** INFLUENCES

Of course, kids learn about real life from their experiences and the experiences of those around them. But today's "new normal" can expose our kids to traumatic, scary, and sometimes life-changing influences. Protect them.

This includes protecting them from *other family members* who are toxic. Step up and discuss bad behavior with your toxic siblings, cousins, grandparents—and, sadly, the myriad of new boyfriends, ex-spouses, and odd live-ins beleaguering your extended family.

Help your kids cope by building healthy boundaries *yourself*, and then teach them to "get ready" for those events when exposure is unavoidable. Arrive late, leave early, and steer clear of interaction while you're at obligatory holiday dinners, birthdays, and family reunions. Teach kids to let hurtful comments or inappropriate remarks land without harm—maturely and lovingly processing the junk that comes up.

And, by the way? Violence and harassment—of any kind—are grounds for immediate and definitive action. Protect your kids from physical and emotional abuse. They are God's gift to you. Don't endanger them. This includes bullying and the negative influences of social media—an easy thing to limit when threats start to appear.

LOOK UP

by Sarah Harnisch

Sometimes you're in a place where you're so weary, there is nowhere to look but up at the face of God. You have nothing left to give anyone. When you cry out, it seems He doesn't hear or listen. One cold, windy Monday afternoon, I yelled at God in my tiredness.

Then this weary mom heard the voice of God, and it changed everything for me.

I'd woken up that morning to the sound of screaming—loud screaming. I have five children who are homeschooled, and our oldest is nonverbal autistic. He was fourteen years old. His siblings were twelve, ten, eight, and six. His littlest brother had tossed a Lego at him to horse around. When I stepped into the living room, he had him by the throat, on the floor, and was shoving dog treats down his mouth until his lips were turning blue. He is not a bad kid—he just doesn't have the words to articulate how he feels, and he used strong, sometimes dangerous methods to communicate. I put my body between his and his little brother's as I was trained, taking the pounding myself, until he got up and walked over to his eight-year-old brother nearby.

He wanted his tablet. When Ben wouldn't hand it over, he slapped his face so hard that the imprint of all five fingers were on the little guy's cheek. And in a flash of forty-five seconds, I had two sons to care for and one to calm down.

Two weeks later, while we were on the way to church, he lost his temper because it was not silent in the van and put a pencil into his brother's knee cap. We were in the emergency room. There was blood everywhere. I had to watch him get charged with a felony and two misdemeanors—my autistic boy, who loves people, but has no words.

This had been going on for more than a decade—we continually consulted and trained with a team of twenty-seven different experts and professionals on how to reign it in. I juggled these daily battles minute by minute while homeschooling and carrying a full-time job that started at 4 AM. How could I do it better? How could all five of my kids feels safe?

I made the toughest choice I'd ever made as a momma: to put him in a school where they could work intimately with him and give him his words back. I would not see him for a year.

On my drive home, my whole world was turned upside down.

I'd not seen the sun for weeks. The song "Worn" from Tenth Avenue North came on the radio. The words dug so deeply into my heart. My soul, too, felt crushed by the weight of the world.

I pulled over to the side of the road and wept. I felt like a failure in all I did. I was a failure at my job. I was a failure as a mom. I was a failure as a wife. Sixteen years of homeschooling, and I felt I was a failure as a homeschool teacher. I was mediocre at all I touched, excelling at nothing and dropping everything to the floor. My family was paying the price for my inability to balance. My family was hurt because I had nothing left to give. I needed rest. I needed deep rest—the kind of rest an afternoon nap doesn't fix.

In that moment of brokenness, a little drop of sunlight touched my leg. In March in upstate New York, that's pretty rare. I saw it move across my leg. I stopped sobbing. Then I saw that little beam of light move across my van. It moved across the farmer's fields to my left and right until the entire van was bathed in sunlight. I got out of my van and looked up at the sky. There was not a single cloud anywhere. It was just me and God and the warm sunshine.

I yelled at the sky. "Why God? Why can't You let me rest? I didn't ask for all of this! I don't like my plate overflowing! Can I quit my job? Can my son be healed?" And loudly, audibly, I heard the words "No."

"I don't understand!"

And then—in my head—I heard "Because when you are weary, you rest in Me. When you are strong, you do it all by yourself. You take glory where glory doesn't belong. And until you learn to release to Me, your plate will be over full. Because in that place, you listen."

I sat for a few moments and realized what all of that meant. I had no release because I had to fix it all myself. But the Lord was telling me that I was carrying burdens that weren't mine to carry in my stubbornness.

I drove back up the hill and got out of my van in my driveway. I looked up. There were clouds for miles and miles and miles. The sun was gone. And I realized I'd seen a miracle in that farmer's field. God had opened the sky to speak to my heart.

A year later, my son came home.

Today, he is an amazing daddy to two little peanuts. He is a gifted graphic artist, with words and without violence. He is close with his siblings, and that makes my heart smile.

I've not learned it all. I'm not the perfect mom. I make more mistakes than I can count. I still hold tightly to too many things. But God in His faithfulness has pulled a few things off my plate. I have learned in small spaces that many of these battles are not mine to fight. I walk a little softer. I pray a little harder to a big God who loves to listen. Sometimes His answers aren't what I want to hear. But He knows the end of the story, and I do not—so I rest in Him. It is the King of

Heaven that we serve! Every trial is a chance to gather a testimony that someone else is going to need to hear on their own journey.

I've learned that broken is the very best place. It means you're ready to grow. I now put fears and doubts and worry for my family in a box and leave it in the arms of Jesus. He already died for all of those things! Those broken, hurt, weary places are where I can learn to love in the deepest ways possible.

Are you carrying burdens that aren't yours to carry? Are you, in your stubbornness, trying to be a Supermom or Superdad—suffering from fatigue, depression, and overwhelm instead? God is here to co-parent your family with you. He *knows* your family needs His protection, care, and wisdom, just as He provided this loving input to Jesus's family on Earth.

HE WAS EXACTLY
WHERE HE NEEDED TO BE

"Why were you searching for me?
He asked them."

—LUKE 2:49 CSB[*]

F rantically, I pushed my way through the crowd. My eyes scanned the sea of people moving in the opposite direction. My young son was lost. As I shouted his name over and over, I hoped that I would hear him respond to the sound of my voice.

How I could have misplaced the Savior of the world? I thought to myself as panic and guilt overtook my thoughts and actions. *What kind of mother was I?* Other, more carefree moms might say, "Don't worry. He'll be okay. He's a preteen and probably off with friends."

Of course, that was the attitude that got me here in the first place. Yes, at age twelve, my boy was on the brink of manhood. But to me, He was still my baby, and I needed to find Him.

For a brief moment, the stress of the situation took me back to when I first found out I was going to be a mother. I was just a teenager when I became pregnant, and the circumstances surrounding my pregnancy were anything but normal.

---

[*] Christian Standard Bible.

Six months after Elizabeth had become pregnant, God sent the angel Gabriel to Nazareth, a city in Galilee. The angel went to a virgin promised in marriage to a descendant of David named Joseph. The virgin's name was Mary. When the angel entered her home, he greeted her and said, "You are favored by the Lord! The Lord is with you." She was startled by what the angel said and tried to figure out what this greeting meant. The angel told her, "Don't be afraid, Mary. You have found favor with God. You will become pregnant, give birth to a son, and name him Jesus.

"He will be a great man and will be called the Son of the Most High. The Lord God will give him the throne of his ancestor David. Your son will be king of Jacob's people forever, and his kingdom will never end." (Luke 1:26–33)

I was honored and felt such an overshadowing of peace in my life that I said "yes" to something that would not only change my life, but also the world that I knew.

Living out that "yes," however, was something altogether different. I was pregnant and had all the emotions of a teen mom who went from planning a wedding to now planning a family. *How would my fiancé react to the news?* I thought. *Would we still get married? Would I be a single mom? What would everyone say about me in our little town of Nazareth?*

The commotion around me shook me from my thoughts and brought me back to the urgent situation at hand.

Please God, I prayed fervently.

"Jesus, Jesus!" I continued to shout as I kept looking for Him. People nearby probably thought I was losing my mind because of the look on my face. Still, frantically, I continued. I must find my son. Joseph was just as concerned.

As the last place we could look, we made our way back to Jerusalem where we'd been staying on our family trip. When I found Him,

I promised myself I would hold Him tightly and let Him know how much I loved Him.

Well, at least that is what I had planned to do.

> *After three days they found Him in the temple courts, sitting among the teachers, listening to them and asking them questions. Everyone who heard Him was amazed at His understanding and His answers. When His parents saw him, they were astonished. His mother said to Him, "Son, why have You treated us like this? Your father and I have been anxiously searching for You."*
>
> *"Why were you searching for me?" He asked. "Didn't you know I had to be in my Father's house?" But they did not understand what He was saying to them. (Luke 2:46–50)*

At first, we didn't understand. A temple? He should be with us! This was one of the last places I thought an adventuresome twelve-year-old would be. Yet He reminded me, "I am in my Father's house." Jesus was obedient to God first.

In that moment, my son taught me that even though He wasn't where I wanted Him to be, He was exactly where He needed to be. I was torn between what I wanted and what I *knew* what was right. And what was right was to start the difficult mom-process of letting go.

Although Jesus was perfect, His family wasn't. In fact, they were probably like a lot of modern-day families with multiple kids, scattered focus, and busy schedules. That's why Jesus *gets it* about your imperfect family relationships. And it's why He's there as a steadying hand in the midst of your daily lives. So how can you live and love like Jesus when it comes to your family?

BE A **SPIRITUAL LEADER** IN YOUR HOUSEHOLD

"Teach children how they should live, and
they will remember it all their life."

—PROVERBS 22:6 GNT

Family is central to our lives with Christ. In fact, God's intention is for families to be together and for parents to train their children in the ways of the Lord. A strong family is just good Oola. And *you* can take a leadership role, not only by growing stronger as a Christian yourself, but also by establishing Christ-centered family traditions such as Bible study, prayer time, regular church activities, saying grace at mealtimes, missions trips for older kids, and pro-active discussions at home about those behaviors and beliefs in which the Lord delights. This goes for dads, too, as well as moms—and especially for households led by single parents.

LOVE WELL

"He must manage his own family well.
His children should respectfully obey him."

—1 TIMOTHY 3:4

Patience, kindness, attentiveness—and even going against what society says is "standard" because you know what's better for each family member—these are the hallmarks of loving your family members well.

But loving well also comes with boundaries—just as Jesus set boundaries of good behavior and right action. Think about it as having *two hands* of love: one to hug, and the other to be firm. As a culture, too often we want to bundle our kids in Bubble Wrap, so they never experience pain. Our role is not to protect them from all pain but to teach them how to appropriately deal with the challenges that life will present.

Loving well also means accepting the things you cannot change—that's the meaning of unconditional love. Fight the good fight, yes. Do the best you can to guide, advise, and discipline. But in the end, you also have to love your child. Don't focus more on inflexible rules than forming a loving relationship and teaching your child to show this same love to others.

TRUST GOD WITH YOUR KIDS

"I will bless you with a future filled with hope,
a future of success, not of suffering."
—JEREMIAH 29:11 CEV

Most new parents don't know what fear is until they have a baby—with childhood providing an endless supply of things to worry about. Rest assured, however: God has good plans for your children's lives.

Unfortunately, however, too often we feel we're not able (or willing) to provide everything *society says* is "necessary" for children. If we don't spend the money necessary or get our kids into the necessary activities or send them to the right schools, then somehow they'll be left behind when compared to the rest of society. But worldly "success" is only man's definition of victory. All the worldly achievements imaginable will not provide the ultimate reward that comes from knowing Jesus: eternal life.

God will provide exactly what's needed for your children to fulfill the role He has in mind for them. And even after you can no longer be an ever-present and guiding force in their lives, God still will be there for them. You can trust Him with their future.

OOLAFIELD

"A man's heart plans his course, but
the Lord determines his steps."

—PROVERBS 16:19 BSB[*]

---

[*] Berean Study Bible.

f you think about what you do in an average week, the majority of your time is spent on the job. And whether you're a senior executive, a part-timer working around your school schedule, a stay-at-home parent—or even the founder of your own company—your career is one of the most defining aspects of your life.

So what does your career say about you?

Too often, modern society seems to push us into a career-driven existence—regardless of whether we're in the ideal field or even whether we enjoy going to work every day. Suddenly, what seems to matter is whether we have the right job title, make a respectable income, or work for a well-known company.

Even worse, sixty-hour workweeks are "impressive" because it means we're important, valued, or simply working to get ahead—even though this unsustainable schedule impacts our marriage, our kids, and our free time for maintaining a committed relationship with God.

JESUS UNDERSTOOD BALANCE
IN HIS WORK LIFE

Though Jesus was here to serve others—and to make the ultimate sacrifice—the Bible tells us that He also spent plenty of time with family and friends over good food and meaningful conversation. While you, too, are here to serve others and add value to this world—to share your gifts with a community of people—at the same time, you have to maintain balance.

Working late, rarely seeing your family, missing key volleyball games or important soccer tournaments, always running late for non-work activities you want to do or friendships you want to cherish—this is a sign that your career has become your focus.

CREATING WORK **BALANCE** AND RECLAIMING YOUR LIFE

While we're not recommending you impulsively quit your day job, stories *do* abound of people who have left their overstressed careers—even downgrading, if needed—and then emerged so much better financially as a result. If you've found yourself on a career path that was society's idea, your parents' idea, or your professor's idea—or if you simply googled "jobs that make the most money" and followed that path—you're likely to arrive at a certain age and say, *You know, that's not what I want. I don't have a life.* There should be no shame or conflict about changing careers or pulling back for the sake of your family, your marriage, and your own sanity.

If there's something else pulling at you—which is really just another way of explaining how God's purpose finds its way into our hearts—it's okay to make that leap to something new and explore a different path, as long as you have a plan to transition.

THE NUDGE

by Sarah MacKenzie

With a deep breath and unwarranted sense of confidence in my next move, I picked up the scissors. I looked in the mirror at the bad hair day that had lasted over a month, and I started to administer a self-cut. I didn't have fancy scissors or any training or experience. I simply felt the urge to cut my bad hair, and I acted upon it. I would love to tell you that as the first locks of hair fell to the sink below that I was concerned about the end result, but I wasn't. It felt like an "Edward-Scissorhands-meets-Paul-Mitchell" moment of pure perfection. The scissors seemed to flow effortlessly to the exact point and angle as I trimmed with surgical precision. With hair blanketing the sink and the floor below me, I looked in the mirror and wondered if Michelangelo felt the same as he looked up at the final painting of Genesis on the ceiling of the Sistine Chapel.

I followed the smell of coffee out of the bathroom and into the kitchen where my mom and her friend were enjoying light weekend conversation and a cup of dark roast. My heart started to quicken, and time slowed, as their eyes drifted away from their conversation and toward my freshly chopped creation. I waited with anticipation for a disappointed response and a "what the heck were you thinking" comment. But, to my surprise, I heard, "Wow, your hair looks great. Did you do that yourself?" Funny thing is that I almost lied, but with an insecure shakiness to my voice, I said, "*Yes!*" and walked out the front door. I returned to university and received similar compliments and questioning. These compliments and my answers turned the remainder of my college years into time split between late-night study sessions, completing my sociology degree, and turning my dorm room into a makeshift hair salon for my friends.

With my sociology degree firmly in hand, I felt the nudge to move across the country. I acted on it and moved to a city where I knew some family and friends. I decided it was time to settle down and become an adult. I quickly put my hard-earned sociology degree to work and got a job in a residential program helping women in crisis. After some time there, the residents learned of my secret skill and asked if I could put my talents to good use and offer them haircuts. I obliged and reopened my makeshift hair salon. I will never forget the look on one lady's face when she looked at herself in the mirror. She had just gone through a rough chapter in her life and was looking for a fresh start. After I had finished, I handed her a mirror, and with a Julia Roberts–sized smile on her face and Bambi tears in her eyes, she exclaimed, "It's me. I'm back; it's me." It was in this moment that I felt another nudge, this time to become a hairstylist. I had no idea how a sociology degree would contribute to that, but I knew I had to do it.

I listened.

Halfway through my cosmetology program, and with the scent of perm solution in the air, I started to question everything. *Why did I cut my hair that boring Saturday afternoon in college? Why did I move across the country?* And most compelling was the question, *Why did I leave my career at the residential program and go back to school to become a hairstylist?* I felt like I was taking a step backwards. While my friends were going back to university to get their master's degree, I was going back to college to do something entirely different. In the midst of this inner personal struggle, I heard a knock at the classroom door. A strange man walked in and asked if he could speak to me. Nervous and confused, I walked over to him. He proceeded to ask me if I would be interested in going on a missions trip to Mexico to do free haircuts for the poor. His words didn't speak to my mind; they spoke to my heart. A familiar nudge penetrated my soul. It wasn't that I wanted to go, but I needed to go. I didn't know why or how, but I knew that this is something I needed to do.

It would be four years before I would go on one of these trips with him to do free haircuts in poor communities, in the prison, and at an orphanage for children with special needs. And four more years before I would find myself in an extended two-month outreach program, traveling throughout Mexico and offering free haircuts to those in need. On one of my stops in Mexico City, I was introduced to the heart-wrenching reality of human trafficking. A salon was set up in the largest red-light district in all of Latin America with the purpose of serving the girls who were forced to work the streets and providing them a safe place to be cared for in a practical, dignified, and welcoming way.

On my third day there, twelve years after cutting my hair in the bathroom, I felt my purpose being lived out. In a moment, it all came together. It all made sense. This is the reason I studied to be a hairstylist. This was why I also studied sociology. This is why I volunteered for missions. This was the reason for all of my random education, work, and volunteer experience—all wrapped up in one incredible package that would make a positive difference in the world. This was God's purpose for my life. Every nudge I felt and acted on, even when it didn't make sense, led to this moment. This is what I needed to do, but how? This would mean that this small-town girl from Brookfield, Nova Scotia, would again have to abandon everything and move to one of the largest cities in the world. I wrestled with this for fourteen months before I decided to once again follow my heart. In May of 2014, I sold everything, grabbed my passport and my one-way ticket, and boarded a plane to Mexico City.

And it is from here, a modest 700-square-foot apartment on the third floor in the heart of bustling Mexico City, that I tell my story. Since arriving, we have set up an employment project to help these strong, brave, and beautiful women find alternative ways to survive. I know someday when their journey of restoration is complete, they, too, will have stories to share that will inspire and change the world.

What started as a bored, impatient girl acting on an urge to give herself a haircut has turned into a calling of fighting on the front lines for freedom and justice and helping the exploited and broken find their own voices. God can take what is literally in our hands and use it to shape the world we live in to reflect more of His love if we listen to the urges in our heart.

What skill or knowledge or expertise have you developed in your career that God can use in unexpected ways? Have you ever thought about the "right livelihood" you would pursue if God were doing your job placement? The Bible is filled with people who played a major role in God's kingdom, though, by today's standards, their skills were not impressive.

Could you be the modern-day fisherman, fruit merchant, or basket weaver who becomes the catalyst for some monumental shift in the world *because you let God lead you in your career?*

FISHING WAS IN OUR DNA

"They left everything and followed Him."

—LUKE 5:11b BSB

I awoke to the sun as it cracked the horizon. Its light shimmered across the Sea of Galilee and into my eyes. I tried to shut them tighter and get more sleep, but the scent of sea air began to awaken all my senses. I licked my dry lips and tasted the salt that had settled on them through the night. The ache in my joints told me it was going to be a humid day at work as I pulled my body up from the cedar-and-oak floor of our wooden boat. This was a very common feeling as fishing for a living was not an easy profession. Through the heat of the day and the chill of the night, we fished to keep our company successful, provide for our families, and feed the people in our community.

I walked around the maze of sleeping fisherman, navigating the fastest route to the trammel net that was cast before we slept. I grabbed onto the net. This moment of excitement never gets old. I wanted to feel heavy resistance of a big catch. I gave it a tug, but it felt light. We had the nets out all night and caught nothing. A light catch happened from time to time, but nothing? *What was going on?* I thought to myself.

My brother John and I had a very successful family fishing company, and fishing came naturally to us. It was not only a way of life for many in our village of Capernaum, but our dad had trained us since we were children. Fishing was in our DNA. Not only did we have the training, we had all the tools we needed to flourish in this industry. We had employees, boats, and customers, but today we didn't have any luck catching what we needed. I looked across the sea and realized no one was having any success, not even our business partner Simon and his crew; their nets were empty, as well.

I started the morning ritual of carefully cleaning the nets so they wouldn't wear out or tear, then started preparing for another day of fishing. *I would rather be cleaning, preparing, and selling fish*, I thought to myself as we brought the boats to shore. We needed a much-deserved break from last night's disappointing effort before we had to head back out to sea.

As we pulled up our boat next to our friend Simon's, we noticed a crowd had gathered on the shore. This was uncommon for so early in the day. But when I saw a man talking to the growing circle of people, I quickly recognized that it was Jesus. As the crowd pressed in on Him to listen to the Word of God, He stepped toward Simon's boat and asked to be taken a little way offshore so He could better address the people. It had been a long, unproductive night, and I'm not sure I would have said yes, but Simon politely honored His request, let Him board, and pushed off from shore.

Jesus sat in the boat and preached to the crowd. We listened intently as His voice echoed over the water, and we watched as His message resonated with so many hearts, including ours. He proclaimed constantly the unconventional message of good news.

When He finished speaking, He made a strange request.

> *When Jesus had finished speaking, He said to Simon, "Put out into deep water and let down your nets for a catch."*
>
> *"Master," Simon replied, "we have worked through the night without catching anything. But because You say so, I will let down the nets." When*

they had done so, they caught such a large number of fish that their nets
began to tear. (Luke 5:4b–7)

Before long, I heard Simon yelling. I turned and saw him waving
in excitement for me to come out to his boat. As I approached, I saw it
filling up with water from the weight of all the fish. I couldn't believe
my eyes. They had more fish than they could handle. The nets were
starting to tear, so I grabbed on to help and realized that my hands
were on the net of a harvest that was beyond my wildest dreams.

Exhausted, we worked to get all the fish into both boats. Our
prayers were answered. This was going to be a great windfall for our
business. And after this catch, you'd think that we would be planning
for business expansion and even more boats. But the next thing I witnessed changed my life forever: Simon dropped to his knees and said,
"Oh Lord, please leave me. I am too much of a sinner to be around you."

My eyes flickered slowly to the face of Jesus as I also began to
realize the magnitude of what had just happened.

Yet Jesus looked down at Simon and replied, "Do not be afraid;
from now on you'll be fishing for people."

We had just pulled in the largest catch of our lives. Our parents
would be proud, and our village would tell stories about this day's
catch for years. But the tearing of the nets and the straining of the
boats were like a breaking down of the traditions and mind-sets we
all had adopted over time. In that moment, we realized it wasn't just
the fish that were caught, but Jesus caught us—hook, line, and sinker.
On the best day of our career, we realized that we needed to quit our
jobs because Jesus was calling us for something greater.

At the same time that the fish had flooded our boats, questions
and self-doubt flooded my mind. As we turned our boats back to
shore, I asked myself over and over if I was worthy of such a purpose.
I knew that I was a hard worker and a great fisherman, but did I have

the skills to follow this man and become a fisher of men and women? What would my family think of me abandoning the family business to follow this new-found calling? My mind told me that I was crazy, but my heart knew that this was what I needed to do.

Our boats listed and groaned as they finally landed on the rocky beach. We got out and—leaving our gains to our family and workers —immediately started following Jesus. I have no idea where this new career choice will take me, but I go in faith that this is exactly what I should be doing.

Praying about your ideal calling in life and stepping out in faith to follow God's lead is one of the scariest—but most rewarding—things you will ever do. While His plan might be for you to simply expand what you're doing in your existing career, it could also be a complete 180-degree turn into another field that will uplevel everything you do—from the people you know, to the money you make, to the satisfaction and balance you achieve in life.

Working in the field that *God calls you* to pursue—now that's Oola.

LOVE IT OR LEAVE IT

"Commit your work to the Lord, and
your plans will be established."

—PROVERBS 16:3

If you're dissatisfied with your current work, welcome to the crowd; an estimated 70 percent of people hate their job.* What could be worse?

---

* Gallup, January 15, 2017: *www.gallup.com/poll/180404/gallup-daily-employee-engagement.aspx.*

Investing eight to ten hours a day in a job you hate and then bringing that misery home and creating a toxic life *outside* the office, too.

Dissatisfaction with your current work might be God's way of nudging you to look for something more meaningful. If you've considered leaving your job or changing careers altogether, our advice is this: *don't do it without a plan.* While it's great to have faith that God will provide, create a transition plan between your current job and finding a new one so your financial life doesn't become a train wreck. Save a year or two of living expenses. Arrange for part-time consulting work while you're building that new business. Pay your utilities six months in advance. And cut back on your lifestyle until you've transitioned and are making ample income again.

But also consider whether this is the right time to make a move. Having faith in God also means having faith in His timing. If it's your season to stay put, find ways to love your job or the people you serve or the work you do. While you may not enjoy analyzing reports or managing processes every day, consider who you're helping or how you can make it more enjoyable—including asking for a promotion, improving the negative energy around the office, or getting permission to bring entirely new operating methods into your workgroup.

ALWAYS BE OF SERVICE

"Work with enthusiasm, as though you were working for the Lord rather than for people."
—EPHESIANS 6:7 NLT[*]

Have you ever wondered about the ultimate purpose behind the work you do? How does your product or service improve people's

* New Living Translation.

lives (if you're an entrepreneur), and if you're employed by someone else, how do people benefit from your work product?

Striving to be of service helps us be more like Jesus who lived the ultimate example of a life of service: healing, teaching, and making lives whole. Whether you're in a technical field or a creative role, whether you're in retail, manufacturing, service delivery, consulting, or something else, consider the service aspect of what you do and strive to be people-focused, first and foremost.

STAY RELEVANT IN YOUR CAREER SKILLS

"Work hard and become a leader;
be lazy and become a slave."

—PROVERBS 12:24 NLT

Today's digital world—and the new technologies that are being developed almost daily—require that we step up and keep up on relevant skills for our industry. This isn't always easy, especially if your job doesn't require using these applications on a daily basis. If you're not a digital native, start looking around for classes you can take—or simply commit to adopting one new technology per quarter to see how far you get.

Of course, we're not talking about getting consumed by yet another social media platform. But think about it: communications devices, modern research methods, new ideas for managing or marketing your business, and today's parenting trends are all ways to improve your skill set without letting your focus be pulled away by society at large.

You can also begin studying "best practices" in your field, industry, or profession. Seek out a mentor who can guide you in what you need to know for your field* or—if you're an entrepreneur—find a noncompetitive company who's doing things right, and take steps to learn from them.

By learning new technology and studying best practices, you'll become more valuable to your employer, clients, and colleagues. This also goes for increasing your industry knowledge, too, by reading the latest books, white papers, and online articles.

---

* One of the best kept secrets for finding mentors is SCORE, formerly the Service Corps of Retired Executives, who will advise you for free. Their 10,000 mentors are active and former executives and business owners who have wisdom and contacts to share. There are 300 chapters across the United States.

OOLAFAITH

> "We must believe that God is real and rewards
> everyone who searches for Him."
>
> —HEBREWS 11:6 CEV

F or Christians, faith isn't just belief in God—it's an active relationship with Him. It's practicing gratitude for what He's given you—sending up high-fives when He helps you win, asking for His grace, help, or comfort when you need it most, and being open to Him bringing good into your life. It's what Jesus taught us to do.

The reality is that God wants a loving and caring relationship with you. He'll show up in ways that are better than you'd ever imagine, but as Hebrews 11:6 tells us, *you have to seek Him out.* Your Christian walk is a two-way street.

WHAT ARE YOU DOING TO SPEND MORE TIME WITH GOD?

Growing up, being "faithful" meant going to church on Sundays. Today, there are tons of ways to stay connected to God the other six days of the week, as well. If you've found yourself too busy to work on growing stronger in your Christian walk, why not look at what you *are* spending time on and then reallocating a few hours a week for a small group meeting, Wednesday night Bible study, morning meditations, or even exchanging vacation time for a missions trip.

Lots of Christians are fans of meditation—spending quiet time every morning with God and choosing a Scripture to contemplate.

In fact, Joshua 1:8 tells us to meditate on God's instruction both *day and night.* One easy way to start is to work your way through Proverbs, choosing one verse every morning or night and then spending ten to fifteen minutes contemplating: *What does God want to show me today?*

Finally, when you consider other ways to spend more time with God, ask yourself, *What did Jesus do to keep in close relationship with*

His Father? The Bible gives us countless examples. As you read, try to find those that not only resonate with you, but which you can also practice in your own life.

SPEAKING OUR FAITH IS ANOTHER WAY TO GET PLUGGED IN

Proverbs 18:21 tells us that "Life and death are in the power of the tongue." So another way to get plugged into the life-affirming force of God's presence is to declare verbally the positive things that God Himself has said over us. *I am chosen. I am beautiful. I am created to do good works*—these are all statements that affirm we are wonderful, special, and loved by God. In fact, *Bible.org* has a Scripture-based list called *Who Does God Say That I Am?* which you can include in your prayers and meditations.*

And there are popular Oola affirmations† that will help you declare your gratitude and confidence to the Lord. *Affirmations* are vividly detailed statements you can recite that help the brain focus on bringing about your desires—in this case, an awesome relationship with God.

Sometimes we just have to speak it to believe it.

REBOOT, RESTART, **RECONNECT**

If you're a Christian who long ago got turned off to "organized religion"—if you'd like to reconnect to God but aren't active in a church—there are still easy ways to get back into relationship with Him and learn more about how Jesus says we should live.

---

* Find the list at *bible.org/article/who-does-god-say-i-am*.

† You'll find Oola affirmations plus colorful affirmation wristbands at *www.oolalife.com/store/bands*.

What can you do?

Start with prayer. It doesn't have to be anything formal: just a heartfelt message that says, *Hey, Lord, thanks for all the blessings you've given me. Thanks for watching out for me in times of trouble.* Prayer is a way to stay connected, and it can be done anytime, anywhere.

Next, add a daily study of some kind, whether it's reading the Bible or a daily devotional or simply a book of insightful teachings. Find one that you can keep on your nightstand and read it every morning and night to learn more about how God supports us and loves us— and how He wants us to live our lives.

Finally, find a church that resonates with you. Attend services at several churches in your town before deciding where you fit in and where you believe you can be an active member.

HOLDING HANDS

by Denette Jacob

stared up at the weathered cross on the top of our old country church. The fresh white paint made it look new again; however, the worn wood told the real story. The cross atop our old country church looked how I felt, shiny on the outside, but tired underneath. I needed to be here today.

My husband held my hand as we walked across the gravel parking lot to the cracked concrete steps. I held onto the steel pipe railing for extra support as I climbed the seven steps that led to the heavy oak front door. I can run up any flight of steps you throw in front of me, but these seven steps, on this day, made my legs feel weak.

I walked in and was surrounded by the beige and light green accents on the ceiling that my family and friends helped to paint. We made our way to our regular pew, six rows up on the left. The warm light from the colorful stained glass windows that adorned both sides of the church filled the space. My husband Rod held my hand the entire way.

With my husband still holding my hand and giving it an extra squeeze as if to say, "It's going to be okay, Hon," I started praying. I needed God. I needed to know He was there and that He's got this. I couldn't believe I was being tested yet again.

Just yesterday, it wasn't Rod holding my hand. I was holding hers. It was Hazel. All I could think about was squeezing her little hand as it rested in my palm. I squeezed it tightly. As I felt her soft skin against my thumb, I turned my hand to study the little creases in her knuckles and her tiny baby fingernails. The dramatic contrast between her warm hand and the cold stainless-steel bedrail in my other hand shook me. I tucked her precious hand into her blanket and cried as they wheeled her to surgery. Hazel is my one-year-old granddaughter, and she has cancer.

It seems the timeline of my life has been dotted with a lot of hand-holding.

As a small girl I held my dad's hand when feeling unsure as he dropped me off for my first night away from home.

I held Rod's hand, though others said we we're too young to marry, as we committed our lives together in marriage when I was nineteen.

With each child we welcomed into the world, I held their tiny little hands in mine while counting all ten fingers and toes and cried knowing they were going to be okay.

Through all these milestones, while I was using one hand to hold the hand of someone I loved, I felt someone holding my other hand. It was God. He was there with me. I could feel it.

These were moments of gratitude and required faith to know that He was there—with me.

But what about the other moments? The moments like today?

The time my husband held my hand in fear that I would fall to the floor after hearing our healthy, seventeen-year-old son had cancer?

Or the time I held Jared's hand as he took his last breath?

Through these tragic life events, although challenging, over time I did learn to be grateful and have faith. Not just in the good moments, but in all life would offer. Trusting Him. Trusting His plan. Trusting He was holding my hand. And trusting He sees what I do not.

But today, it is different. She's one year old. I don't get it, and I don't know if I can feel Him holding my hand.

As I try to pray, I feel anger moving in as if working to force the faith out of my body. I repeat what I have told myself countless times before: "Be grateful and have faith." God has a plan for this. But does He? Is He there? How could a loving God do this?

I thought back to a poem from my childhood that hung on the wall of our old farmhouse. It was a poem about a man who had a dream that he was walking along a beach with the Lord.* As he walked, scenes of his life were flashing across the sky. For each scene, he noticed footprints in the sand, one belonging to him and one to the Lord. After watching his life play out in the sky, he noticed that when he was going through good times, there were two sets of footprints in the sand, but when he was going through difficult times, there were only one. Confused, he asked the Lord why He left him during the bad times—moments when he needed Him the most. The Lord answered him and said, "I didn't leave you during the difficult times; I carried you."

I needed the Lord to carry me right now, to prove that He was there, because my body was weak, and my faith was waning.

I remembered the words spoken in church on the day we buried our son Jared. Through the tears, confusion, and questions, I heard, "These precious gifts that we call children are on loan to us from God. They are His children and not ours. It is our job to love them, feed them, clothe them, and care for them. But, at any time, God might call his children back home, and then it is our job to let them go."

I prayed over that statement from years ago, trying to latch on to something, anything, that would restore my faith. Nothing came. I was confused. I had questions.

---

* The poem is called "Footprints in the Sand."

This isn't the first time my faith had been challenged. When God took Jared from me, I had endless questions. Why him? Why now? Why have you put me on this path? God took Jared, but I didn't leave God. Instead, I grasped His hand harder. I held Him in gratitude and stayed with Him in faith. I stayed, knowing that He sees things and understands things that I never will, like the marriage that should have broken apart after losing a child but has been made stronger than ever by faith. Like the family that should have drifted apart because of the pain of a lost son and brother and yet was brought closer because of our faith.

As I left our old country church that day and descended the steps for the short trip home, I realized that God has held my hand and will carry me when I need it the most.

Today, our precious Hazel, through constant prayer and with the dedication of countless people to her healing, has overcome the odds and is cancer-free. I know He was there through it all, and will always be there—holding my hand.

Was there ever a time when *you* could have lost all faith but didn't? Those are times when God holds our hand. We survive and grow in faith as a result.

But what about situations that stretch out for years, causing daily pain and anguish? What if you've tried everything to get past it, to the point where your faith—*in anything*—is waning? As we'll learn in the next story, sometimes having faith and turning to Jesus is our last resort.

FAITH WAS MY LAST RESORT

"Go in peace. Your suffering is over."

—MARK 5:34b NLT

pulled open the flimsy door and felt the morning air rush into my humble home. I looked up at the heavens to get a quick judge of the weather and to say a silent prayer before I went out into the world. The knots in my stomach called cadence to the army of goose bumps that were standing at attention on my arms.

I was scared.

It was as if I was going into battle. I had one foot in the house and one foot out. The contrast of the warm stale air inside and the cool fresh air outside amplified my internal question of going back to bed in fear or stepping outside in faith. If this was going to work, I had to go all the way. I took a deep breath as I covered my disheveled hair in an attempt to make myself invisible and began walking down the pebbled street.

What I was doing was illegal, and it was against what my religion had taught me, but I didn't have a choice. This wasn't about dishonoring my family, religion, or the laws but about getting the chance to live.

I was sick with an illness I'd had for more than a decade. Of course, I'd tried all the cures, but no one had been able to help me. It wasn't my lack of asking—in fact, I consulted every doctor and tried every

97

man-made remedy I could find. I spent everything I had to get well. And because I'd exhausted my resources, defying the law was my only option.

Afraid, but with a hopeful heart, I put one foot in front of the other—despite the dire consequences of being seen or being caught.

We all have issues: illnesses, relationship issues, past guilt, hidden addictions, and more. Some of us are able to sweep them under the rug, some issues are elephants in the room, and some issues are held so close that not even the people closest to us are aware of them. I had a bleeding issue that wasn't my fault, and yet it disgraced me. The rules of society said I was unwelcome, that I was underserving of love, wholeness, and acceptance.

Eventually, I found myself alone and fighting to fix this issue. I'd become financially and emotionally bankrupt. The daily pain and discomfort, the hopelessness, and the seclusion had brought me to the end of my rope.

But I'd heard of a man named Jesus who was traveling through my town on his way to heal a sick twelve-year-old girl. Rumor had it that nothing scared Him. From sickness and disease to even hanging out with a mischievous bunch who didn't always have a good reputation, it seemed Jesus didn't care about people's scary issues; he cared only about the people themselves.

I was desperate to find Him and ask Him to heal me.

Up ahead, in a crowd of people, I saw Him.

The closer I got, the harder it was to move. The crowd was closing in on me. Step after step, the fear became insurmountable, but I persisted. What would people think if they saw me, and what would happen if my only chance to get well actually failed?

I was afraid. But my faith was stronger.

In that moment, I realized that faith isn't the absence of fear—it's believing in something despite it. You can't see the wind as it pushes the dust across the desert, but it is there. My faith is the same as that wind, and I felt it pushing me toward Jesus.

With each step closer, my faith grew. And with everything in me, I pushed my way through the heavy crowd. I could see Jesus up ahead. There were so many people, but I was determined. If I could just touch the hem of His garment, I knew I would be healed. But as the crowd suddenly pressed in on me, I stumbled to the ground. I couldn't miss my chance, so I reached for His cloak. And instantly I felt healed.

> *At once Jesus realized that power had gone out from him. He turned around in the crowd and asked, "Who touched my clothes?"*
>
> *"You see the people crowding against you," his disciples answered, "and yet you can ask, 'Who touched me?'"*
>
> *But Jesus kept looking around to see who had done it. Then the woman, knowing what had happened to her, came and fell at his feet and, trembling with fear, told him the whole truth. He said to her, "Daughter, your faith has healed you. Go in peace and be freed from your suffering. (Mark 5:30–34)*

I stood there in wonder, with a clean and healed body, as the crowds slowly moved away and continued following behind Him. By simply trusting my faith and touching the cloak of Jesus Christ, my life was forever changed. I had to break the law and go outside the barriers of man-made rules to get to Him.

But the beauty of what I discovered in that moment was more than a healing. Jesus affirmed my faith. He didn't call me unclean or judge me; He showed me that faith and trusting Him were more than a religious act. Faith is hope, an understanding that He is there with me at all times, even in seasons of complete isolation and despair.

◎ ◎ ◎ ◎

What's chronic in your life? Whether it's an illness or a bad habit or a crazy relationship or some other cross to bear, realize that simple everyday faith goes a long way. As you work toward Oola and toward getting closer to God, here are some ways to actively live your faith.

The results may surprise you.

MAKE IT **PERSONAL**

"Listen! I am standing and knocking at your door."
—REVELATION 3:20 CEV

This isn't your parents' Christian walk. As our modern-day world has gotten more and more complicated, being in relationship with God has actually gotten easier. It's less fearful, more loving, and more forgiving than the fire-and-brimstone religion of our forefathers. It's fun and a lot less serious. And anyone who's attuned to the damage caused by random violence, broken marriages, and financial ruin through covetousness can see that His commandments are protective, not punitive.

God has a loving nature, and—as Scripture tells us—He wants a *personal* relationship with us. He's simply waiting for us to show up and create this bond in whatever way works for us. So whether you get up early to read the Bible, practice daily gratitude, or feel His presence when you're out in nature, appreciating what's around you, God is available and eager to connect with you. When you do, Zephaniah 3:17 says, "He will rejoice over you with gladness."

Remember, too, that your faith is *your faith*. We're not dictating anything here. Whatever form your relationship with Jesus takes is between the two of you.

LISTEN UP

"Be still, and know that I am God."

—PSALM 46:10 NIV

How often do we ask God for something, but don't stop our hectic pace long enough to listen to His answer? While this beloved Psalm is a favorite of many Christians, most don't know that *Be still,* literally translated, means *Shut up!*

When you ask for wisdom, help, mercy, or anything else but then keep lurching forward with your own solutions, you're not allowing God to show up for you. When you bring your problem to God but then still hold onto the fear and anxiety of the situation, you're saying, *Lord, I trust you—but not really.* You're losing ground in your faith walk.

To truly practice *being still,* try quieting your mind through meditation. The Christian meditation app called Abide* has meditations for all kinds of topics (all based on Scripture), as well as bedtime stories that help you sleep better in the midst of worry. It's used by church leaders, Christian therapists, and even Grammy award-winning singers.

ACTIVATE IT

"Faith without deeds is dead."

—JAMES 2:26 NLV

Think back to the day you received Christ. You accepted Him as your Savior and, to the best of your ability, you began living and loving like Jesus. While it may have been recently or decades ago, in

---

* For iPhone, iPad, and iPod Touch. Supports iOS Family Sharing. Annual subscription required.

the days immediately after your baptism, you probably wanted to "do everything right." You actively practiced your faith in Jesus. You probably prayed regularly, belonged to a small group, read the Bible, and looked for other ways to be around other believers.

Well, how is your faith walk today?

If it could use a little more activation, why not invite Jesus even more into your life with a simple prayer like: *God, today I recognize that You love me and that I need You. Thank You for sending Your Son Jesus to die for me. I know that I have made mistakes. Please come into my life and make me new.*

You can also shake things up with one or two new faith practices each quarter. Sign up for the church outreach in your community. Register for the women's retreat in the spring or the men's houseboat trip this summer. Do an organized couples' night out with other believers. Join a deep-dive Bible study on the Old Testament or Revelation. Or, subscribe to a podcast or streaming service for lectures from Christian leaders and noted authors.

Get active beyond just going to church on Sundays and studying the Bible during the week. It might even mean changing churches to one that resonates more with you and your new outlook. There's no right or wrong. But considering the sheer variety of worship styles, messages, teaching methods, fellow parishioners—even music— there's a church home where you'll feel inspired to not only grow as a Christian but to create a closer relationship with God, too.

CHAPTER
8

OOLAFRIENDS

"Friends always show their love."

—PROVERBS 17:17a NIV

One of our friends is Willie Morris, the founder of Faithbox, a monthly subscription of Christian reading material and inspirational décor. When we first met Willie while rolling the OolaBus through Manhattan, collecting dreams, we incorrectly assumed the Faithbox team would be an elitist group of hard-core Christians. Nothing could be further from the truth.

"We dig your vibe about Christianity because we've had some mixed experiences," Troy pointed out. "What's your philosophy on doing it right?"

With a confident smile and a friendly gaze, Willie picked up his electric longboard, walked toward our VW Surf Bus, and replied. "It's pretty simple," he said. "Don't be a Richard."

Uh, he didn't say Richard, but you know what we mean. And so true, right?

Isn't it easier to model Jesus's friendships—and befriend people in the first place—when you're kind, loving, and helpful?

REAL FRIENDS DON'T KEEP JESUS A SECRET

To further the point—*let's be candid*—some of the most judgmental people around are actually devout believers. They know the Bible backwards and forwards. They've read every Christian advice book. They're fans of all the top Christian talk shows. But while that's amazing—and something to be admired—what *isn't cool* is their disdain for others who aren't quite there yet.

Our advice is this: you be you. Be authentic and bold in your Christian faith. But don't put others down for taking baby steps toward Christ right now.

Besides, who did Jesus hang out with? The Pharisees and leading scholars of the day? Did they all sit around the synagogue declaring, *You're amazing. No, Dude, you're amazing. Guys, we're all amazing.*

Hardly.

Jesus hung out with prostitutes and criminals and gamblers *because they needed His message.* He reached out to ordinary people and said, "I love you, and I believe in you. Let me show you *another path* than the crazy way you're trying to do in this life right now."

Ultimately, we believe this is what Oola friendship is all about for Christians: challenging each other as believers to love and befriend others as Jesus would do.

Of course, it's great to have Christian friends—surrounding yourself with positive people who reinforce your message and growing spiritually together. But, *man,* you are missing out on *why you're on this planet* if you're not reaching out to people who are struggling in a way that loves them unconditionally and shows them on a daily basis what living God's way looks like. Be generous, be kind, be loving, and be supportive. Don't just hang out with the "cool" kids. Love everyone. Reach out and talk to people you wouldn't normally talk to and show them what a Christian lifestyle looks like in a way that encourages them to think, *Wow, I want what you have.*

When they get to the point where they want to find out more, you can say, "Hey, I know. I struggled, too. But I found Christ and He taught me some principles to live by."

That scenario will bring more people to Christianity than pounding Bible verses into their head and making them feel bad about the choices they've made. Think of kindness and openheartedness as outreach. It's you bringing people to God just by being a good human being.

◎ ◎ ◎ ◎

522 FRIENDS

by Stephanie Jones

'm an introvert. Give me a good book, a blanket to snuggle up in, a mug of tea, and I'm a happy girl. I could go weeks without leaving my home and be content. Interacting with strangers and small talk causes me anxiety and pushes my boundaries.

It was during one of my snuggle-up, grab-tea, and crack-open-a-good-book days that I started to feel a nudge that maybe I need to push outside of my comfort zone. Maybe I could benefit from expanding my social circle. As 2010 came to a close, I wrote it down on paper, stared at it, felt nervous, prayed, and took the leap.

What I wrote down was inspired by a book I was reading. The premise of the book was: what would happen in your life if you just gave randomly, without conditions or expectations, to people for twenty-nine days? I was intrigued and excited.

I thought to myself, *So, go up to random strangers and give them a gift?* That sounds insane. I tried to drown out any words that were coming off the pages before they could take root. I'm an introvert. I'm not sure if I even like people. People will think I'm crazy, but it's a new year, a new beginning, and a perfect time for getting outside of my comfort zone. With anything new comes doubt. How do I approach strangers? What if they reject me? What if I thought they needed help and they didn't? With the megaphone from God nudging me to go on this journey and insecurities trying to stop me from taking this leap, a little tug in my heart spoke louder. "Just do it Stephanie! Trust Me and trust yourself," I heard.

So, on December 31, 2010, I wrote, *My goal is to go beyond the twenty-nine days and do an entire year of giving. I want to stop being focused on self and strive to make serving others a priority.*

I started small and safe.

DAY ONE: I called a friend and gave her the gift of my time. I didn't even tell her what I was doing. I felt a little anxious to call because this is a friend I'm not really close to but felt I needed to check in on her. I'm trusting this is what God wanted me to do. Day One complete. It was a little win. It felt easy, and I was ready for Day Two.

DAY TWO: Hershey Kisses for a friend. He loves chocolate, and it is still in my comfort zone. Day Two complete.

DAY THREE: *I* broadened my horizons and gifted recycled Christmas cards to St. Jude's Ranch for Children. I'm learning gifts don't have to be to people. This gift helped the environment and would impact children I'd never meet. Day Three complete.

DAY FOUR: On Day Four, I made homemade treat bags for the ladies who clean my home. I felt a little silly, but they loved them, and it made for more friendly hellos and goodbye's when they are at my house. This one felt good and got things rolling for me.

Next up, the Dunkin' Donuts for the nursing staff (and, of course, I saved one for my husband), the diapers and canned goods for the local food pantry, and a box of chocolates for the UPS man were simple gifts that were all accepted with a smile and a warm connection, even if only for a moment. As the momentum kept building, my confidence in me—and the process—was growing. I became empowered, and I started to see God's purpose for me starting to take hold. Making other people's day and brightening the world around me—*I can do this!*

Day 29 passed in a flash, and I blew by a year. Sadly, on Day 522, my journey ended. Or so I thought.

I took a little break and have been giving a daily gift ever since. When I felt that little tug to walk sixty miles for a friend who was diagnosed with cancer, I signed up, raised over $2,500, and completed the Susan G. Komen sixty-mile walk. When I was at the Big House for a Michigan University football game, out of the 100,000 screaming fans, I felt the pull to walk up to a soldier and ask if he needed a hug. He said, "Yes." This was completely outside of my comfort zone and slightly crazy, but when I gave him the gift of a hug, he whispered, "I needed that today."

On another day, I found myself at the starting line of the Chicago Marathon with my sixty-year-old mom. She dreamed of running a marathon, and I wanted to train and complete the marathon with her as my gift. Each mile, I ran for a different person who had impacted my life. I ran a mile for Lauren and Molly, college students who went missing and have never been found. I ran a mile for Scott Patrick, an Indiana State Trooper, who was killed in the line of duty. I ran a mile for Emily, a high school senior with so many dreams ahead who was killed texting and driving. And I ran the last 0.2 miles for my mom and me. My relationship with my mom has been forever changed by giving her the gift of being her running partner in that marathon, crossing the finish line at the exact same time. Our friendship forever deepened.

And maybe the craziest of all gifts was when I found myself on a flight to Alaska with a group of strangers heading on a missions trip. I wanted to go to Alaska to give the gift of love and hope to people in need, but I also wanted to give the gift of the Word of Jesus Christ and how he'd changed my life through giving. On that trip, I met three college gals who charmingly referred to me as Mom and have become close friends. Over the last three years, I have driven to Oklahoma to visit them, and they have visited me in Indiana several times.

Throughout this journey, I've made 522 friends and counting. Some of them for a moment and others for a lifetime. Sometimes the interaction changed the course of their day, and sometimes it changed their life. When this all started, I thought my mission was to make a difference to others. What I didn't realize going through this giving journey was that God had a plan to change me. By trusting His plan, my whole life changed. But that wasn't the ultimate lesson that I learned.

The ultimate lesson I learned was that Jesus is my unconditional loving and caring friend. He is the ultimate giver. He gave His life for us. He'll be there in your time of need. He'll show up when you least expect it. He will push you to your limits, and He will be there for you when you fall. He will bring the right people into your life if you let Him, and He will work through us to be that person for someone else. He answers prayers through us, and He speaks through our words and our actions. But like any complete and true friendship, it starts and ends with trust. The more I have trusted the relationship that I have with Jesus, the more I feel connected to a higher purpose for my life and the more I feel connected to Him.

Stephanie found 522 friends but discovered that Jesus is the ultimate friend—giving, wise, supportive, and unconditionally loving. So if our duty is to live and love like Jesus, what does that say about how *we are supposed to show up* in our own friendships? The Bible gives us plenty of guidelines.

Of course, we'll probably make lots of mistakes, but luckily we can always get things back on track with a friend using Christ's real-life friendships as an example.

ONE COLOSSAL MISTAKE COULD NOT END THIS FRIENDSHIP

"Love each other as I have loved you."

—JOHN 15:12

For years, we'd been so close. Yet in a moment of fear, I had turned my back on the best friend anyone could ever have. The truth was, I knew Him probably better than anyone else.

He'd been wildly popular during the previous three years. As we traveled together throughout Galilee, He was constantly surrounded by fans. People were calling Him the Son of God, yet everywhere we went—the merchants, the old people, the children—everyone spoke to Him as if they knew Him personally. His effect on people was uncanny. Of course, He could always be counted on to stop for those who needed Him, even when it wasn't convenient and even though we complained.

"I will make you fishers of men," Jesus had told me and several of my friends on the shores of Capernaum three years earlier. We hardly knew Him at the time, yet, without hesitation, we dropped our nets and joined Him in His work. Though I was a rough and headstrong fisherman, I—Simon Peter—had found my way into His inner circle because Jesus of Nazareth had chosen me.

We spent nearly every waking moment together, eating meals, sharing stories, and traveling from town to town. What crazy times

we had: boat rides in rough seas, fish dinners on the beach, and even a little dancing on the water. Within months of joining His ministry, the twelve of us who made up His crew of disciples were consumed with excitement and adventure for each new day.

Of course, He was on good terms with all twelve of us. But over time, He and I developed a kindred spirit that was unique. It was the kind of friendship where, in one breath, He called me the Rock—and in the next, He ordered, "Get behind me, Satan."

Jesus spoke to me like that because he saw *who I really was*, not who I sometimes pretended to be. It was a friendship of honest transparency, the friendship of a lifetime.

And only He knew it was all about to end.

I remember our last meal together. He hosted it for us just after His triumphant entrance into Jerusalem. It was Passover. Our spirits were high. We hadn't a clue it would be our last night together.

If we had, maybe I would have expressed so much more gratitude, support, admiration, and empathy.

It was an intimate dinner, just for the crew. As the meal progressed, Jesus quietly got up and filled a wash basin. Kneeling before us, He began to wash our feet.

Seriously? I thought. He was the Messiah—the man I looked up to and had followed.

"You'll never wash my feet," I told our Lord.

"You do not realize now what I am doing," Jesus said, "but later you will understand." That night, He taught me what it was to be a true servant to others. Only later did I realize He was preparing us for a greater life of service one day.

Jesus then broke bread and gave thanks to God—something we'd seen Him do many times before—but this time, He explained that the bread is His body that would be broken for us. He handed us the wine and said it is His blood that would be shed for man.

Looking back, I think He knew even then the kind of violent death He would suffer. But in the emotion of that moment and at the benevolence in His voice, I was moved as I'd never been moved before.

"Lord, I will lay down my life for You," I vowed.

But Jesus knew better.

"Before the rooster crows," Jesus said, "you will deny three times that you even know Me."

Incredulous, I bristled over His reply. *I would never,* I thought. *And if that were true, why doesn't He kick me out right now?*

I'm so glad He didn't.

As Jesus continued sharing, I realized He was voicing His love for us from the depths of his soul. He wanted us to know how to be true friends. And He wanted to give us a glimpse into our future.

> *My commandment is this: love one another, just as I love you. The greatest love you can have for your friends is to give your life for them. And you are my friends if you do what I command you. I do not call you servants any longer, because servants do not know what their master is doing. Instead, I call you friends, because I have told you everything I heard from my Father. You did not choose me; I chose you and appointed you to go and bear much fruit, the kind of fruit that endures. And so the Father will give you whatever you ask of him in my name. This, then, is what I command you: love one another. (John 15:12–17)*

The supper ended and I went out into the night. This is where my fear took over, and I started to deny my best friend. *How could I betray this man who completely changed my life?* I regretfully thought to myself.

Somewhere nearby, a rooster crowed ominously as the local guards in Jerusalem continued their shakedown.

I said, I don't know Him, I insisted for the third time that night.

As we now know, later Jesus laid down His life for me—the friend who'd denied Him—just as He laid down His life to cover the sins of the world. He openly and publicly gave up His body to be broken and gave up His blood to be shed for man.

Yet, I, in my fear, had denied that I even knew Him. I had refused to acknowledge our friendship to the authorities. But none of that mattered to Him. One colossal mistake could not end our friendship. While I could never fully grasp the pain that He endured at His death, I do know the anguish I felt as I saw my friend die, knowing He loved me to the end.

Are you that kind of friend? Are you the kind who can sustain the hurt of a lifetime yet still return—as Jesus came back after death—to comfort and soothe your closest friend? When Jesus appeared to the disciples following His resurrection, He was standing on the shore of Lake Tiberias as they brought in their fishing boat. Approaching Peter, Jesus was full of compassion.

"Take care of my sheep," Jesus urged the rough fisherman, handing the early Christian church over to the man who had betrayed Him but to whom Jesus had still stayed true.

Today, as the most benevolent and loving friend imaginable, Jesus is there for you.

But what about your non-churched friends? They need Christ, too. Can you hang with them without being threatening yet still deliver the message: *I struggled. I found Christ. I was transformed, and here's what happened?*

What's it like to have friendships where you live and love like Jesus? Here are some ways to get there.

CHOOSE YOUR INNER CIRCLE **WISELY**

"The righteous choose their friends carefully."

—PROVERBS 12:26 NIV

Just as Jesus assembled a crew to befriend and become His inner-most circle, so we should exercise care in choosing our closest friends. These are the people we trust with our plans and secrets. They're the ones we call when disaster strikes or when we need someone to talk us off the ledge. They're the ones who know us inside and out—including our dreams, fears, blind spots, and most likely our daily schedule. They are few in number and usually closer than some family members.

If your inner circle could use an upgrade—including some new confidantes—start reverse-engineering the friends you want. Would they be smart, successful, positive, reliable, and trustworthy people? Would they be artistic, talented, interesting, worldly, or sophisticated? Look around and start plugging those people into your life. While reverse-engineering is common when you move to a new city, you can also start where you live now and begin nurturing new friendships that matter.

Of course, when it comes to just our acquaintances, coworkers, and the moms we chat with during the morning school run, we can be less cautious; they're not necessarily people we rely on for help, listen to when making decisions, or trust with our future life plans.

With anyone we're considering befriending, however, Proverbs 22:24–25 (NLT) does caution us: "Don't befriend angry people or associate with hot-tempered people, or you will learn to be like them and endanger your soul." Toxic people bring down our energy and can make us feel bad about ourselves. They affect our mindset and can be domineering in their demands. They can be manipulative in getting their way. And have you ever heard that famous quote: "We become like the five people we spend the most time with"? That's the real danger. It's just human nature to take on the thinking, actions, and even mannerisms of the friends we're closest to. Avoid the toxic ones.

CHOOSE FRIENDS WHO WILL **CHALLENGE** YOU

*"As iron sharpens iron, so a friend
sharpens a friend."*

—PROVERBS 27:17 NLT

One of the best ways to amplify your life and steadily move toward Oola is to surround yourself with positive people who will give you wise counsel, cheer you on, and also challenge you to do better, achieve more, and stay focused. True friends don't have an agenda. They're not interested in keeping you small in order to make themselves feel bigger. They *want* to see you succeed.

Additionally, smart, successful people like to hang out together. Find the possibility thinkers in your circle and cultivate those friendships. These are the people—Christians and non-churched friends— who can give you a broader perspective about anything you want to do.

Last, be grateful and thank God for those friends who elevate *and celebrate* you. These selfless and generous friends are worth their weight in gold.

BE AN **AWESOME** FRIEND IN RETURN

*"One who loves a pure heart and who speaks with
grace will have the king for a friend."*

—PROVERBS 22:11 NIV

A good friend can be life-changing for the better. As Christians, it's our calling to be that friend to others. So what are you doing daily to be a better friend and encourage those around you?

One way is to simply stay connected. In our fast-paced, modern existence, simple things like texting a word of encouragement, calling the night before a big presentation, FaceTiming when you're out of town, getting together after work, or biking over for a quick coffee on the weekends are ways to stay connected, informed, and involved. But don't just rely on social media. A recent study by the National Institutes of Health* said social media use was "significantly associated with increased depression" among young people age nineteen to thirty-two years old. And the *New York Times* recently reported on the heartbreaking epidemic of social isolation among seniors: as many as 46 percent of those over age sixty suffer from loneliness.† While these older friends may not be in your inner circle, they still have rich lives to share and can bring wisdom and the joy of companionship to your life. Check in, visit, and bring some love to those you know who are isolated.

Additionally, decide—in each instance with a friend—whether it's better to be an advisor or a listener. You can provide a new perspective, dispense ideas for solving problems, or simply listen when friends vent their fears, anger, and frustration. The discernment God gives you in knowing the difference, and your ability to sometimes keep your opinions to yourself, will make you the wise counsel in a close friend's life.

Finally, pray for your friends—both Christian and non-Christian ones. While we often know the outward struggles that our friends are facing, we don't always know their inner battles. Praying for both gladdens God's heart. It puts others above ourselves. God hears a prayerful friend.

---

* Read more about it at *https://www.ncbi.nlm.nih.gov/pubmed/26783723.*

† *https://www.nytimes.com/2016/09/06/health/lonliness-aging-health-effects.html.*

OOLAFUN

"There is nothing better for people in this world
than to eat, drink, and enjoy life.
That way they will experience some happiness along
with all the hard work God gives them."

—ECCLESIASTES 8:15b NLT

N ow here's some intelligent design: God wired us—body, mind, and spirit—to actually benefit from having fun. Did you know? Laughing with friends, relaxing at a church barbeque, taking the time to get away for a girls' weekend or "man camp," or simply sitting on a beach enjoying His beautiful creation actually boosts your *physiological* health.

For one thing, it reduces production of the stress hormone *cortisol*—making it easier to cope with tension, fear, and overwhelm. It also boosts *serotonin,* the brain chemical that regulates mood, memory, and sleep. And it positively impacts your key relationships; sharing good times with others helps you form bonds and social connections, which is one of the fundamental needs of humans. Even the American Psychological Association says that having fun is a good thing.

It's no wonder that *fun* is one of the seven fundamentals of Oola.

But while Christians often get a bad rap as being stuffy and uninteresting, the reverse is actually true; being a Christian is super fun. In fact, you're plugged into a network of people, events, and memorable moments that can add a whole new dimension of joy and camaraderie to your life.

So what are some ways you can kick off the stodgy reputation of yesteryear and start bringing Jesus along for the party?

ISSUE YOUR OWN
INVITATION TO THE FUN

If you belong to a megachurch, chances are you're a little overwhelmed by the thousands of people—and the equal number of activities available. If you're feeling a little lost and, even worse, don't feel included, it's up to you to invite yourself to the fun. Step up. Check things out. Ask questions. You'll find that everyone is welcome. And if you're a singleton participating in these activities, have no fear. You can contact the organizers in advance so they're already acquainted with you and can be ready to welcome you when you arrive.

The alternative is staying on the periphery and a Christian life that's compartmentalized—with a Sunday life and rest-of-the-week life—going to church but not engaging further. That's not the Christian life that God wants for you.

Of course, where things really get fun is when you bring *your own time and talents* to the mix and actively serve as a volunteer—not just an attendee. Can you join a ministry, organize a food pantry for needy families, or launch a blanket brigade for the homeless? Can you assemble a speaker series, teach an Oola Bible Study, sing in the worship team, or help on administrative committees? Can you connect outside of church with other believers who are starting charities or humanitarian programs? When you do, the sense of satisfaction you get from working with others to transform something lends an extra margin of fun.

Remember that God's Kingdom is made up of *people*, and the more energetic and committed they (and you) are, the better.

YOU DON'T HAVE TO SCHEDULE
FUN ON YOUR CALENDAR

While Dave has fun all the time, Troy—who used to schedule travel as his main source of fun—had to learn ways to have spontaneous fun every day. Now, as they tour the country in the OolaBus, the guys add fun by seeking out the best donuts in a city, grabbing some lobster rolls on the Atlantic coast, getting splashed on a detour to Niagara Falls, and racking up hours of fun in out-of-the-way restaurants, coffeehouses, and oyster bars.

Better yet is when the Oola tour takes them overseas where they've ridden camels in Dubai, visited an elephant sanctuary in Thailand, gone surfing in the Pacific, and even gotten stranded at a remote *Policia* station in Cuba after their taxi driver was arrested. Now that's some serious OolaFun.

GIVE YOUR BUCKET LIST A **CHRISTIAN** FOCUS

When a friend of ours took her first trip to Italy, she planned six weeks of solo travel just to take in the Christian monuments, small-town churches, and towering basilicas she'd always read about. She wanted to go—by herself—to sit in the dusty pews and stroll through the quiet gardens, eager to experience the combination of history and God's presence in sacred spaces. From the majesty of St. Peter's Basilica to the quiet beauty of the Sistine Chapel to the haunting sounds of a vesper service in a hillside church above Florence, she soon realized how different her experience would have been had she been traveling with a friend, a spouse, or a tour group.

Perhaps you, too, have something on your bucket list that will bring you closer to God or help you better understand His plan for your life. Of course, if you haven't yet compiled a list of ultimate life experiences you want to embark on, start one now. Shoot for at least fifty things you want to do, be, and see—places you want to go, people you want to meet, and things you've always wanted to do. It might be something outside in nature, attending a rare event, training with the top instructor in your sport, or meeting a notable person. No matter what it is, ask yourself how you could grow as a Christian through the experience. And as you compile your bucket list, make sure you add some uniquely church-related activities that matter greatly to you.

◎   ◎   ◎   ◎

SEEKING JOY

by Avonlea Roy

At age twenty-nine, I made one of the most difficult choices I've ever had to make in my life.

For eight years, I had fought to save my marriage, praying to God to help me honor my commitment. Domestic violence and abuse had ravaged our home and our family, but instead of getting better, things kept getting worse. Finally, I made the painful but courageous decision to leave.

As I sat across from a notary at her kitchen table, signing divorce papers—heartbroken—I thought of all the years I had endured. I felt peace in my decision and something I hadn't felt in years: hope, not only for more than a life to endure, but hope to also find joy again. I realized that God loved me enough for me to have joy in my life and in my marriage, too.

I lived the next five years in survival mode. I put myself through college while working part-time and raising two little boys. But I sought joy in any way possible. I found cheap ways to have fun with them, renting $1 Redbox movies, holding game nights on the weekends, and taking them to parks and playgrounds. But, at the same time, I was laser focused on getting my life back together. Even while working to have fun again, my mind would wander to bills I had to pay or the rush-hour traffic I would have to face Monday morning.

In those five years, I drifted from my faith and the religion of my youth. When I attended my first OolaPalooza, I realized that both my faith and fun, once so strong, had become weak areas in my life. Although I was trying to have fun with my kids every week, fun became just another responsibility; another task on my to-do list. Joy was still a distant memory and I was not a "fun" person.

I spent a year applying the principles I had learned from Oola, including reestablishing a relationship with God and attempting to be more present in the enjoyable moments in life, but at the end of that year, I felt like my life was even worse than before. I was still single, exhausted, between jobs, and struggling to raise my boys. I felt like I had hit rock bottom.

What I didn't know was that God was doing some heavy demolition in my life so that He could build something new and better.

I cried and I prayed like crying and praying was a part-time job. But then, one by one, miracles began to appear. First, I got an interview for my dream job. That same week, I met the man I would eventually marry. Before my job interview, Josh texted me something that made my heart skip: "I'm sure you did great. But I did say a little prayer for you." I got the job. And before long, Josh and I shared one of the happiest days of our lives when we exchanged wedding vows in front of our loved ones. People noticed my smile that day. It was real, instead of the fake one I had been wearing during my season of struggle.

I believe that God intends for us to "enjoy" life more often than we "endure" it. Even in the Scriptures, we learn that God wants us to have joy. Now we pray and study the Bible together as a family. We recently read in Leviticus about the Israelites after they had escaped from Egypt. God established holidays, seasons, and festivals for His people—for rest, celebration, and worship. Of the seven holidays described, five were for *celebration*.

God wants us to have fun, sing, dance, play, relax, be creative, have adventures, and appreciate the world He created. Now that I have a strong marriage based on shared Christian values—and with Oola as a guide to keep my life balanced—I have more fun, happiness, and joy than I ever could have imagined. Fun is not something on my to-do list, but something to provide joy. Josh and I regularly make time to have fun as a family—we play games with our kids, practice sports, go see fun movies, and spend time at the pool. We have fun together as a couple, too, going to concerts and the theater, trying new restaurants, hiking, and snowshoeing. Recently, we checked off a bucket list item and went to Mexico to volunteer at an orphanage and then made time to zip-line, hit the beach, and enjoy some amazing Mexican food.

As much fun as we have together, we also take time to pursue our individual dreams of fun and support each other in our unique interests. Josh loves surfing and Olympic lifting, while I enjoy acting and yoga. We find little ways to have fun every day, while dreaming of the types of fun that we can add to our bucket lists, then mapping out a plan to achieve them.

Oola reminds us to find joy in the life God has given us and that joy isn't a destination, but a pursuit—one that is discovered on our journey to becoming our best self.

Just as with other aspects of your life, God plays a part in you having fun, too. If you've ever scored last-minute tickets to a sold-out concert or gotten a rare opportunity to take your hobby to the next level or walked in the park on a beautiful spring morning, you know that God is there—smiling right along with you.

INVITE JESUS TO THE PARTY

"Fill the jars with water."

—JOHN 2:7b BSB

Weddings are always kind of fun. The food, the drink, the music, the dancing. It's a celebration, not a funeral, after all. I enjoyed being there even if I was just a lowly servant. And this wedding was a doozy, a weeklong event. Seven days and nights of fun that started off with great promise three days before. The ceremony was beautiful, the décor was on point, and the food was at a level that everybody would be talking about for years to come.

It wasn't until the day of the actual wedding ceremony that things went south. The biggest snag that could ever happen at any wedding happened. We can debate whether it was the unexpected guests or lack of funds that caused this dilemma, but the cause really doesn't matter. The reality was that this "happily ever after" celebration was in trouble.

This party had run out of wine.

This may not seem like a big deal to you, but it is very important that the hosts—in this case, the family I work for—keep the food and wine flowing freely during a wedding. Not only would this look thoughtless on the part of our household, but it's a big part of the tradition and fun. Running out of food or drink is considered a disgrace to the host.

And while everyone truly did feel bad for us, people are still people and behave just like people do: the guests took turns feeling genuinely bad for the family while alternately huddling in groups—gossiping and speculating just how this unforgivable problem might be solved. We, me included, had no idea what to do. I saw people around me whispering while pointing to empty glasses. I could see the look of panic on the faces of the wedding planner and the other servers as they hurriedly looked for a solution.

Thankfully, Mary, who was closely connected to this wedding and truly the sweetest, most selfless lady ever, wanted to help. She calmly asked her Son to do something to make this problem go away. He seemed rather uninterested but, probably because it's hard to say no to your mother, He appeared to agree to help. He started walking toward me.

Whoa, Guy! I wanted to say. *Don't look at me. I'm not in charge. I'm just a server.* But He kept coming anyway. And when He approached, He asked me to do something that didn't make any sense. I listened, shrugged, and with nothing else to do, I did what He asked. I walked over to the stone purification jars that held twenty to thirty gallons of water. I could see the dirt floating on the surface of the little water that remained in the jars. *How many guests had washed their hands in them?* I wondered. *What was He thinking?*

But like I said, I was there as a server, and I did what I was told. I could see Him watching me as the other servants and I began filling the jars with water. After the jars were filled with water, we looked at Him for our next command. *What now?* I wondered. *How are these massive jugs of bad water going to help with the problem of running out of wine?* I thought to myself.

I looked around dumbfounded as this man asked me to do the unthinkable. *I was going to lose this job. What was my boss going to think?* What I was asked to do was gross and made no sense. But because I was a servant, I couldn't really chime in with my opinion, and I reluctantly complied.

I drew the water out of the jars and cautiously walked across the room full of guests to my boss. I don't know how I got chosen for this task; I guess I was in the wrong place at the wrong time. I slowly raised the dirty water up in a goblet and offered it to my boss. He took it from my hands and raised it toward his lips. I looked down toward the ground and slowly closed my eyes, hoping to avoid his angry response. I clenched my fists and stressfully squeezed my eyelids together as I waited for my fate. I heard my boss take a sip of the water. What I heard next was unexpected:

> When the master of ceremonies tasted the water that was now wine, not knowing where it had come from (though, of course, the servants knew), he called the bridegroom over.
>
> "A host always serves the best wine first," he said. "Then, when everyone has had a lot to drink, he brings out the less expensive wine. But you have kept the best until now!" (John 2:9–10)

I opened my eyes to see the smiles and approving gazes of the guests. Instantly, people focused back on the party and started having fun again. The celebration went on. I watched as the dancing continued, the laughter resumed, and because of Jesus, a couple, a family, and a community had the best day ever. No one thought anything of what had just happened, except me.

I knew that I had just witnessed the first miracle performed by Jesus. This miracle launched the ministry of Jesus. He added joy to the celebration of two becoming one under God. What would come later would forever change the world.

◎ ◎ ◎ ◎

The wedding at Cana proves that we're guaranteed a crazy good time whenever we invite Jesus to the party. Just because you're a Christian doesn't mean you need to lead a boring life. Jesus didn't just sit in a synagogue—He went out and lived life to the fullest.

But most of the time, people believe they can't have fun if the get-together is a "Christian thing." Somehow, it needs to be buttoned-up, sobering, and dull. Far too often, we end up living two separate lives—our Christian-on-Sunday life and our rest-of-the-week secular life—because, well, being Christian isn't fun.

But put yourself in the Judea of 2,000 years ago. Not only was Jesus the biggest celebrity around, He was super fun. Seriously. Walking on water? Working miracles? Turning Evian into vino blanco? How many of your non-churched friends can do that?

To bring Jesus along, here are some tips that will boost the fun factor.

BE YOURSELF AND MEET **NEW** PEOPLE

"Love your neighbor as yourself."
—GALATIANS 5:14b

Jesus met people who weren't necessarily just like Him. While He never compromised who He was, He ventured out by interacting with people beyond His small crew. Whether you're going on a missions trip or talking to the high school student bagging your groceries, you can find joy in the people around you.

Too often, we're so overwhelmed with the have-to-do's of our day that we rush through life not talking to people. Enjoy the moment. Notice others. The fun happens when you connect and create a new friend. But don't worry that you have to be focused on evangelizing or winning people for the Lord—it will happen naturally as people get to know you and see the impact of Christ in your life. Be yourself and meet new people. You might discover a new best friend.

JOIN A MISSIONS TRIP AND **CHANGE** YOUR LIFE

"Let's go back to every city where we spread the Lord's word. We'll visit the believers to see how they're doing."

—ACTS 15:36b

Whether you build a school, educate women, establish safe water sources—or something else—making a tangible difference in the lives of local people counteracts their commonly held views derived from decades of famine, war, poverty, and illiteracy.

And, by the way? It's a blast to participate. Plus, the lifelong memories will transform you—permanently.

Most people come home from a missions trip with greater gratitude. While we often think we need so many "things" to live our lives, a missions trip helps you identify what's really necessary. It helps you step outside your own needs and be unselfish. You learn what life balance is all about.

You also form lifelong friendships with those participating with you. And you emerge stronger as a person: compassionate, worldly, seeing things from Heaven's perspective, and less fixated on your own challenges. Finally, missions trips require faith: you have to raise the money to travel and assist with the project, which requires you to believe that God will show up to provide.

One good way to get started is Missions.Me—a California-based organization that mobilizes thousands of missionaries from dozens of countries to descend on a single nation for a week to give aid, train small business owners, provide medical services, teach sports, and more, all culminating with a country-wide series of stadium events that mobilize that nation's own people for further self-growth and continued Christ-centered work on their own.* They make it easy-breezy for church teams and individuals to participate, even arranging for travel, housing, and meals, plus providing online tools for fundraising.

MAKE THE **MOST** OUT OF EVERYDAY THINGS

"A pretentious, showy life is an empty life;
a plain and simple life is a full life."

—PROVERBS 13:7 MSG[†]

Taking the dog for a walk in the woods, helping the kids make spiced peaches from your own tree, and packing a picnic for a day at the beach—these are the simple pleasures that make life fun. And you don't have to spend a ton of money or assemble a group of people or even go anywhere if you don't want to.

Being in the habit of researching and finding simple things to enjoy is part of the OolaLife. So, what can you do to add more fun?

Start by making your household a tranquil and restorative environment where you and your family love to be. Tidy up. Declutter. Add some candles, and push play on your favorite playlist. Limit screen time, and establish quiet hours and "no electronics" days. When you're done, begin discovering what's fun about being at home—whether it's making homemade cheese from locally sourced

---

* Visit *1nation1day.com* for details. In 2020, for the first time, Missions.me will bring their week-long outreach to the United States, organizing thousands in the Los Angeles area for their 1DayLA campaign.
† The Message Bible.

goat's milk, watching a documentary series on something fascinating, or starting a new craft or hobby. Next, find out what's fun to do locally that's free or doesn't cost a lot: movie night, lectures, hiking, concerts in the park, readers circles, or a classic board game to play.

Finally, start a folder or Pinterest board of things you read about or find online that sound fun for you, your family, and your friends. Whether it's a community festival, scenic drive, or recommended lunch spot, finding fun things to do takes research and planning. Don't be boring; get out there and enjoy life to the fullest—always being careful not to diminish these simple pleasures by wishing you were doing something "better" or more posh. Ecclesiastes 6:9 tells us, "Enjoy what you have rather than desiring what you don't have."

One final thing: don't let your focus on tomorrow rob you of enjoying time with the family and friends who are right in front of you. Jesus lived thinking about the future, but you'd always find Him present in the moment and enjoying the company of people. He stayed on course, but made beautiful "pit stops" along the way.

OOLABLOCKERS

*"Woe to the world because of the things
that cause people to stumble!"*

—MATTHEW 18:7 NIV

n addition to the 7 F's of Oola, there are habits, beliefs, and attitudes that will either hold you back or propel you forward. We call these OolaBlockers and OolaAccelerators. And while your blockers and accelerators may be different from ours, you'll likely recognize a bit of yourself in the responses, traits, and self-talk we'll discuss in Sections Three and Four of this book.

Blockers, which start in the next chapter, quite simply are the traits and characteristics that get between you and your dreams. It is the junk that keeps you from showing up fully, thinking of yourself as worthy, or asking for what you need in order to be happy. Not only have we experienced these Blockers *ourselves* over the years, but we see them time and again in the lives of OolaPalooza attendees and those we meet on the OolaBus. Blockers like *guilt, self-sabotage,* and *anger* can keep you from going for what you want—even holding you back subconsciously. They're the negative head game that will keep you from living the life you dream of and deserve.

While we'll go in-depth about each Blocker over the next seven chapters, there's a formula that works for *all* Blockers to help you eliminate them and move forward toward your goals.

It's called the Ready-Set-Go Formula, and it works like this:

First, if you're facing a blocker such as fear, guilt, self-sabotage, or lack of focus, get *ready* to move past it by calling it out: *I'm too angry at my spouse to even discuss marriage counseling. I'm afraid people at the gym will be looking at me. I'm not qualified for that job—they'd never hire me.* Call it out. Simply identify your Blocker.

Next, *set* your blocker in its place by putting it in proper perspective. Ask yourself, *What will my life look like if I give into my (fear, self-sabotage, anger, etc.)?* Will your life get better or become worse? Will you be wealthier, less stressed, more influential, slimmer, or some other positive change—or will your life be diminished? If so, how? Additionally, ask yourself, *What will my life look like if I overcome this OolaBlocker—if I do the work and take action to push through?* Will your life be better or worse? Will you get the promotion, heal the relationship, feel better about yourself, or experience some other positive change? Set your blocker in perspective.

Finally, *go!* Determine one gutsy step you can take now, in this moment, that requires only twenty seconds of courage, but that will help you overcome what you're feeling and help you move closer to your goal. Whether it's to send an email, make that call, research the solution, or write down your talking points, determine the one courageous action you could take—then *go do it.*

Ready, set, go.

And in this next chapter, we'll apply that formula to the very first Blocker: *Fear.*

FEAR

"She is clothed with strength and dignity,
and she laughs without fear of the future."

—PROVERBS 31:25 NLT

n a recent interview, television personality Joanna Gaines—
founder of the Magnolia home-decorating empire and *Magnolia
Journal* magazine—admitted growing up with fear.* Born a Korean
American, she was bullied at school as a young girl because she
is half Asian.

She learned that "Who I am isn't good enough." She was never
completely confident in her skin. Later in high school—eager to make
friends—she would walk into the lunchroom and, seeing other kids
already grouped at the tables, turn around and leave, hiding in the
girls' restroom until class resumed. Her fear, she says, "just took over."

When a chance internship at the television news program *48
Hours* took her to New York City during her last semester of college,
she finally began to tackle her insecurity. Instead of wondering *Am I
good enough,* she began to ponder, *What's my purpose?*

Well, how about you? Have you been living with fear?

While many people will say, "Oh, I'm afraid of snakes" or "Yeah,
I'm afraid of heights," some of the most limiting fears are actually
the ones we don't readily identify but have still internalized over the
years: the fear of success, the fear of failure, shyness, the hesitancy to
try new things, the fear of change, or fear of making a decision—fears
that have a daily grip on our ability to create the future we want.

JESUS, TOO, FACED **FEARFUL** SITUATIONS

Suppose you knew from childhood the terrible death you would
meet on this earth. Imagine spending weeks in the desert, surrounded
by wild animals and repeatedly assailed by Satan. Think about being

* Read the interview at: *https://darlingmagazine.org/joanna-gaines-darling-interview/*.

in your mid-twenties and starting out in a new career—speaking in public for the first time, ministering to ever-growing crowds, and standing up to the religious authorities of your day.

As a young man, Jesus experienced many situations in which He *should have been* afraid. His disciples certainly were. And so were the everyday people to whom Jesus ministered. Even the Bible tells us, during that fateful Passover week, that Jesus wept as He prayed in the Garden of Gethsemane—full of anguish, distress, and sorrow at His coming crucifixion.

While we may never know if—as a man—Jesus was truly afraid, the one thing we *do know* is that Jesus had something more powerful than fear: *He had faith.* In the midst of fearful situations, He knew His Father was always with Him.

Well, shouldn't we have that same level of assurance when faced with fearful situations on our way to creating the ideal life?

WHAT **FEAR** LOOKS LIKE
FOR CHRISTIANS

For Christians (and everyone else), fear is a normal human emotion. But, as human beings, we're actually born with only *two* innate fears: the fear of falling and the fear of loud noises. All other fears are learned. And the good news is: they can be *unlearned.*

If you've lived in a secular world, fearful of being judged by others for abstinence, parenting boundaries, turning down job offers from unethical companies, sharing a Christian post—or *anything else* the world seems not to respect or understand—those fears can be unlearned, and boldness can take their place. If you've ever hesitated to evangelize, afraid to speak your faith and invite others to church, that fear can also be replaced with confidence and self-assurance. Luckily, we have Jesus as a role model for overcoming fear. And, in addition to prayer, there's also a practical exercise you can use to overcome fear in the moment.

READY, SET, AND
LET GO OF YOUR FEARS

While we've already taught you the Ready-Set-Go Formula for overcoming OolaBlockers, by far the most limiting Blocker we see among our readers and audiences is *fear*: fear of going to the gym, fear of eliminating debt, fear of getting counseling instead of a divorce, fear of leaving an abusive marriage, fear of promoting your business, fear of traveling to an exotic country, and so many more fears. The Ready-Set-Go Formula works perfectly on fears like these.

But the key is to summon up—with God's help—those twenty seconds of courage.

Let's say you've set a goal to lose some extra pounds and get into shape. Awesome! You know you'll need to hit the gym at least three times a week and probably add some resistance training, along with logging some time on the treadmill. It's something you've never done, and knowing you'll be uncomfortable, you run into fear.

To apply the Ready-Set-Go Formula, follow these steps.

First, get ready to face your fear by simply calling it out: *I'm afraid of being judged. I don't know how to use the equipment. I'm afraid people will be looking at me.* You're simply identifying your fear.

Second, set fear in its place. Ask yourself, *What will my life look like if I give into my fear?* If you've ever carved out time in your schedule to go to the gym, then gotten ready, but simply just didn't go, did you feel better about yourself or worse about yourself? If you persist in not going, will you get stronger or weaker? Will you get into better shape or even more out of shape? Then, ask yourself, *What will my life look like if I push through this fear?* What if you open the gym door and hop on the treadmill. Would you feel better about yourself or worse about yourself? What if you continue for three months without fail? Would you feel more fit or less fit? Set fear in its place.

Finally, decide what your twenty seconds of courage will be—that one action step you'll take to move forward. Maybe it's putting on your running shoes, pushing away the junk food, or pulling open that gym door. Then, simply take action and *go do it*.

This is how the simple Ready-Set-Go Formula can break the hold that fear has over you.

GOOD VIBRATIONS
by Emma Faye Rudkin

magine not hearing everyday sounds: a refrigerator humming, a microwave beeping, or cars honking. You may think it would be an amazing gift to silence the noise around us. But imagine not hearing the simple sounds of nature: birds chirping, water running, or rain falling. That would be sad but manageable. Now imagine not hearing the sounds of people around you, such as a sweet compliment, your parents telling you they love you, or simple everyday communication. That would be unimaginable. All sounds silenced, unheard.

At three years old, my ears were shut to the world. Silence.

The world can be a scary place when you are experiencing it and feeling it through all five senses, but it becomes terrifying when your sense of hearing is taken away, especially at three years old. The doctors recommended to my parents that I enroll in a school for the deaf to navigate this new world. They thought it would be best for me to be surrounded by others like me and learn sign language to communicate. My parents were devastated and afraid themselves, but they prayed and trusted the answer they heard: "Enroll Emma in a mainstream school." They enrolled me in a Christian school and hired a speech therapist so I could learn how to communicate with other kids. I worked extremely hard for years to become proficient at reading lips and learning how to speak. I would study the positioning of my lips in a mirror and place my hands in front of my therapist's mouth to feel the vibrations produced by certain sounds. Eventually, I learned how to speak.

Even with all the hard work, my speech wasn't perfect, and kids at school noticed. I was teased and became horribly insecure. The more I tried to hide and blend in, the more I became a target. It became something for others to point out, draw attention to, laugh at, mock— and worse. This world became scary, and I woke every day in fear of what the day would bring.

I coped by becoming great at pretending. In groups, I pretended that I could hear what they were talking about. When everyone else was laughing at a joke, I pretended I understood and laughed with them. I pretended that I belonged and that I was happy, but I was in my own quiet world. The only voice I could hear was the one in my head questioning God, my self-worth, and the fear of what I would face next.

Every day felt the same. I played pretend until school ended and the car door closed. Then, in the safe sight of my mom's unconditional love, the tears would flow. I would cry all the way home and many nights into the evening. My mom would tell me that it is okay to be sad today and cry tonight, but tomorrow is a new day. Tomorrow I needed to love myself, love others, and trust God's plan for my life. I wanted to believe her and trust God, but part of me questioned if she too was playing pretend.

Over time, and repeating this painful cycle, I found myself in a place of darkness and great anger toward God. Why did He make me like this? If God loved me, why couldn't He make me normal? If He was the big God of miracles in the Bible, why couldn't He heal me? I wanted the pain to stop. I desperately wanted to be normal and to fit in. I became angry, anxious, depressed, horribly insecure, and so lonely I could hardly stand it. I wanted to find answers, and I wanted to be healed.

I started desperately searching God's Word for why He had allowed this and how He could heal me. Instead of finding the answers I wanted, I started seeing what God intended. I discovered Psalm 46:1, "Be still, and know that I am God; I will be exalted among the nations, I will be exalted in the earth." I saw that God has a greater purpose for our hardships in this world, way beyond our human reasoning. He can see what we can't.

I continued to dive into the Bible for answers. I discovered James 1:2–4, "Consider it pure joy, my brothers and sisters, whenever you face trials of many kinds, because you know that the testing of your faith produces perseverance. Let perseverance finish its work so that you may be mature and complete, not lacking anything." I realized that my life may be a constant struggle (and may always be so), but I wouldn't be the person I am without these hardships. I wouldn't be the person He needs me to become.

When I heard *"God closed your ears to the world, so that you may hear His voice,"* my life was changed forever. Now I hear, not through longing and desire to be like everyone else, but through acceptance. God allows me to hear what He's called me to hear. The world is full of darkness and can be a scary place, but God has protected my heart through this filter of deafness so I would long for the light that leads me from the world.

This understanding of my deafness became the purpose of my life. It helped me push through all my fears and start to truly live my life for Him instead of for the opinions of others. I started to follow my heart instead of trying to fit in. I began to intensely study piano and music theory, which led to guitar, ukulele, singing lessons, and actively performing in my community. Yes, a love of music grew in me, and I can't hear. I experience music, not through hearing like the rest of the world, but through the vibrations and feeling it with my body. My faith in Him started to drown out the fears in the world around me. The more I studied music, the more my love of music grew. This passion in me pushed me through my fears. I fully trusted Jesus and that this was His purpose for my life. This was why He made me the way I am. It wasn't a mistake; it was a perfect plan. I needed to be a voice for the deaf community, especially the young girls, to show them that He doesn't make mistakes, they have a purpose, and they can follow their dreams.

The statistic that completely touched my soul was that 98 percent of the deaf community has no contact with a church and limited ways of knowing Jesus, making them the third largest unreached group with the Gospel. This was it! This was the purpose for my life: to bring the deaf community to Jesus—uniting the hard-of-hearing, the deaf community, and the hearing world together through music, art, and His Word. Using live captioning, synchronized vibrating backpacks to feel the beat, and a light-up dance floor, we could create a musical experience for those who can't hear.

This fall, I was reflecting on my journey while enjoying a gorgeous day in South Texas, a day He created. Over a sea of smiling faces, I could see the drummer beating away on the drums, the lead guitarist moving his fingers across the strings, and I could feel the energy of people dancing to the music all around me. Their customized back-packs vibrated in synchronicity to the music and the light show on the stage. The joy and confidence in the crowd was palpable. Many in the crowd were experiencing music for the very first time. But I couldn't hear anything but silence—the silence that for much of my life left me sad, fearful, and angry. However, not today. Today, I was grateful for the gift of silence He has given me. I felt the presence of God. I felt Him smile on this event as if to say, "Atta girl. I knew you could do it."*

---

* Emma is a former Miss San Antonio, the founder of Aid the Silent, and the originator of Good Vibrations Music Festival dedicated to inclusion and equality for all.

Even when we're experiencing fear, God is smiling over our growth, especially when it's something that will create the awesome life He wants for us. And, as we'll discover in the next story, when we learn an important lesson that brings us closer to Him, that's an even bigger payoff for us. Take a look.

TEACHER, WHAT DO *YOU* SAY?

"The sinless one among you, go first:
Throw the stone."

—JOHN 8:7b MSG

D ust filled my eyes as their feet shuffled around me. I took in a deep breath, scared it could be one of my last few. My mouth was dry, and dirt had caked my lips. The whispers I once heard now became booming accusations. I was completely surrounded and completely alone. The fear was crippling. My heart was beating faster and faster as I glanced at their hands. I could see their knuckles turn white as they each gripped their stone. My life was flashing before my eyes, and everything around me was happening in slow motion.

I had committed adultery—a crime punishable by death—and the growing crowd surrounding me were my judge, jury, and executioners. My fate had already been decided, and my death was soon to come. The thoughts of dying this way had never crossed my mind before. I was afraid of dying, but I was more afraid of the physical pain and family humiliation that comes with this kind of death.

Through all the chaos and chanting, I realized that I wasn't the only one on trial. The Pharisees were attempting to get the attention of a man who was speaking to a group of people nearby. They were trying to involve Him in my stoning. He completely ignored them at first and kept teaching. Why wasn't He afraid like me? Of course, He saw them, and of course, He could feel the tension in the air. But, He softly interrupted His teaching and calmly started to write in the dirt as the mob grew and grew.

> *"Teacher," they said to Jesus, "this woman was caught in the act of adultery. The law of Moses says to stone her. What do you say?" They were trying to trap Him into saying something they could use against Him, but Jesus stooped down and wrote in the dust with his finger. They kept demanding an answer, so He stood up again and said, "All right, but let the one who has never sinned throw the first stone!" Then He stooped down again and wrote in the dust. (John 8:4–8)*

After He spoke, I heard the sound of stones dropping to the ground one by one. The stones that were meant to slowly and painfully kill me were now innocent, simple rocks resting in the dirt. Still crouching, I slowly opened my eyes and peeked through my fingers that were protecting my face; the mob was dispersing and getting smaller by the minute. I removed my hands from my face and stood on my feet.

> *When the accusers heard this, they slipped away one by one, beginning with the oldest, until only Jesus was left in the middle of the crowd with the woman. Then Jesus stood up again and said to the woman, "Where are your accusers? Didn't even one of them condemn you?"*
>
> *"No, Lord," she said.*
>
> *And Jesus said, "Neither do I. Go and sin no more." (John 8:9–11)*

As we parted ways, my mind replayed this moment over and over. What did He write in the dust? Was it a list of their indiscretions? Did He write their secret sins in the ground in front of them? Or was it simply, "Where is the man?" All were very valid estimations.

The truth is, it didn't matter what He wrote.

The truth is that He didn't have to defend me. He could have ignored the situation and gone on with His teaching, but He didn't. He could have simply agreed with them, and it would have been over for Him. It would have been over for me. His act of courage was all it took, and the bullies scattered. His courage in the face of fear set me free.

Most people thought He gave me a free pass that day to get away with a crime, when according to the law, I should have been put to death. If you really knew me or had lived even a small portion of my life, you would know that wasn't the case. There is no excuse for what I'd done, but instead of condemning me, He forgave me. He didn't say that what I did was okay, but He allowed me to go live my life and sin no more.

I once heard that the wages of sin is death. It isn't always the death we imagine. Any time you allow sin into your life, big or small, whether it is exposed or not, it can eat away at who you really are. I had been putting myself to death way before the crowd started picking up rocks.

It wasn't a free pass, but He did give me a second chance.

Not only did He convince others to put down their stones, He convinced me to put down mine. He was not only brave enough to save my life, He was brave enough to see the real me and allow me to live life renewed.

In the face of my greatest fear, He showed me the greatest gift.

◎ ◎ ◎ ◎

Like the life-threatening circumstances in which Jesus found this woman, dangerous situations are very real and should be avoided.

Everyday fear, on the other hand, is a choice. It's simply easier, less uncomfortable, less confrontational, and less work to stay as we are—*and where we are.* But that's not Oola. It's not the balanced and growing life that God wants for us.

In the Old Testament, God commands us to be strong and brave.*

"Don't ever be afraid or discouraged!" He says. "I am the Lord your God, and I will be there to help you wherever you go."

With that kind of assurance in your back pocket, overcoming fear and moving forward on your goals should be easy, right? Here are some tips to help you stay bold and fearless.

HAVE **FAITH** OVER FEAR

*"Peter started walking on the water
and came toward Jesus."*

—MATTHEW 14:29 CSB

The book of Matthew tells us that Peter had enough faith to walk on water, but as soon as the wind picked up, he lost his focus on Jesus, became fearful, and—starting to sink—cried out, "Lord, save me!"

Well, how often do *we* start out with confidence, only to let fear sink our plans when the going gets tough? Even worse, how often do we fearfully stop our own progress once we figure out what's coming next? In the garden of Gethsemane, Jesus *begged* His Father, "Get Me out of this. Take this cup of suffering away from Me."†

One way to increase your faith in these moments is a favorite quote of Christians: *If God brings me to it, He will bring me through it.* At times like these, you can also pray for stronger faith and, especially, for discernment. If you're truly pursuing a path that God has inspired you to take, you can pray, *Hey, Lord, if this is the right thing to do, then smooth my path and show me the next steps.*

---

* Joshua 1:9 CEV.
† Matthew 14:36 MSG.

BE **FEARLESS** WHEN
HELPING PEOPLE MEET JESUS

"I tell you," He answered, "if they remain silent,
the very stones will cry out."

—LUKE 19:40 BSB

If we're all disciples of Christ, then helping others meet Jesus is an important homework assignment that God has given each one of us. While that obligation might seem replete with fear, the truth is that bringing even one person to Christ during your lifetime is a huge deal and cause for limitless celebration in Heaven.

So how can you have less fear around introducing Jesus to people you know? Start by inviting them to less threatening, more welcoming activities than Sunday church services, such as a church barbeque or kids' activities around the holidays. Once they're there, a good time and a great message will go far toward bringing them back on their own to experience the love of God's people.

If it's a family member, consider Susie Bradley's approach. After growing up in a salt-of-the-earth household with parents who only occasionally attended church, Susie's father was diagnosed with terminal cancer. He wanted to spend his final months with family, and Susie—who had returned to the church in her twenties—was soon faced with a fearful task: talking to her dad about Jesus. He was angry and terrified of the diagnosis he knew would lead to death. He didn't want to leave Susie's mom or their family. He wanted to know why he'd been given this death sentence. But mostly he proclaimed that he wasn't finished on this earth yet.

As God breathed confidence into Susie, she left her journal with Scriptures by his bedside. She got friends at church to send him cards and letters. She talked frequently about the beauty of even one person being brought to faith, and the beauty of her dad surrendering and finding God's peace. As he slowly began to accept Jesus as his personal savior, Susie realized her twenty seconds of courage had paid off. When he was finally ready to go home to be with Christ, Susie was glad that God had put a mission in her heart that would last for eternity.

LEAN INTO YOUR **FEAR**

"Be determined and confident!
Do not be afraid or discouraged, for I, the Lord your God,
am with you wherever you go."

—JOSHUA 1:9 GNT

Going through a fearful activity can often be the game changer that will transform your life. In order to overcome your fear for something you know you have to do, can you lean into it and test the waters? Can you attempt one task, then do something more, and then do something else? By leaning in, you get familiar with the environment, the people, the activities, the tasks, and other elements needed to fully move forward in this area.

By going where your fears are, then leaning into them, you'll emerge braver and more informed about the next task you need to complete. But also consider that what you're most fearful about is probably an area where God is challenging you to grow anyway. By not stepping forward and taking action, your own limitations are keeping you from living the full potential that God has planned for your life. Whether the fear is confronting your financial situation or having that uncomfortable conversation with your spouse or deleting that toxic friend, lean into it. And be sure to call in the comfort of Christ—through prayer—while you're in the middle of it.

GUILT

"When you are guilty,
you must confess the sin."

—LEVITICUS 5:5 GNT

A s a Christian, you've probably heard about free will. The fact is, part of our journey in this life—and a big part of human nature—is that we're allowed to make our own choices, decisions, and judgments.

But can we get real here?

Sometimes those choices hurt ourselves and other people. And all too often, guilt is the ultimate result.

If you've been carrying around guilt for something you've done, realize that its effects are far-reaching. Guilt creates low self-esteem, shows up in our relationships, makes us feel unworthy, stops us from taking advantage of opportunity, plus so many other costs that stem from the original act, which may have happened decades ago.

Alternatively, we can also carry around guilt for something that happened *to us*, even though it was no fault of our own. Whether it's physical abuse or maltreatment that was inflicted upon us, an incident from our childhood, or something horrible that we were wrongly blamed for, oftentimes—even as the victim—we still feel guilty: *If only I hadn't talked back to her, if only I hadn't gotten into his car, if only I hadn't worked late that night.*

No one escapes being hurt. But you don't have to continue punishing yourself through guilt. Similarly, no one escapes making choices, using words, or pursuing actions that hurt others. Mistakes get made. Accidents happen. But you don't have to continue punishing yourself with guilt over something you've done.

ASKING FOR **FORGIVENESS** IS KEY

The reality is that we've all hurt someone we love. So how do we deal with that? How do we erase the guilt and move on? The key is to ask for forgiveness, *then forgive yourself, too.*

STEP ONE: ASK GOD FOR FORGIVENESS. Psalm 86:5 NLT tells us that the Lord is so good, so ready to forgive, and so full of unfailing love for all who ask for His help. Admitting you did wrong and asking forgiveness is something that God has instructed us to do. When we come to Him with genuine regret for our transgressions, the Bible assures us that He will give forgiveness willingly. The reality is that He knew you'd screw up and forgave you before you were born.

STEP TWO: ASK FORGIVENESS FROM THE PERSON YOU'VE HURT. To the best of your ability, address the matter as soon as you can—offering genuine remorse without excuses, explanations, or opinions, which only muddy the water and tend to weaken our admission of fault. If it's too dangerous to approach the other person, communicate your request for forgiveness in some other way that's safe, such as by voice mail, text, or email. Realize that asking for forgiveness doesn't mean you have to renew your relationship with the person (unless you want to). Your responsibility is only to ask for forgiveness and is in no way linked to how they respond. They do not need to forgive you. The goal here is to release guilt's hold on you.

STEP THREE: TRY TO MAKE IT RIGHT. If you stole something, pay it back. If you damaged someone's reputation, own up to it with those you spread gossip to. Right the wrong as best you can. Make the effort, even if you have to ask the person you hurt how they would like to see the matter resolved.

STEP FOUR: WORK ON FORGIVING YOURSELF FOR THE PART YOU PLAYED IN THE SITUATION. Even after you ask for forgiveness from God and the one you harmed, and rectified the wrong to the best of your ability, sometimes we still carry shame and guilt for the hurtful thing we did. Our action was a complete disappointment to ourselves. *How could I do that?* plays on auto-repeat in our head. You're human. No one escapes sin. Learn from what you've done, don't make the same mistake repeatedly, and then let it go. And when the guilt returns, repeat this four-step process.

THE **GIFT** OF GRACE

Just as we can't escape life without hurting others, people—including those we love—hurt us. If someone has hurt you, it's your responsibility to forgive them. You're not saying that what they did is right. And it doesn't make what happened okay. You're just taking steps to release the hold their transgression has over you.

It's also you stepping up maturely and recognizing that, by withholding forgiveness, you could be keeping *someone else* from releasing their guilt and living with a clear conscience. Now, they are able to reach their God-given potential and live free of guilt. Don't we all need the gift of forgiveness from time to time? Show grace. Be the bigger person and allow someone else to move on, too.

GUILT, GOD, AND WISDOM

by Jonathan Harte*

My wife refers to me as her "Beloved." It's from Song of Solomon 6:3 *"I am my beloved's, and my beloved is mine."* She honors me, and I am beyond grateful that I have the opportunity to try and live up to that title. Many days, I struggle to feel deserving of her love because, it's simple really: I messed up colossally.

I made a singularly devastating choice to "step outside" of our marriage and jeopardized everything I held dear in this life. There's no excusing it, and you will never hear me try to justify my behavior. I owned it, including the equally immense guilt that came with it. I broke the heart of the woman I loved more than life itself, and the guilt nearly broke me. The urge was to hide it, but I confessed to her because I knew I needed to take responsibility and fix this.

So, how do you get past guilt of that magnitude? Honestly, I believed this burden was mine to carry for the rest of my life. As far as I was concerned, it was a life sentence, and I deserved it. I told myself, "This was the deal," and I was prepared to live with the guilt forever.

God, it seems, had other plans.

My wife was a devout Christian from the very beginning of our

---

* Pseudonym used to protect contributing writer.

marriage. I, on the other hand, was not. I valued and respected my wife's faith. I appreciated her prayers and was grateful to her for raising our daughters as Christians, but I was not inclined to become a believer. There were many times my wife would tell me I could not keep living off of "borrowed faith," and I would one day need my own. She had no idea just how prophetic her words would be. During one of the early days following my admission, she was having a particularly hard day, as one with a broken heart would, and collapsed in my arms. It was at this moment that the enormity of what I had done to her hit me like a freight train. It was at this precise moment I knew I could not fix any of this on my own. I called out to God, searching for answers, and I promised that, if given a second chance, I would truly honor both my wife and our marriage as I should have done from the beginning. This was the day my wife unknowingly spoke of.

My wife and I sought the help of a Christian counselor to begin the task of rebuilding our marriage. There were times my guilt took over, wore me down, and put distance between us. During those weeks, we often went for drives to be able to talk privately, while my mother-in-law watched the girls for us. On Good Friday, 1999, we found ourselves outside the location where it all went terribly wrong, where I took a road I should never have even considered. As we sat there talking for hours, our conversation turned to faith. I was familiar with who Jesus was, the Christmas story, and Easter. However, there was something different about this conversation; my wife told me it was Jesus knocking on the door, asking me if I wanted Him to come in. There, in the very place where I nearly lost all that was most precious to me, I gave my life to Christ. I cannot explain how or even why I was extended such grace, love, and hope, but I was. I have never been the same since and am deeply grateful to God for that. Hope is a powerful thing, and it should never be overlooked when digging out from under whatever has buried you.

It wasn't magic; my new Christianity did not instantly restore our relationship, but it did give us hope that we had a greater chance to turn it all around. Eventually, we would have more good days than bad. We started to embrace the healing and the joys in our life. However, even with my newfound faith and hope for the future, my guilt continued to nag at me and my struggles to overcome it became arduous. I had accepted that God forgave me, and I had accepted that my wife forgave me, but I could not forgive myself. So how did I deal with the guilt?

First, I took complete responsibility for my actions and owned them. There is no negotiating this. Second, I recognized that I needed God to intervene, not just in the immediate situation, but also to continually work in me. I do not believe I would be the man I am today without God's intervention. Yet, guilt was still my teacher, continually reminding me to never take for granted the most precious things in my life.

In sharing her view of my infidelity with others, my wife said, "Our marriage is better now—not in spite of the infidelity but, in truth, because of it." Even though I wish it could have happened some other way, I do agree with her. However, beyond the restoration of our marriage, I know I would not have been open to a relationship with Jesus had I not been completely burdened with the guilt and consequences of my own actions. I had to be broken for Him to build me into the man He desired me to be.

Ironically, writing my story brought guilt to the surface again and had me reaching out to my wife. We started talking about how God can use guilt to draw us closer to Him, but once its lesson has been learned, guilt is no longer useful and must transform into something else, lest we live in its shadows for the rest of our lives. We discovered that guilt can be transformative. When guilt is filtered through love, which is God, and through faith, which is our relationship with God, guilt becomes wisdom.

The wisdom I acquired through processing my guilt has made me stronger and smarter. I am 100 percent committed to my wife and to our marriage. Although I am still working on becoming the man God designed me to be, there is no doubt I am no longer the man I was. With guilt now transformed into wisdom through love and faith, I know I have a greater chance of being all that God created me to be.

Is there something you've done that has hurt someone but, in the process, also made you wiser? Hurting someone often comes with two kinds of lessons: wisdom and guilt. But while wisdom often keeps us from repeating the mistake, guilt can keep us stuck in the past, unable to move forward and live a normal life.

As the next story shows us, nothing we do, however, is so unforgiveable that Jesus cannot intercede with us—even when the transgression was *against Jesus Himself.*

THE GUILT I CARRIED WITH ME

"This man truly was the Son of God!"

—MATTHEW 27:54 NLT

t was early morning. The sun was already blazing down upon His tortured body. His fresh wounds were now being scorched by the sun's potent rays. Standing at attention, I took a drink of water but could barely swallow because of the tightness in my throat. I was a soldier and had trained for years for this duty. I had achieved the highest honor a Roman Centurion could. But no amount of training could prepare me for this task so different from the rest, nor for what I was currently witnessing. My fellow soldiers had been hardened by years in the military. Compassion was not a common trait in our line of duty. As I watched them in this moment, they were rowdy and their heartlessness was evident.

Forcefully they carried this high-profile criminal into the Prae- torium. His body fell to the ground, unrecognizable. He didn't even look like a man anymore. The blood was no longer red but black, and his wounds were caked with dirt. He'd been whipped to the edge of death. Looking at what was left of Him, I have no idea how He held onto life. My fellow soldiers began to strip Him down, exposing Him in a way that revealed the extensiveness of the wounds. They took some thorns and, weaving them into a crude circle, placed the painful crown upon His head. Then they found a purple robe, which signified royalty, and tied it around his neck, just so they could shame Him even more. As they placed a staff in His hand, I watched them mock and spit on Him, calling Him the King of the Jews.

This man, who they felt so free to humiliate, was the most high-profile criminal I had ever dealt with. He was the man they called Jesus. And He had just been condemned to death.

Through the streets of Jerusalem we escorted Jesus, along with two others, who were criminals and who would be crucified with Him. In those days, the condemned were made to carry the rough-hewn crucifixion crosses on their backs and shoulders—a staggering demand after the beating He'd had. Any healthy Jewish man would struggle to carry the weight of the cross, but what I didn't realize at the time was that Jesus was carrying the weight of the world.

Slowly we wove our way through the streets, and people came out of their homes to see what their so-called king was reduced to. A week earlier, they'd been honoring Him with a parade, and now these same people were shouting *Crucify Him!* Wretched with pain, He struggled to carry the cross. I instructed a Greek man just arriving from the city of Cyrene to help Him.

When we got to the place they called Golgotha, the prisoners stopped and fell to the ground exhausted. On the place where they fell, the company of soldiers nailed the men to their crosses. Jesus twisted in agony as they drove the nails through His hands and feet. When the soldiers were done, I positioned a sign above His head that Pilate had made. It read: *This is the King of the Jews.*

Together, we lifted the crosses from the ground. As each one rose to its upright position, we heard a popping sound as the weight of the criminals, held only by the nails in their hands, dislocated their arms from their sockets. The blood, the bruises, and the pain were so extensive that I couldn't look at Him. I turned my head toward the ground.

The crowd shouted louder and louder, "If you are the Son of God, come down from there." The man was hanging on the cross, suffering, and still they mocked Him.

Then I heard Jesus begin to speak and raised my head. Looking out over the crowd of people and soldiers, He said, "Father, forgive them for they know not what they do." Out of the corner of my eye, I could see my heartless fellow soldiers gambling for His clothes. The crowd continued to mock Him. Yet in the midst of this indignity, Jesus asked His Father to extend forgiveness to them.

And in that moment, the guilt of carrying out these orders began to take a deeper and deeper hold of my heart. This was my job, but how could I be part of this agony?

Then, the unthinkable happened.

At noon, darkness fell across the whole land until three o'clock. At about three o'clock, Jesus called out with a loud voice, "Eli, Eli, lema sabachthani?" which means "My God, my God, why have you abandoned me?"

Some of the bystanders misunderstood and thought he was calling for the prophet Elijah. One of them ran and filled a sponge with sour wine, holding it up to him on a reed stick so he could drink. But the rest said, "Wait! Let's see whether Elijah comes to save him."

Then Jesus shouted out again, and he released his spirit. At that moment the curtain in the sanctuary of the Temple was torn in two, from top to bottom. The earth shook, rocks split apart, and tombs opened. The bodies of many godly men and women who had died were raised from the dead. They left the cemetery after Jesus's resurrection, went into the holy city of Jerusalem, and appeared to many people.

The Roman officer and the other soldiers at the crucifixion were terrified by the earthquake and all that had happened. They said, "This man truly was the Son of God!" (Matthew 27:45–54)

I thought it was like any other day. I thought He was like any other criminal. Yes, I followed my orders, and brutally nailed Him to the cross. But, when I realized He was the Messiah, everything changed.

What had I done?! Who had I become? I couldn't take back what I had done; it was unforgiveable. Then I realized what Jesus had said while He hung on the cross. *Father, forgive them for they know not what they do.* If He could forgive me, how could I not forgive myself? I couldn't change what had happened that day, but I could change myself. He took every sin I ever committed, and He paid the ultimate price. He thought I was worth dying for, and so, I chose to live a life worth living for.

Oftentimes, we, too, think that what we have done is unforgiveable. But Jesus died on the cross so that our "unforgiveable" sins could be erased, deleted—eliminated. It's not necessary to carry guilt about our sins, when God freely offers forgiveness. Here are some tips to help you move on.

WRITE A LETTER TO SOMEONE WHO HAS **HURT** YOU

> *"Remember, the Lord forgave you,*
> *so you must forgive others."*
>
> —COLOSSIANS 3:13 NLT

If someone has hurt you, it's not necessary to carry the weight of the situation anymore. Approach the person and offer forgiveness. If that's impossible—because they're no longer living, you can't locate them or it's simply too dangerous—you can use a technique we like called *The Total Truth Letter,* an exercise we got from success coach Jack Canfield.*

---

* Read more about The Total Truth Process in Jack's awesome book *The Success Principles: How to Get from Where You Are to Where You Want to Be.*

When we're hurt and upset, we usually fail to communicate *all* our true feelings to the person we're upset with. It also becomes difficult to resume a normal relationship with them if that's what we choose to do.

Take out a piece of paper and complete the following statements as you work through the steps—one or more statements for each step:

1. *Express your anger and resentment.* I'm angry that…I resent…
2. *Express your hurt.* It hurt me when…I felt sad when…
3. *Express your fear.* I feel scared when…I was afraid that…
4. *Express your remorse, regret, and accountability.* I'm sorry that…
5. *Express your wants.* All I ever want(ed) is…I deserve…
6. *Express your love, compassion, forgiveness and appreciation.* I understand that…I forgive you for…I appreciate…

When you're done writing, you can deliver the letter, burn it, or otherwise destroy it. The key is to express *for yourself* your emotions and pain. This doesn't condone what they did to you, but it helps you forgive the person completely and allows you to let go of any guilt anchored in the past situation.

LOSE THE WEIGHT OF **GUILT**

"For day and night your hand was heavy on me. My strength was sapped in the heat of summer."

—PSALM 32:4 WEB

When we talk about guilt at our live event, OolaPalooza,* we usually ask the biggest, strongest guy in the audience to come up on stage and hold a twenty-pound bag straight out to the side while we're

---

* Read more about it at *oolalife.com/oolapalooza*.

teaching to everyone else. After a while, even though the weight of the bag is light relative to his size and strength, he fatigues and his arm drops to his side. This is a simple way to illustrate that you can hold guilt for a while, but over time, even if you think you are strong, guilt literally weighs you down. Perhaps that's why many people say, *I've had the weight of this pressing on me for years.* You just can't move on. It's too heavy. To lose this weight, take steps to forgive and move on.

PREVENT GUILT FROM MANIFESTING AS OTHER **BLOCKERS**

"When I did not confess my sins,
I was worn out from crying all day long."

—PSALM 32:3 GNT

Guilt is a choice. You can take steps to eliminate it from your life, but if you choose not to process the guilt, realize that it's likely to show up as *other Blockers* on your way to creating the OolaLife.

How does this happen? You feel guilty about something that you did years ago, then become fearful about pursuing something new because it might end up the same. You disappointed yourself with your mistake, so you lash out in anger at someone you love, who doesn't deserve it. Your guilt convinces you that you don't deserve to be happy or successful, so you self-sabotage a terrific new opportunity to advance your career. You feel guilty that, as a teenager, you somehow attracted the wrong man, and now your self-esteem keeps you from getting into another relationship.

Are you holding onto guilt and letting it manifest as other Blockers? Identify it, and do the work to push through.

ANGER

"Stop being bitter and angry and mad at others.
Don't yell at one another or curse
each other or ever be rude."

—EPHESIANS 4:31 CEV

Have you ever heard of *the ripple effect*? It's the idea that, just like dropping a stone in the water, your actions create a ripple of energy—either good or bad—that touches millions of people you may never meet. Two thousand years ago, Jesus created the ultimate ripple effect. And today, you may see people like medical researchers, missionaries, talk-show hosts, or church leaders use this phenomenon for good on a grand scale.

But you have access to this ripple effect, too. What about eye contact and a simple smile, holding the door for someone with their hands full of kids and groceries, or buying a coffee for the person behind you in the drive-through?

And what about the ripple effect of *negative energy*—something horrible and lasting like anger? History is filled with examples of the mass impact on millions of people that anger once produced: the 9/11 tragedy, the slaying of Dr. Martin Luther King Jr., and more historically, the anger of those who crucified Jesus. Smaller events, too, create lasting anger, like cutting off someone in traffic, being rude to a server when your order isn't to your liking, or callously dropping an inflammatory comment on someone's Facebook post. *The ripple effect* works both ways.

WHERE DOES **ANGER** COME FROM?

Anger starts with its distant cousin, *frustration*, a perfectly normal response to life's crazier moments. But when uncontrolled frustration continues or escalates into heated arguments, obscene language, violent outbursts, accusations, manipulation, or worse, that's when the real damage happens.

While it's hard to think about prayer or any other God-centered remedy during such episodes, experts do recommend steps to tame your temper in the moment: step away, think before you speak, focus on resolving the issue at hand, practice relaxation skills, or get some exercise to cool off.

But in the long run, work with Jesus to find out where the anger is coming from. Was it learned during childhood? Does it stem from just one incident? A trained Christian counselor can help you consider your past and present triggers and then help you prayerfully calm the rage for good.

WHAT **SIXTY** SECONDS OF ANGER CAN DO

You might have heard the Ralph Waldo Emerson quote that says: *Sixty seconds of anger robs you of one minute of happiness.* Well, the reality is much worse than that. Anger robs *others* of happiness, too. Think about the effect of your anger on your spouse, kids, family members, friends, and even strangers. And when you act out at the office, you set the tone for your workplace.

But there's an even more sobering risk: erupting in fury makes you unsafe, untrustworthy, and someone to be avoided when the going gets tough. People sense that they can't bring their problems to you for fear that you'll explode with rage. Those aren't the kind of trusting relationships God wants for us. Anger keeps us disconnected from the close loving bond of others.

GET A **GRIP**

Of course, anger doesn't just affect our emotions. It affects our physical body, too—by putting us into "high-alert mode" and initiating many physical changes. For one thing, our adrenal glands release two potent stress hormones: adrenaline and cortisol. These powerful chemicals prepare our body for action—either fight or flight—which means our muscles tense, our heart rate accelerates, and our breathing becomes faster and shallower. Our blood pressure goes up. We may begin to sweat. And psychologists say it takes the body twenty to sixty minutes to calm down and return to normal.

If this is what happens with just one angry outburst, can you imagine what damage occurs from long-term, ongoing anger? Insomnia, stroke, heart attack, skin conditions, and gastrointestinal distress are just some of the risks. Get a grip on your anger, or it will take its toll on you.

ALONE WITH YOU NEXT TO ME

by Lauren Crews Dow

t was nearing midnight. Exhausted, I fell into bed and quickly rolled over to my right side. I turned off the lamp and thought that falling asleep would be the perfect remedy for a very difficult week. I had an aching feeling inside me of being utterly alone, even though I wasn't. He was lying right next to me, but I felt like he wasn't there at all. *Why doesn't he just know how I feel?* I thought to myself.

"Good night, babe. I love you!" Thomas said as he touched my left shoulder, signaling me to give him our routine good night kiss.

"I love you, too," I responded as I slowly turned around, gave him a peck on the lips, and quickly rolled back over.

My body language said it all.

As I waited in the silence and darkness, I closed my eyes tight and cleared my throat. I longed for him to say something, anything, but I dreaded the words I knew he was going to say. Finally, the words, "What's wrong?" fell out of his mouth with a concerning tone.

"What's wrong? What's wrong, Thomas?" I exclaimed. "I feel alone in this and that's what's wrong."

"What do you mean you feel alone? I am right here," he calmly responded.

How could he not see this? How could he not feel what I feel? I thought to myself.

After a heavy sigh, I snapped back, "Thomas, I can't bear this pain. I feel at times that I can't breathe because of the weight of this hurt, this anger, and this sadness. It's just too much. And I feel like I am carrying it all by myself."

The anger further boiled up inside of me as only seconds passed by. I pushed off the covers because my body was getting hot. I sat straight up, looked at him, and yelled, "Aren't you sad? Aren't you angry? Anything? Show me any kind of emotion! Please!!"

With a calm but shaken voice, Thomas said, "Lauren, of course I am! I am heartbroken. That was my baby, too!"

I started to sob as I quickly got out of bed and walked towards the bathroom. I locked the door behind me and started to fill the bathtub. I turned off the lights to be alone with just me, my bath, and my thoughts. As I climbed into the tub, I noticed the water was way too hot, but it actually balanced out the pain I was feeling in that moment, so I slid my body and pain deep into that water. As I laid there in silence, the only thing I could hear was the sound of my tears dripping into the tub as they rolled down my face.

We had been trying to conceive for eight months. Then, to our surprise one day, "it" happened.

After eight months of prayer, and a little bit of pixie dust scattered on a Disney cruise, we were finally blessed with the gift of life. The feeling was overwhelming—knowing that a little baby was growing inside of me, and knowing that my body was providing this little human with everything it needed to grow and develop. I was so thankful to God for picking Thomas and me for this perfect, special gift.

In deep gratitude, Thomas, Kyleigh, and I would pray over my belly every night. Thomas loved the idea of becoming a father again, and Kyleigh was so excited to be a big sister to Cookie. Yeah, she named the little baby Cookie. Maybe it was because she knew this baby would be sweet like her. Either way we went with it.

I was nearing the end of my first trimester when I lost Cookie. I never thought it would happen to me, but no one ever does. The miscarriage led me to a downward spiral of pain, anger, and depression. The pain of feeling that my body couldn't support this baby, and the anger at God for giving me this child, letting me get my hopes up—and then taking it all away—crushed me. Why did this happen? Why would God do this to me? And why am I feeling so alone in this? Why doesn't anyone understand, especially Thomas?

As I laid in the tub, I brought my knees up to my chest, closed my eyes, and began crying out to God like never before. I was so mad at Him, and kept blaming Him for taking my baby away. However, in this time of anger, I also felt intense guilt that I was mad at God and at Thomas. Everything around me and inside of me felt like it was being ripped away and I was losing control. As I felt the anger and guilt polarize my mind, I suddenly felt a strange sense of peace flood over me in my brokenness. I saw His light shine through all of my hurt, sadness, loneliness, anger, guilt, shame and fear.

I remembered a friend told me once that God welcomes your anger at Him, because He knows it will bring you closer to Him in a way you've never known before—that He will use the pain and anger to bless you in ways that you can't imagine. It was in that moment the weight lifted off my chest, and I realized He is able to give me everything I truly need.

God is no stranger to anger. In fact, He's visited His wrath upon individuals and entire populations throughout the history of man.

But what happens to our relationship with God when *we're angry?* If we look to Him for relief, healing, and restorative calm, anger can actually bring us closer to God in a way we've never experienced before.

THE STORM

"You will know which one to arrest when
I greet him with a kiss."

—MATTHEW 26:48 NLT

He looked older than His years. The lines on His face were more pronounced, and His anguish was obvious. Jesus was sorrowful and troubled as we walked toward the urban garden of Gethsemane. While on our journey, I thought that it would be more helpful for me to walk right beside Him. But I didn't have the courage. So, instead, I paced myself a couple of feet behind Him to His left. I was hoping that my presence was comforting to Him somehow and that He knew that I was there for Him.

When we finally arrived at the garden, He told Zebedee's two sons and me to come with Him while He went to pray. I had never seen Jesus this overtaken by distress. Seeing Him this way frightened me and made me distressed, too.

"My soul is overwhelmed with sorrow to the point of death. Stay here and keep watch with me," He said. I watched Him walk a little farther into the garden; then He fell with His face to the ground and began to pray intensely. This was painful to watch, and I felt even more concerned now. It was hard to look away. But as worried as I was, I could not keep the exhaustion that I felt from the long journey from overtaking me. I tried to fight it, but I was unable to stay awake.

Finally, promising myself that I would only rest for a minute or two, I allowed my heavy eyelids to close, and I fell deeply asleep.

I don't know how much later it was when I felt a nudge on my shoulder. Feeling foggy, it took me a moment to realize that it was Jesus waking me up.

"Couldn't you men keep watch with me for one hour?" He questioned. I was embarrassed at my lack of strength and again promised myself and Him that I would remain awake and keep watch like He asked. I remember watching as He went back into the garden to pray. My intention was to stay awake and pray for Him, but again, with my eyes burning, I gave into sleep.

I was mortified when He woke me up the second and third time as He interrupted His praying to rouse me from slumber.

Finally, after awakening me for the fourth time, Jesus said, "Rise! Let us go; here comes my betrayer."

Jumping up, I stood, then began to follow Him.

In the darkness of the night they arrived. Shamefully, they used the night as cover for this unlawful event that would transpire, so things would not be fully exposed to the public. But even if the world did not see this tactic, I certainly did. Though Jesus announced in advance his betrayer's arrival, I still couldn't believe my eyes when I saw this despicable person coming closer and closer through the thickness of the dark. The moon peeked through the trees, almost as a spotlight for the travesty that was about to take place.

It was Judas!

And remarkably, he had the audacity to walk right up to us like it was any other day and to greet Jesus with a kiss on the cheek. Nothing could prepare me for the feeling I had—realizing a person we had recently broken bread with was now a traitor. Jesus had told us at dinner that this would happen, but we couldn't believe that Judas would actually do it. True, Jesus had had multiple attempts on His life throughout our time together, but it did not seem likely that Judas would be the one orchestrating the next attack.

But Jesus had known. As soon as Judas kissed Him on the cheek, He replied, "Do what you came for, friend." Judas stepped aside, and guards seized Jesus.

Friend! I raged inside. *Why would He call Judas His friend?*

Judas was certainly no longer a friend of mine. How could Jesus be so calm while I was beyond distraught? *How did we not see this coming?* I thought. *How could Judas do this? We trusted him!*

Had he been planning this callous act the entire time, and we didn't know it? This guy—he had been our brother. For years we traveled, worked, ate, and played on the same team of world changers. After all we had experienced together, how could Judas turn his back on the One who believed in us the most? The One who believed in him. The One who showed us a better way to live. Why would Judas do this? What was worth selling his soul for?

The questions fed my anger like a carnivorous animal.

I looked over at Jesus, who was being restrained by the guards. His face was calm. And was it my imagination or were the lines in His face less pronounced than they had been on our journey here? How could He not seem to be angry about all of this? I know Jesus taught us to turn the other cheek, but this was too much. There were times past when Jesus had seemed angry, like when He chased the money-changers out of the temple. He would also get upset when He saw injustices. But even then, He never allowed anger to rule Him because He saw the bigger picture.

But wasn't this different? How could even Jesus not be infuriated and fight back now?

I couldn't hold back any longer. My anger overtook the grace in me. I could see Judas through the sea of armed guards, the posse of the religious folks, and the high priests who had gathered. The smug satisfied smirk on Judas's face seemed to be personally provoking me to come after him.

Blinded by my feelings of hatred and disgust for Judas coupled with my feelings of love and loyalty for Jesus, I became enraged. I once told Jesus I would lay down my life for Him. Was this that moment? Ensnared in the anger that had been building in me, I took action. The anger surged through me, I grasped my sword as tightly as the anger was grasping my heart, and I blindly swung it.

At the instant sight of blood, I stepped back. I looked at Malchus, the servant of the high priest, bleeding from the side of his head. I had taken off his ear. It wasn't Malchus's fault; it was Judas I was after. I should have stopped, but I couldn't. My anger toward Judas was so great that it had a life of its own. In my rage, I did not discriminate who I would hurt. With the fire in my eyes unrelenting, I couldn't get control of myself.

"Put away your sword," Jesus told him. "Those who use the sword will die by the sword. Don't you realize that I could ask my Father for thousands of angels to protect us, and he would send them instantly?" (Matthew 26:52–53)

Put away my sword? If I did, how would the Scriptures be fulfilled that described what must happen now?

What's more, how could Judas have been the one who betrayed Jesus, yet I was the one getting the reprimand? It took me a moment, but once again, I saw the true heart and spirit of the Lord and Savior Jesus Christ as He reached out to Malchus, laid His hand upon his severed ear, and healed him.

In one moment, Jesus could have allowed Himself to be as angry as me, but instead, He was an example of control—an example of how an act of revenge was counterproductive to His larger cause.

I lost a piece of myself that day as my actions hurt an innocent man. What I experienced was the fruit of a lack of knowledge and understanding. Jesus, in one moment, could have taken control of the situation, but He wasn't reactionary. He understood His purpose and the power He possessed. If He would have reacted in a fit of anger like me, He could have disqualified Himself from His true purpose and the victory He would have later as King over the rest of humanity.

When your anger hurts innocent people, it hurts *you* in the long run, too. You can never get back those sixty seconds of fury, particularly if you damage a relationship, ruin your prospects, physically injure someone, or actually commit a crime. If anger is present in your life, start praying fervently for God to help you get past this OolaBlocker.

SOLVE YOUR **TRIGGERS** BEFORE THEY ANGER YOU

"Also get rid of your anger, hot tempers, hatred, cursing, obscene language, and all similar sins."

—COLOSSIANS 3:8 GWT

Anger is usually triggered by one of two things: a situation that pops up unexpectedly or a recurring problem that gets on your last good nerve. Going ballistic over either one is never acceptable—*particularly* when you have 100 percent control over solving, containing, managing, or eliminating virtually all *recurring* triggers.

If you're continually late getting out the driveway or dropping the kids off at school, for instance, there are things you can do to de-stress your morning routine: lay out clothes the night before, put together backpacks and set them by the door, keep cut fruit in the fridge, and get to bed thirty to sixty minutes earlier so you wake up refreshed and prepared to take on your day.

If your triggers are related to your money, household responsibilities, technology, bills, taxes, office politics, work deadlines, or something else manageable, schedule time on your calendar to take care of these recurring issues—even asking a friend or coworker to help you if necessary. Don't give in to anger. It's never a lasting solution anyway.

COMMUNICATE YOUR **PASSION** FOR CHRIST WITHOUT ANGER

"The anger of man does not achieve
the righteousness of God."

—James 1:20 NASB[*]

Not a day goes by that breaking news programs *don't* carry stories about religious fervor causing violent confrontation. It seems that it's the "new normal" in our world. But does it have to be?

Religion today divides people through anger. But there are better ways to communicate your passion for Christ. Do good works. Love unconditionally. Be an example of what living a Christ-centered life looks like. Establish boundaries for interacting with others. And prayerfully consider how to best represent your beliefs to others.

You're not going to bring anyone to Jesus through anger. You can disagree with non-Christians and boldly profess your faith, but don't let that disagreement escalate into rage.

---

* New American Standard Bible.

BE A **VICTOR**, NOT A VICTIM

"Sensible people control their temper; they earn
respect by overlooking wrongs."

—Proverbs 19:11 NLT

Joel Osteen is famous for saying: *Be a victor, not a victim.* Far too often, anger comes from a feeling that we've been wronged—whether that's actually true or just imagined. Someone has hurt us, and that's grounds for continually beating up the rest of the world.

But who's *really* the one being hurt on an ongoing basis by holding on to this anger? That's right—us. Instead of focusing on having been wronged, why not focus instead on taking action to overcome the past? Instead of staying stuck in victimhood, why not take steps to move forward toward victory? If you want to take it to the next level, what if you could find gratitude in that bad thing that happened? Maybe it made you stronger, more independent, or turned you toward Jesus. When you're consumed with achieving the OolaLife, victimhood will be part of your distant past.

SELF-SABOTAGE

"I don't understand why I act the way I do.
I don't do what I know is right.
I do the things I hate."

—ROMANS 7:15 CEV

God has designed each one of us for greatness. Yet all too often, instead of stepping into the magnificent role that He's planned for us, we stop ourselves. We get in our own way.

In the Old Testament, God chose a prophet named Jonah to go to the city of Nineveh, the then capital of the Neo-Assyrian Empire and a major metropolis with more than 120,000 people.

"Announce My judgment against it," God said, "because I have seen how wicked its people are."

But Jonah would have none of it.

Instead of following God's path, which would eventually see Jonah transform this great nation, Jonah fled to the coast where he boarded a ship for Spain.* While you've probably read what happens next—Jonah gets thrown overboard by the crew and swallowed by an enormous fish—what's more important to this story is what often happens to all of us: despite Jonah's self-sabotage, God keeps nudging Jonah until he goes to Nineveh and turns the population from their wicked ways.

Jonah fulfills his calling.

WHY DO WE KEEP OURSELVES FROM **MOVING** FORWARD?

Think about how a three-year-old approaches the world. They don't stop themselves when reaching for a toy they want. They don't tell themselves, *I'm not smart enough* to play blocks with the other kids. They don't procrastinate before walking straight toward the polar bear enclosure at the zoo. They don't hold back, delay, procrastinate,

---

* Read this story in the four chapters of the Book of Jonah—we like the New Living Translation. Nineveh is on the outskirts of modern-day Mosul in northern Iraq.

stress-eat, overanalyze, self-medicate, overwork, seek retail therapy, gamble, or otherwise prevent *anything* they want to do. They simply don't behave or act in any way that keeps them from getting what they want.

But what happens as they grow? They hear two critical words that change that eager, confident, loving, and exceptional image of themselves: *you are.*

"*You are* acting crazy in the back seat," their mom begins. *You are* mean to your brother. *You are* too clumsy to play that sport. *You are* not ready for that class. *You are* lazy and won't get anywhere in life. *You are* not cut out for that career.

Later, the criticisms become even more direct and—sadly—originate from more and more places: *You are* irresponsible. *You are* less qualified than we need. *You are* not the one I want. Eventually these statements pile up and create a self-image that works hard to live up to exactly what we've been told: *you are not good enough to have the life you want.*

Is it any wonder that our subconscious mind remembers this information—and stops us—every time we want to move forward?

SILENCING "YOU ARE" WITH "I AM"

If God were speaking to you right now, what would He say? *I love you just the way you are. I believe in you. You can achieve the great purpose I have planned for you. I've instilled in you everything you need to create an amazing future in My Kingdom.*

Real different, right?

So one way that we can overcome the limiting messages we took on from our past is to take a page out of God's playbook and start *talking to ourselves* the way He would talk to us. By using the words, *I am,* you can undo the years of negative reinforcement that are causing you to build roadblocks between you and the OolaLife: *I am smart enough. I am worthy and deserving. I am beautiful and unique. I am capable of being loved. I am worth it. I am enough.*

"I AM DESIGNED BY GOD FOR **GREATNESS**"

When we travel around the country on the OolaBus, we meet people who have been living with self-sabotage for *years*. On our journey to more communities than we can count, we've noticed of all the Blockers, *fear* and *self-sabotage* are the most common. In fact, in just a few minutes of conversation and interaction, we often see more beauty and potential in the people we meet than they see in themselves. This is heartbreaking—especially considering that you have *amazingness* inside of you. Yet the person who most frequently tells us that we're not good enough—is *ourselves*.

To start eliminating self-sabotage, first identify where it's showing up for you. Do you overeat under stress? Do you hold back in your career? Do you stay disconnected from romantic relationships? Where are you sabotaging what could be an amazing life?

Next, ask yourself what your life would look like if you continue to give into this self-sabotage. Alternatively, what if you pushed through the self-sabotage? Finally, what's your twenty seconds of courage? What action step can you take today?

VOICES

by Hannah Crews

The only thing I could see was a bright light, a light so blinding that it made everything around it invisible. My heart was pounding; my breath was shaking. But slowly, the sounds of hand claps and whistles started to echo throughout the auditorium. My twelve-year-old face kept staring at that spotlight, my cheeks and lips covered in bright pink stage makeup while wearing a 1940s costume gown. My singing solo was finished—and the play was almost over. I stood there, with a sense of purpose draped over my awkward prepubescent stage body, like a warm blanket of confidence and belonging.

I quickly exited stage right. I muted my microphone to get ready for the final bow, only to hear the murmurs of two of my fellow classmates in a nearby corner: "Why did *she* get this part," said the first girl. "She's not even that good," replied the second. The girls snickered together, thinking I couldn't hear them. But I did.

My heart sunk down to my stomach. The sense of purpose I felt just seconds before was now replaced with a seed of doubt. *Maybe I'm not that good after all.*

Fast-forward five years. The lights in our AP English class were turned off. The television was turned on, as all thirty of us high school juniors waited for our campus's weekly news broadcast to start. Lively music played through the speakers, the school mascot flashed on the

181

screen, and the picture faded to a seventeen-year-old me. "Thanks so much for tuning into this week's Cardinal Report. I'm Hannah Linn."

As the show started, I sat up tall, daydreaming about a career on *Good Morning, America*—but my ears were listening harder than ever to any voice that whispered doubt around me. Sure enough, I heard the sigh of a girl two rows behind me, "Please, I'd rather claw my eyes out." It was followed by the stifled laughs of the posse next to her.

I sunk down in my chair, wanting to become invisible. Her words and their laughter watered the doubt growing inside me. *Maybe my dream is a dumb idea.*

Fast-forward another eight years. I sat in front of my computer, finishing up the final touches of a video filled with speaking parts, graphics, music, and fancy edits. With a tremoring finger, I clicked "post," and the video went live on all social media sites. That same sense of purpose and accomplishment suddenly fell over me and gave meaning to all those years of reporting and television training.

As quickly as the sense of accomplishment came, I grew to expect it to flee within a moment's notice. Sure enough, within minutes, the comments started. And through all the support, all I could see was the negativity and criticism.

My body sunk so deep in the couch that I couldn't get up. Instead, I lay down, covered my face, and wept. Every tear that fell from my eyes that day felt like the final remnants of my purpose leaving my body.

Maybe this isn't God's plan for my life, after all, I thought.

I was so tired of it all—so resentful to this "purpose." Every time I pursued it, it resulted in the backbiting words or finger-pointing voices of criticism and shame. I was experiencing death by a thousand cuts. All I wanted to do was to remain quiet, complacent, and hidden where it was safe. But in that space, I started losing myself. Shunning the things I loved was driving me to a place of emptiness. All those years of education, training, creating, reporting, editing, speaking, singing, articulating, and performing—at times it seemed they were all for nothing.

During this dark moment in my life, I craved change. A friend recommended the book, *Oola for Women*. When it arrived, I tore open the FedEx package with such vigor, you would have thought it was chocolate. I turned to the first chapter on a beautiful spring day. I'd put on yoga pants and my favorite monogrammed ball cap. As I sat in my back yard, leaning against a chain-link fence on a bed of deep green St. Augustine grass, I began to read the stories of incredible women. It felt like I had dived into another world—a world that was challenging me, calling me out, and revealing things about myself that I had no idea existed.

It challenged me to look at the others in my life whose voices weren't as loud, but who were always there for me: the life-breathers in my circle who spoke over me with unconditional encouragement, wiped my tears, and gave me insight on how to gracefully handle myself when I was hurt. They were those who flicked me in the forehead with loving words, reminding me of my gifts and my purpose.

Why had I let the negative few drown out the positive many?

After reading for well over an hour, I gazed up at a bright blue sky with tear-brimmed eyes and a repentant heart. I had just finished the chapter on self-sabotage, and seven words smacked me in the face: *I am designed by God for greatness!*

I paused and reread that sentence over and over.

Those seven words brought clarity to my heart and cleared out the built-up negativity in my mind that had been growing since I was twelve. I realized that I was allowing the opinion of others to control my life, my decision-making, my self-worth, and my purpose. Not only was this unfair to me, but it was unfair to God. I realized from this point forward, I would not live for them but for Him.

My heart was convicted and lovingly corrected, the negativity erased from my mind. The purpose had been placed back in my heart. No longer was I going to blame others for my fears. No longer was I going to point the finger and play victim. No longer was I going to stay stuck in a place of self-pity. It was time for me to move out of People-Pleasing City, USA, and step into the woman God designed me to be. I knew in this moment that I would place my self-worth in God and my purpose in His hands.

Years of self-examination and Christ-seeking later, I stand in a hotel room next to one of my closest business partners. The video crew is clipping on my lapel microphone and the photographer is snapping some behind-the-scenes shots. The lights are on, and the camera is rolling. As I gaze at the teleprompter, all of a sudden I feel a familiar emotion—the feeling I first felt when I was only twelve years old. That same warm blanket of confidence and belonging is back! But this time, I realize that it isn't just a feeling; it's the love, the mercy, and the goodness of God.

In today's culture of judgment, jealousy, and criticism, it's easy to believe we're not capable, not lovable, or somehow not worth a successful future. Fortunately, Jesus has a 50,000-foot view of our lives and capabilities. He sees us not only as we are, but *who we can be.*

LIVING WATER

*"They couldn't believe He was talking with
that kind of woman."*

—JOHN 4:27b MSG

The sun blazed through the clear sky from its highest point and dissipated the few clouds that tried to offer protection. It was hot—the kind of heat that pulls moisture and energy out of your body. I felt it as I made my way through my town of Sychar to Jacob's well to get water. Although the Samaritan sun was bright and hot, the painful part was that it lit up the village, and everyone could see me. The sun felt like a spotlight on me as I took my daily walk of shame, moving past the mean girls and judgmental men and religious folks. The constant judgment of others—and my past—made me feel "less than" as a woman and had me questioning my self-worth constantly.

I wanted to avoid hearing what they had to say about me, but their whispers seemed amplified, and their glances spoke volumes. They didn't know my heart, but they all had their opinions. They had no clue who I really was, the challenges I have endured—they only knew the failures of my past decisions. Was it really so unforgivable to love and want to be loved?

For some, it seemed they could make marriage work on the first try; I hadn't been so lucky. I thought that with persistence, it would have stuck on at least the second or third attempt, but it didn't. Why did this keep happening to me? Why did I keep falling into the same cycle in my relationships? Was it my family upbringing? Did the first husband ruin me for a second, third, fourth, or fifth marriage?

Maybe marriage wasn't for me, and that is precisely why Matthaeus, my current significant other, was my roommate and not my husband. Maybe it was for the best. The heartache I felt from each broken relationship left me with nothing more to give. I was empty and broken.

As I approached the stone well, I saw a man resting there. I had never seen Him before. *What kind of guy hangs out at wells in the middle of the day?* I thought as I moved swiftly and tried to avoid eye contact. As I began to lower my bucket down the well, grasping the rope firmly and looking into the deep black hole, I felt like I was looking at my life. What was it that caused me to keep living in this Groundhog Day where I never moved forward, just the same cycle with different players? With a big tug, I started to pull up the bucket filled with water. It was then that He spoke to me—His words broke the trance I was in as I reflected on my dismal life.

"Will you give me a drink?" the man asked.

I glanced over and noticed that He was a Jewish man who appeared to be tired from a long journey. Since Jews don't associate themselves with Samaritans, I wondered, *Why is this man talking to me?*

I was also taken aback. *Did He really just ask me for a drink? Seriously, who is this guy?*

I looked at Him in disbelief. Didn't He realize that talking to me could cause Him problems? Of course, I had nothing else to lose, but by the looks of Him, *He did.* Did He not get the memo that His kind don't talk to my kind? I mean, not only was He not supposed to talk to me because of where I was from, but I was also the kind of girl who could ruin one's reputation just by being seen with me. Then He said, "If you knew the gift of God and who it is that asks you for a drink, you would have asked Him and He would have given you living water."

What's this? He shows up without a bucket or rope, and now He's offering me something that seems impossible. *Does He think He has better water than the person who gave us this well?* I thought to myself. I replied, "Sir, you have nothing to draw with and the well is deep. Where can you get this living water? Are you greater than our father Jacob, who gave us the well and drank from it himself, as did his sons and his livestock?" Bewildered, I stared at Him for a response.

"Anyone who drinks this water will soon become thirsty again," He replied. "But those who drink the water I give will never be thirsty again. It becomes a fresh, bubbling spring within them, giving them eternal life."

I wanted this living water, and replied, "Sir, give me this water so that I won't get thirsty and have to keep coming here to draw water."

"Go and get your husband," He told me.

"But I'm not married," I replied.

"You are right when you say you have no husband," the man said. "The fact is, you have had five husbands, and the man you now have is not your husband. What you have just said is quite true."

How could this man already know my mistakes yet still speak to me? But more than that, His tone was different. He wasn't judging me like the others did, but His voice seemed to challenge me—in a good way. He didn't see me as my sin but—instead—as *who I was created to be.* I had made so many mistakes over and over, but He put aside everything and broke protocol to speak to me.

Who is this man who speaks of Living Water? I thought to myself. *A prophet?* Confused, I finally replied to Him, "I know that Messiah (called Christ) is coming. When He comes, He will explain everything to us."

The Man declared, "I, the one speaking to you—I am He."

In that moment, I realized that I was speaking to the Savior of the world. Moments earlier, I didn't feel worthy to talk to anyone in my town, and suddenly I was speaking to the Lord Jesus Christ. A feeling of confidence flowed through my body and spirit. I put down the water jar that I had just filled from the well and went back to town. I wanted to tell everyone that our long-awaited Messiah was at the well. The same people who avoided me, as I avoided them, were now listening to me as I told them about my experience. The people of Sychar started walking to the well to see for themselves. When they met Jesus, they convinced Him to stay and teach the good word. And He did for two days.

Many of the Samaritans from Sychar came to believe in Him because of my testimony. Before, I was the woman who avoided everyone and tried to drown out the gossip around me. But now I felt whole.

Just like the woman at the well, we, too, can fall into a pattern of failure. Whether it's in our relationships (as she experienced) or in our career, finances, fitness goals—wherever you are sabotaging your future—God has a plan to help you move past this cycle of disappointment.

LISTEN TO THE VOICE
THAT CREATED YOU

"Jesus answered… 'You people judge by outward appearances; I do not judge anyone.'"
—JOHN 8:14–15 NET

What often brings down our self-esteem to the point of self-sabotage is that we listen to the voices who are judging us, instead of listening to the One who created us. All too often, what we hear on social media, in our workplace, throughout our extended family, the neighborhood, or even in our church community is that we don't measure up.

But God is *ecstatic* about us and our future. He's thrilled to be the driving force behind what we're doing. He *wants* us to become stronger, more talented, more successful and more capable *because that's who we are destined to be* within His Kingdom. This is the voice we need to tune in to: the One who created us.

STOP **SABOTAGING** YOUR HEALTH

"No one hates his own body but feeds and cares for it,
just as Christ cares for the church."

—EPHESIANS 5:29 NLT

Binge eating, junk food, drinking more than "a few" during the game or after work—these are all ways that we self-sabotage our health. Combine this self-sabotage in our diet with procrastination about going to the gym, and you've got a recipe for a future health disaster.

God designed our bodies to support us in anything we want to do. Prayerfully ask Him to inspire you to get into shape, increase your stamina, and keep your cool new image, so you have the energy and vitality to serve Him and pursue your purpose.

CONSIDER HOW **SELF-SABOTAGE** KEEPS YOU FROM LIVING YOUR LIFE FOR CHRIST

"Why do you keep on saying that I am your Lord,
when you refuse to do what I say?"

—LUKE 6:46 CEV

Jesus always shows up for you. Now He needs *you* to do the same for His Kingdom. If you're beginning to see a unique role for yourself in growing the church, ministering to other believers, teaching Sunday school, community outreach, or some other passion, start identifying what's holding you back.

Pray for help getting past your self-sabotage, so you can pursue the unique calling God has placed on your life. See your role on this planet as more than about you, but as an active and fearless team member for a much greater cause—His cause.

LAZINESS

"No matter how much a lazy person may
want something, he will never get it.
A hard worker will get everything he wants."

—PROVERBS 13:4 GNT

T here's no question that a lot of us are lazy. Maybe not as a whole, but definitely lazy parts. It's just human nature, right? We're too "busy" to go to the gym, too "distracted" to pay our bills on time, or too "triggered" to keep hurtful comments to ourselves.

We look at the changes we want to make in our life and say someday I'm going to lose those fifty pounds, someday I will get off my diabetes medication, someday I'm going to put my marriage back together, someday I'm going to build that business or side hustle, and someday I'm going to crush it in all 7 F's of Oola. But what happens? We lounge and procrastinate, watching Netflix and endlessly scrolling on our phones, then explain away with excuses our lack of progress in nearly every area of our lives.

The world makes it easy to be lazy, and we are happy to comply.

SPIRITUAL **LAZINESS**

But have you ever wondered what laziness looks like in your Christian life? Do you skip prayer because you've had a long day? Is the only time you grab your Bible on Sunday mornings on the way out the door? Do you justify harmless lies to get out of prior commitments?

Not only do these lazy habits keep you at arm's length in your relationship with God (and dishonest about your integrity as a Christian), but lazy habits can also lead to far more serious consequences with your family. Where can spiritual laziness show up in your life?

◎ Delegating your children's spiritual upbringing to others (school, church, etc.), and not teaching and leading by example
◎ Skipping church for the big game
◎ Eating in front of the TV or computer and skipping grace

⊚ Making a New Year's resolution to tithe, read the Bible, join a small group, participate in community service, or attend church weekly and then throwing in the towel by February

Whatever you have to do to carve out the time, whether it's give up an activity you like, hold a weekly family meeting, or let something else slide, find the energy to look after the spiritual growth of your family.

HOW YOU DO ANYTHING IS HOW YOU DO EVERYTHING

When you're lazy with the little things, that laziness often shows up in more critical areas, too, producing bleak outcomes in your finances, relationships, and health. Ouch.

To start overcoming laziness in trivial matters, the Ready-Set-Go Formula works perfectly. Pick an area where you're lazy—say, the discipline of consistently posting on social media to grow your business—then, call it out: *I don't have time to post. I don't know what to post. I'm embarrassed that people haven't heard from me in months. I'd have to take a photo to go with my idea.*

Next, *set* laziness in its place: *If I post consistently, my audience may grow and sales might pick up. If I don't, I will not introduce my business or product to new people.*

Finally, find twenty seconds of courage and simply *go for it.* Write a post, take a picture, grab your smartphone, and do a fun video on a new product or service, or find some older inventory you can discount for a special sale.

⊚ ⊚ ⊚ ⊚

THE LAZY CHRISTIAN

by Dave Braun

We were driving ten miles per hour up a mountain pass between Missoula, Montana, and Spokane, Washington, in late September. I was in the passenger seat and the OolaGuru was behind the wheel. Locked into first gear, our fifty-eight horsepower engine was screaming, and although the engine was hot, the inside of the bus was freezing. It was unseasonably cold, and I was desperately scraping the windshield with my debit card to keep it from frosting over. Halfway through the mountain pass, I looked over to the OolaGuru, and I questioned, "Seriously, why are we doing this?"

I was thinking that he would speak words of wisdom that would inspire me to stay the course of collecting a million handwritten dreams on the side of the bus. And, maybe that inspiration would somehow warm my fingers and toes. But, that's not what happened. He slowly looked over at me with a tilted beanie on his head, subtle frost clinging to his beard, and said, "I have no idea."

Gripping the wheel with the strange white Michael Jackson gloves he purchased for $2.99 at the previous gas station as an attempt to keep his hands warm, he continued with a smirk and a chuckle, "I can't believe I left retirement, palm trees, and sunny weather for this old bus with no air and no heat. I guess there is no room for lazy on the road to Oola."

He then looked straight ahead and just kept driving. I looked straight ahead and mumbled, "Yeah man, no room for lazy on the road to Oola."

For the next thirty minutes, the OolaBus was filled with shivering silence and condensation. Nearing the top of the pass, we heard the sound of a horn honking behind us. We assumed they wanted us to go faster. As they prepared to pass us, we were getting ready to look over and give them our best, *Sorry Bro, 10 mph is all we got,* when we saw smiles and waves. Through the frosted window, an enthusiastic guy in a warm car gave us a big smile and thumbs up as he sped past us. As he passed, we noticed a newer model Subaru with Minnesota license plates and a LIVE OOLA car decal in the back window. We instantly felt inspired, laughed, and said at exactly the same time, "That's a God thing."

We reached the summit of the pass and started our first-gear, emergency-brake-pulling descent into Idaho. Every mile brought a little more sunshine and warmth, and the view of Coeur d'Alene Lake in the distance encouraged our travels. We pulled out of the pass and into the crisp fall air as we chose the longer, more scenic route around the lake. The sun was forcing the freshly fallen snow out of the pine trees. The reflections of the fall colors off of the lake were awe inspiring. The pain from the mountain pass was quickly forgotten, and we chatted about how easy it could have been to give into our own laziness and quit on our dream.

It seems we're not alone.

In the countless submissions for stories to be included in this book, we didn't receive a single story about laziness. Not one. "Maybe they're too lazy to submit a story," we laughed. So, I dug into it. Instead of waiting for a lazy Christian to come to us, I would actively seek one out. My search started where all journeys begin—with Google. A simple search immediately revealed a blog called The Lazy Christian.

Perfect. *Wow, that was easy,* I said to myself. Excited, I dug into the blog. I noticed that Rachel started the blog in 2012, admitting that she was a lazy person and an even lazier Christian.

Gold mine! I thought, *the perfect story for our book.*

But then I noticed that she'd written five blog posts, quit writing years ago, and no longer responded to her 147 followers.

Hilarious.

She was too lazy to keep her blog going and even too lazy to shut it down. I emailed her; I subscribed to her mailing list—nothing. No Rachel.

It's not just Rachel. We are all prone to laziness, whether it's overcoming the challenge of a cold mountain pass or sticking to a blog. In fact, our editors recommended that these stories for our book be at least 900–1,200 words each. Currently this story is 737.

We weren't put on this Earth to sit still but, rather, to actively pursue God's purpose for our lives. You can't do that watching endless reruns of *Friends* or mindlessly scrolling Instagram. What's more, the Gospel is filled with numerous warnings about laziness, which—as we'll see in the next story—showed up in unexpected ways during Jesus's ministry. Take a look.

IT'S A VALID QUESTION

"Someone else always gets there ahead of me."

—JOHN 5:7b NLT

was so close to the edge of the water that I could see my reflection in the pool. Seeing my own image caused me to reflect upon my life. Although the image of what I wanted in life was clear, the likelihood of my hopes and dreams becoming a reality felt a million miles away—a million miles that I could never reach. I looked around as people came by the pool each day; none really paid much attention to me. Some were here for the festival, and some were here for a miracle. This place was called Bethesda—*the pool of mercy*—which is odd because it never had mercy on me.

Five covered porches with colonnades divided the place where I lay. I knew every inch of this space because I had been studying it for almost four decades. In fact, it had been thirty-eight years to be exact, but who's counting? Some might imagine me laying out by the pool relaxing or even working in this beautiful space designed by a former king. Perhaps you can see me as an architect or artist appreciating the beauty while living my best life. But the truth is, I didn't have a life. Nobody really bothered to know my name. Most likely, I would have gone down in history as the man at the pool of Bethesda. I was not retired or on an extended vacation, either.

I was homeless and paralyzed.

Every day for thirty-eight years, I lay on my decaying mat waiting.

My time here started with a rumor that circulated when I was a much younger man: that an angel would occasionally stir the waters, and whoever made it into the water first would be healed. I faithfully lay by this water day in and day out, but no one ever helped me to get in. I sat, watching others take their turn in this blessed body of water, hoping that one day things would change, and I would be healed.

Then one day it did.

When Jesus saw him lying there, and knew that he already had been in that condition a long time, He said to him, "Do you want to be made well?"

The sick man answered Him, "Sir, I have no man to put me into the pool when the water is stirred up; but while I am coming, another steps down before me."

Jesus said to him, "Rise, take up your bed and walk." And immediately the man was made well, took up his bed, and walked. (John 5:7)

Standing on my own two feet for the first time in decades, this Man's words hit me like a ton of bricks. The miracle I had been waiting for was not in a pool at Bethesda, but in this Man who stood before me.

When He asked if I wanted to be healed, I wanted to shout, "Don't you think I want to be healed? I have been laying here for so long and wasting so much of my life!"

Looking back, however, it was a valid question. *Did I want to get better?* I had stayed in the same position because of a rumor I'd heard years earlier. Though I sat by the water, I never really thought my life would change. I got comfortable being crippled because then I didn't have to live. Most of all, I had accepted a truth that I could never be healed because no one would help me. Though a miracle happened that day, I still had to *do something*. When He found me that day, He didn't pick me up and help me into the water, He simply told me to get up and walk.

After thirty-eight years of laying poolside, I was now walking and moving through the village. The mat that had been supporting my limp and paralyzed body was now in my hands. Strangely enough, I was immediately approached and asked why I was carrying my mat on the Sabbath. This was unlawful. I told them that a man healed me and told me to take up my mat and walk. Furious, they wanted to know who this man was who was healing people on the Sabbath. That, too, was unlawful. Though I looked around, I couldn't find Him. He had slipped away into the crowd.

Later in the temple, the man approached me again and said, "See, you are well again. Stop sinning or something worse may happen to you." It was Him, and His name was Jesus.

I left and told the Jews immediately that I'd found Him, and His name was Jesus. The Jewish leaders began to persecute Him, but Jesus said, "My Father is always at his work to this very day, and I too am working."

I realized that this man called Jesus never stops working. He ate, drank, slept, and socialized, but he never let Himself become lazy because His mission was too important. He got persecuted for going against the grain of society, but He followed God's plan for His life, and because of that, my new life starts today.

Just as the man learned in the story above, sometimes we can become immobilized because of something—a rumor, an experience—that we think is true. It can stop us from moving forward and literally make us lazy.

But God's Word can be our guide to conquering the habit of laziness. And once we do, this new take-action posture will propel us further *and faster* toward our goals. Get over your laziness and go get your OolaLife. These tips will show you how.

DECLUTTER YOUR SPACE AND
LESSEN THE OVERWHELM

*"Look at the crows! They don't plant or harvest, and they don't
have storehouses or barns. But God takes care of them."*

—LUKE 12:24 CEV

If we don't continually tend to our surroundings, clutter builds.
Emails can overwhelm, magazines and books can pile up, workspaces
can become unrecognizable, and closets can soon overflow. Clutter
creates a burden on us—it weighs us down and holds us back from our
potential. In an article at *Psychology Today* magazine online, researchers said that decluttering makes you feel good because it creates confidence.* It gives you energy because you don't feel so overwhelmed
with your stuff. It decreases anxiety and helps overcome stress in your
relationships because there are no more messy kids' rooms to argue
about or a kitchen that looks like a bomb went off in it.

Dropping off clutter at the local thrift store, walking through tidy
new rooms, having a clear and creative workspace, and seeing an
email inbox that's manageable again gives you such a fresh, light feeling that increases productivity and makes it hard to fall back into laziness. By contrast, when our household and workspace are cluttered
with papers, projects, and bills—all screaming, "Handle me!"—we
don't feel like we have time to do anything productive, so we end up
immobilized—doing nothing, instead of working on our goals.

One book on decluttering we like is *The Life-Changing Magic of
Tidying Up,* by organizing guru Marie Kondo. In her Netflix show,
Marie gives some great tips for keeping only those things that bring
you joy and minimizing the rest. Take a look:

---

* "6 Benefits of an Uncluttered Space" by Alice Boyes, PhD. *Psychology Today* blog. February 12, 2018.

◉ For each item or pile of clutter, ask, "Does it spark joy?" If not, deal with it, delegate it, delete it, or donate it.

◉ Start by choosing what to keep, not what to get rid of.

◉ Don't dump excess items on family members and friends—a sneaky way to part with things that *doesn't really* part with them.

◉ Get rid of gifts and free swag that you don't want or haven't used. This goes for trial-sized toiletries, gadgets, and other items you've always said you'll use "someday."

◉ Store household products in your own attractive containers so that brightly colored retail packaging—with starbursts, banners and "buy now" messages—doesn't visually disturb your tranquil home.

◉ Don't buy storage containers before you decide what you need to store. More storage is not the solution—decluttering is.

As Marie wisely notes, when you tidy up, have clothes in good repair, and know that everything just *works,* you'll have more confidence in yourself. Plus, your gratitude for what you *do have* will soar. We agree.

DON'T KICK THE CAN DOWN THE ROAD

"She carefully watches everything in her household
and suffers nothing from laziness."

—PROVERBS 31:27 NLT

If lazy is the disease, procrastination is an early symptom. If you have a problem in a specific area of your life, don't just kick the can down the road. One of the biggest areas of stress that laziness can cause is a financial problem or health problem that—because of laziness—we simply don't handle. We let the debt pile up, we can't find extra money for retirement savings, and we buy more stuff than we can afford. We slowly gain weight, we don't cut out the sugar, and we don't get that bad tooth taken care of.

Then, before we know it, we reach a certain age and are forced to spend huge amounts of time living paycheck-to-paycheck and managing our diabetes, heart condition, knee and joint pain, and other ailments.

If there's already a siren going off in some area of your life, don't be lazy. Confront it and create a plan to resolve it—then get after it.

DON'T CONFUSE COMPLACENCY WITH CONTENTMENT

"Fools are destroyed by their own complacency."

—PROVERBS 1:32 NLT

It's important as Christians to differentiate complacency from contentment. While contentment is biblical and good, complacency is linked to laziness and is bad. Please don't confuse the two.

Doesn't God want me to be satisfied with my life? you might ask.

Of course. That is contentment. But sometimes Christians get stuck in complacency, then confuse the two and say, *I'm content with my life.*

Contentment is being grateful for what you have and joyful about where you are with your life but still challenging yourself—knowing there is more in you. It means not settling for an ordinary life because you understand that God has created you for *extraordinary.*

Complacency means you're not using your God-given gifts. God placed you in this life for a reason. He doesn't want you to just sit here and park. He wants you to use the skills, gifts, ability, and calling He has placed in you to best serve others and His Kingdom.

To overcome complacency—which is just a sneaky form of laziness—always have one hand grasping gratitude while the other hand is reaching for growth. Be grateful for what you have, but challenge yourself frequently, saying, *What more can I do? Then follow it up with action.*

ENVY

"A heart at peace gives life to the body,
but envy rots the bones."

—PROVERBS 14:30 NIV

W e've all done it. We scroll through Instagram and see that someone else got the promotion we wanted. We check a friend's Facebook page and see a photo of their amazing new kitchen remodel. We get an alert that someone has updated their status and realize they're now in a fairy-tale romantic relationship. Yep, we wanted that, too. Gradually, a feeling of jealousy begins to overtake us.

But just like frustration is normal (but anger is a sin), jealousy is the starting point for envy. It's wanting what someone else has—that terrific house, that vacation in Bali, that cool piece of art. As long as the feeling of jealousy passes through us, it's harmless.

But where envy is different—and why envy is dark—is that not only do you want what someone else has, you *don't want them* to have it. You covet their life when you should be grateful for yours and *inspired* to keep crushing it on the way to your own OolaLife.

THE OPPOSITE OF **ENVY**

Every minute you spend focused on someone else's accomplishment is a minute you've wasted working on yours. So why not let someone else's win inspire you? Don't be envious from a distance, but be inspired from up close. Ask them to mentor you on your way to getting what you want.

Think about how you can live the *opposite* of envy: gratitude for what you already have, admiration for the hard work that someone else put in to earn what they have, and joyful enthusiasm about what is possible in your own life if you apply the same enthusiasm and effort.

◎ ◎ ◎ ◎

FRONTLINE MOM

by Ashelyn Downs

The novels and the movies made it seem so romantic. Falling in love with a soldier and waiting for him to return from battle made beautiful films, but it made me miserable. Though deep down I recognized how incredibly blessed and fortunate we were, my perspective was skewed by the distance and the time between us. The year we spent apart had been marked by "less." While a deployed husband meant less laundry, food to cook, fuel to buy, and people competing for my attention, in almost every other situation, less wasn't positive. Less celebrations, less family time, less hugs, less kisses, less help around the house, and less bedtime stories for the kids—it all took a toll on our family and an even bigger toll on my emotional well-being.

Scrolling through social media to see friends on dates with their husbands or on family vacations as I sat at home alone watching sitcom reruns night after night became a self-destructive pastime. I found myself distancing myself from my friends' happiness instead of celebrating with them in their joys. I was jealous of the dads picking up their kids from school, the wives holding their husband's hand in church, and above all, the fathers that got to be there for the birth of their new babies. That pain cut all too deep as my little bump grew bigger and bigger each week, and I waited to welcome our new bundle of joy into the world while my husband was on the other side of the globe, serving our country.

While my envy for those around me didn't completely mask my ability to recognize how truly blessed and fortunate I was—healthy kids, the ability to stay home to raise them, the loving support I received from others—the feelings of resentment I felt toward my husband during deployment were a constant uphill battle. I fought back jealousy as he excitedly told me of the unique places he'd been. I faked enthusiasm as he gushed about the amazing local foods he'd been able to try. These were things we were used to doing together. But my current reality was that I wiped boogers and butts all day, and cooked chicken and broccoli for the third evening that week, while he had the adventures—without me and seemingly without a thought of me. I envied his experiences, his sense of purpose, and his freedom to do as he pleased. And I desperately yearned for the adult conversation he was surrounded with day in and day out.

My envy began to feed into feelings of fear that I wasn't needed, wanted, or missed. Without conveying these feelings to my husband, I allowed myself to slip into a sense of worthlessness. My days at home with three kids, aged six and under, dragged on continuously and ran into nights of loneliness sprinkled with anxiety.

While the envy seemed like a perfectly natural feeling to have, considering the circumstances, I was struggling with an inner spiritual battle that told me I was wrong. I attempted to justify my feelings over and over, but all those Sundays in church and Wednesday afternoons spent at MOPS (Mothers of Preschoolers) kept nudging me to dive deeper into my spiritual disciplines and challenge myself to find peace and seek wisdom outside of the black-and-white stories of the Bible. Baring my soul is tremendously difficult for me, but I committed to confiding in a couple of spiritual friends I knew would not only be safe to talk to, but who could pray for me, support me, and counsel me. Friends who would give me the *right* answers would be more valuable than friends who would give me the validation I *wanted.*

At first, it was extremely hard to commit to sharing my negative feelings. I had avoided "dumping" my problems on them for fear that the burden would weigh down our friendships and define them as the "givers" and me as the "taker." However, what I realized very quickly was that in my vulnerability and trusting, I enabled them to use their gifts, as well as opened doors for them to confide in me. They fed my soul through conversation, quick texts, and Scripture, letting me know they were lifting me up in prayer, and most importantly, turning me toward my husband when I wanted to turn away and hide my ugly feelings.

This opened the door to honest conversations with my husband on the other side of the world, revealing the strength of our marriage and not the weakness that I had secretly feared. I had never wanted him to feel guilty or responsible for my personal feelings. I was truly happy for him to be given the wonderful opportunities he had and thankful that he was able to unwind after long and stressful days.

As I opened up and expressed my feelings of resentment, it knocked down the walls in my husband's heart. He showed me his seldom-seen vulnerable side. I was surprised to discover that he had been struggling with envy as well. He shared how difficult it was for him to not have the comforts and simple joys of reading bedtime stories to our kids, snuggling with them on weekend mornings, or having family dinners each night. As we communicated more openly, we grew together in our support for one another's struggles and pains. Instead of harboring the envy we felt toward each other, we now talk about what we are feeling and pray for one another.

We have learned that giving into envy only adds emotional distance to the physical miles between us, while working through it pulls us closer together.

Are you, like Ashelyn, envious about someone else's charmed life, when you don't know the real picture? Could you go to God in prayer and ask for wisdom and courage to begin dissolving your envy and covetousness? Can you use the process of eliminating envy—as she did—to grow closer in your most important relationships?

Could you read what the Bible says about envy? Jesus encountered it frequently throughout His ministry in Judea. And toward the end of His life, envy played a crucial role in bringing about God's plan for His Son.

ENVIOUS HEARTS

"Pilate spoke to them a third time, 'But what crime has he done?'"

—LUKE 23:22a CEV

The bloodthirsty crowd was closing in and getting louder by the minute. As the Roman governor of Judea, the growing unrest made me uncomfortable. Before me, they presented the man they called Jesus yet again. I had already sent him to Herod to be dealt with, but here He was again, back in my jurisdiction. I tried to remove myself from this spectacle because of the warnings my wife had given me earlier that day.

This whole situation didn't feel right. Jesus's accusers held their heads high, looking indignant as they tried to hide their jealously behind their man-made rules and regulations. Their mouths were moving with well-scripted and articulate convincing arguments, but their words didn't seem to line up with the somewhat obvious motives they were trying to hide. I could see right through them as each pious statement flowed naturally from their lips. The jealousy toward this man before me was growing from the religious leaders accustomed to the attention and respect of the people.

I glanced out among the sea of people; some of the faces I recognized, but most were strangers to me—not to Jesus apparently. Just one week ago, these same people were singing this man's praises and waving palm fronds. Now they were demanding that He be punished.

Looking back, I knew I would end up with this situation on my plate. Caiaphas, the high priest over the Sanhedrin, along with other Pharisees spearheaded this circus. They had been trying for years to take down Jesus. I had never seen such disdain for a man who helped so many people. It was obvious that for the Pharisees, it was never about the people; it was about their own fears, insecurities, and envious hearts.

When Jesus spoke, He captivated every ear. His message effortlessly seemed to reach and inspire souls. Rumors of His miracles, His teachings, and most recently His raising Lazarus from the dead had reached even me. One of my guards even called upon Jesus to heal a servant. They didn't think I knew about it, but word travels fast in this community, and it was my job to know what goes on.

I wondered if it was the fame or the massive crowds He attracted that they desired for themselves. Or, maybe it was the miracles from Heaven that drove them to this level of crazy.

I remember the first time they became furious. It was when Jesus healed on the Sabbath—then later, they were disgusted as He stood up for a woman caught in the act of adultery. He had called them out—challenging them that the person without sin should cast the first stone. They had never been put on the spot like that before. They felt above such things.

But the last straw seemed to be recently when a woman who was known as a sinner brought an expensive alabaster vial of oil with which to anoint Jesus's feet, then worshipped Him unashamedly. What these so-called holy men really wanted was to be looked upon as gods—not just turn people to God. Jesus threatened these religious leaders' entire way of life as He put them in their place, time and time again.

Now, I was face-to-face with this man Jesus. Would He defend Himself or fight back against these accusations?

Pilate asked Jesus, "Are you the king of the Jews?"

Jesus replied, "You have said it."

Then the leading priests kept accusing Him of many crimes, and Pilate asked Him, "Aren't you going to answer them? What about all these charges they are bringing against you?" But Jesus said nothing, much to Pilate's surprise.

Now it was the governor's custom each year during the Passover cele-bration to release one prisoner—anyone the people requested. One of the prisoners at that time was Barabbas, a revolutionary who had committed murder in an uprising. The crowd went to Pilate and asked him to release a prisoner as usual.

"Would you like me to release to you this 'King of the Jews'?" Pilate asked. (For he realized by now that the leading priests had arrested Jesus out of envy.) But at this point the leading priests stirred up the crowd to demand the release of Barabbas instead of Jesus. Pilate asked them, "Then what should I do with this man you call the king of the Jews?"

They shouted back, "Crucify Him!"

"Why?" Pilate demanded. "What crime has He committed?" (Luke 23:3–22)

But the mob roared even louder, *"Crucify Him!"*

On that day, a man was sentenced to death, not because of His wrongdoing, but by the fear spread throughout the province stemming from the envy of others.

How often in your life have you been like the Pharisees—envious of someone whose existence seems larger than life? Realize that we're all here for a *unique* purpose—one that God has planned for us. Envying someone else's path is like trying to exchange your own customized life plan for a different size, style, or color. Creating an authentic and awesome life is up to you. Here are some tips that will help.

RUN YOUR **OWN** RACE

"Ask the Lord to tell us where he wants us to
go and what he wants us to do."

—JEREMIAH 42:3 CEV

Comparing your life to others'—through TV, Facebook, and staged Instagram photos—robs you of appreciation for what you've achieved in your own life. It takes focus away from your goals, and too often, it leaves you feeling insignificant. President Teddy Roosevelt said it best: "Comparison is the thief of joy."

Your job is to run your own race. In Section Five of this book, you'll be creating a plan for getting exactly what *you* want from life. Don't try to live someone else's.

TURN **ENVY** INTO INSPIRATION

"Follow my example, as I follow the
example of Christ."

—1 CORINTHIANS 11:1 NIV

If there are godly people around you who've achieved tremendous fitness goals or who have great marriages, try to look at them as inspiration, rather than a source of envy. Stop comparing your "beginning" to someone else's "end." It ruins your self-worth (which eventually leads to self-sabotage).

Instead, turn your envy into inspiration. If they have the lifestyle, possessions, activities, faith walk, relationships, or finances that you want, be inspired. If possible, ask to sit down over a cup of tea and learn how they achieved that success. They might even agree to mentor you. Another way to be inspired and learn how top achievers get there is to read biographies of inspirational people. In a simple read, you'll learn more about how to get what you want than you would by being envious for years.

BE REALISTIC ABOUT SOMEONE ELSE'S **SUCCESS**

"To worry yourself to death with resentment would be a foolish, senseless thing to do."

—JOB 5:2 GNT

You don't know the whole picture about someone else's life. While that coworker may be going on a girlfriends getaway to Paris, she may not have the best marriage. While that guy in your men's group at church might be super successful, he might have worked years to get where he is.

We're all human. Everyone is going through trials and challenges. No one has the perfect life. You might be envious about one part of someone's life, but you probably don't know the whole story. For instance, many people work long hours for a decade or more to build a business or reach the top of their field. Some moms miss a lot of childhood moments with the kids to pursue their career. Those you are envying likely sacrificed a lot on the way to success—things that you *may or may not be* willing to sacrifice.

But also, realize that with maturity comes wisdom. Years from now, you may laugh at the idea that you wanted certain things, considering the cost, time, headache, or impact on you, your finances, health, relationships, or your family's lifestyle. Be realistic.

FOCUS

"Let your eyes look directly forward, and
your gaze be straight before you."

—PROVERBS 4:25 ESV

"Oh, look, a squirrel," Dave finds himself saying more than a few times a day. Whether it's a text from a friend, a documentary on the History Channel, or something he forgot to grab in the next room, Dave is—admittedly—a guy who struggles with lack of focus.

Yet one of the most damaging OolaBlockers of all is *misdirected focus*. Whether it's concentrating on the wrong thing at the wrong time—or getting pulled away from activities that don't move you forward—*misdirected focus* can mean months of delay from going in the wrong direction. It keeps you from getting what you want. And sadly, many people we meet who are off-course in following their God-given purpose are *recovering from addiction,* the most extreme example of *misdirected focus*. Addiction often results in losing years that could have been spent creating an awesome life.

BE A **LASER**, NOT A FLASHLIGHT

If you focused your time and energy on just those things that would get you closer to your goals, what would your life look like? For one thing, the daily "noise" of your life—such as hanging out on social media, watching TV, or spending unnecessary time on the phone—would be easily recognized as a distraction and avoided whenever possible.

Instead of starting ten things a day, you would focus on completing three or more high-priority tasks that are directly in line with the goals you have for your life. Instead of agreeing to serve on one more committee, help one more charity, or add one more stop before that important meeting, you would drive straight there, say "no," and politely tell the committee chairman that other commitments have hijacked all your available time.

See what we mean? Be a laser, not a flashlight. You get what you focus on.

DO THE **WORST** FIRST

To combat any lapse in focus, we have a simple remedy for you (Dave uses this one): jot down a daily to-do list with the *tasks you hate* at the top of the list. We call this "doing the worst first"—a technique that Troy learned years ago from his successful brother, Tim. A fan of 3x5 notecards, Tim lists his must-do tasks—whatever is needed to get him closer to his goal—but he starts off his day tackling the stuff he knows he needs to do but hates doing.*

AVOID THE OOLA A-BOMB

Unlike a simple lack of focus, *misdirected focus* is where addictions live: shopping, alcohol, drugs (including prescription medication), gambling, pornography, and social media. These aren't just Oola-Blockers, they're Oola destroyers. It's like dropping an atomic bomb on your OolaLife.

It's rare to find a family not affected in some way by addiction—an environment where there is no energy toward goals. In fact, all available energy is spent feeding the addiction and doing damage control as things unravel. God doesn't want that life for you or those you love.

Help exists if addiction is holding you back from your OolaLife. Call it out, and deal with it. You are stronger than you realize. You deserve it, your dreams are worth it, and your loved ones are likely praying for it every single day.

---

* Later, in Section Five, we'll give you a complete strategy for staying focused on your goals. Part of that strategy is a simple 3x5 card where you'll write down your important tasks and errands.

I WALKED INTO A BAR, AND IT SAVED MY LIFE

by Carlie Young

My heels kicked up dust as I carefully navigated the gravel and random beer bottles in the back parking lot, headed for the front door. The sun rising over the horizon caused me to squint and added a pulse to my familiar morning headache. As I pulled open the door, it felt heavier than the countless times I'd opened it before. My body felt weak and my emotions restless. As I walked inside, the familiar scent of stale beer and last night's cigarette smoke oddly blended with the aroma of fresh coffee and donuts. It was early on a Sunday morning as I walked into the Busted Shovel Biker Bar. I wasn't there for the liquor. I was there for a message.

I made my way past the newly re-felted pool tables and the old jukebox and through the ocean of leather-clad bikers to find a seat. With a forced smile, I hugged and small-talked my way to a vacant plastic barstool I spotted in the front. I sat and rested my heavy head in my hands. The sounds of people walking, moving, and talking echoed in my ears and drowned out the surrounding music. Then the crisp sound of boots striking the black-and-white checkered dance floor and a subtle sound of a chain swinging side to side caught my attention. I lifted my head from my hands and saw a man with a grey beard walk past me. He was wearing boots with a chain that linked the belt loop on his faded jeans to an oversized wallet in his back pocket. He had a leather vest on his back and a Bible in his hand. He got to the front of the random group that had gathered in the bar and said, "I am Pastor Jim, also known as the biker preacher. Welcome to Common Ground Church."

I became uncharacteristically emotional as soon as I heard those words. I felt comforted and very tuned into the moment, like I was exactly where I needed to be. As I listened to him speak, he talked about having faith in God and not earthly things. He said to give your problems and your fears to God, and that is where you will find peace, grace, and salvation.

He then opened his tattered Bible to a bookmarked page and read the verse 2 Corinthians 7:10: "For Godly grief produces a repentance that leads to salvation without regret, whereas worldly grief produces death."

When I heard that verse, intense emotions came rushing out of me in a flood of tears. I knew I was there for a reason, and the reason was to completely shift my life. As he continued, it was like he knew exactly what I was feeling, what I had gone through, and what I was currently going through. The more he spoke and read from the Bible, the more I cried. I felt love, forgiveness, and a sense of peace that I have never felt before. I saw the glimpse of a better way, a life lived differently.

Why all the tears? Why the release? Why all the emotion? Every word he said brought back painful memories of the way I had lived my life the last twenty-five years and the craziness of a week earlier when I received a call from my cousin.

She was hysterical. With a shattered voice she said, "It's Shaylee!" My heart sunk and I asked, "What happened?" I wasn't sure I wanted to know, but she continued. Shaylee was the daughter of a dear friend of mine. I loved her energy and her spirit. She was a beautiful, strong, and athletic seventeen-year-old. She had blonde hair like mine, and we always had a very special connection. But moments before that call, she was riding her bike along the road and was killed by a drunk driver.

When I hung up the phone, the pain in me was heavy and deep. I knew what I needed to do because I had been doing this since I was a teenager—start drinking to kill the pain. That is how I cope. I am a very passionate and driven woman, and whatever I put my mind to, I go all in. That includes drinking. What my mind wanted was to be numb. I saw my mom deal with her pain and problems this way, and I saw my stepdad do the same thing. I grabbed a bottle of whiskey off the shelf, and I poured myself a shot. Still wincing from the burn in my throat, I quickly followed it up with two more. The rest of that day and evening, I found myself at a bar ordering drinks in an attempt to unload some of this pain. I drank until I was completely numb. Then, I drank some more. I went blank.

I woke up three days later.

I reached for my phone and noticed messages from the last three days from friends and family who were worried about me and wondering if I was okay. I grabbed my phone and staggered to the kitchen, opened up the fridge and reached for an ice-cold Chelada Tomato Beer. This was my regular prescription to cure my hangover and ease my anxiety. I leaned over the sink with the beer in my hand, cracked it, and replayed the phone call from my cousin over and over in my mind. I tried to remember the last three days but couldn't. I reflected on my upbringing and how my parents tried to find salvation in a bottle. My stepdad drank to be happy and drank to escape from simple life stressors or serious problems. Whatever the occasion, he had a beer in his hand. Sometimes alcohol turned my stepdad into a monster. I thought back to all the times I had to call the police to stop my stepdad from beating my mom, and how when the police left, that drunken anger turned toward me. I thought back to the times I would try to find safety in my mom, then see her turn a cold shoulder and reach for the bottle herself. Alcohol took my grandmother, my aunt, and an uncle from me before I got to know them. And now alcohol had taken this precious seventeen-year-old girl from everyone who loved her and had left her on the side of the road. I saw pieces of my stepdad in me. I saw pieces of my mom in me, and I saw pieces of this drunk driver in me—I was disgusted and ashamed.

With determined and focused frustration, I turned the beer over and poured it down the drain. I was done. This will not be the legacy for my son.

"I will never drink again!" I screamed out loud to the empty house around me. That was my last drink.

I walked into a bar, and it saved my life. I have been sober for over eight years, and I have completely turned my life around. All the energy I once put into alcohol and the problems it created I now put toward working on being a better version of me. I am happy. I am fulfilled, and I am living my purpose by helping people every day. I still have stress, pain, and problems, and I always will, but instead of finding salvation in a bottle, I now find salvation in Jesus Christ.

Are you consumed with misdirected focus? Are you spending time managing an addiction or doing damage control as things unravel? What about a simple lack of focus on what really matters to your future?

Simon Peter took his eyes off what really mattered: his faith in Jesus. In this next story, we learn that focusing on what's truly important will not only grow our faith, but help us become wiser, more mindful, and more able to bring about our goals. Take a look.

EYES ON HIM

*"Set your mind on the things that are above,
not on the things that are on the earth."*

—COLOSSIANS 3:2 WEB

W
e were exhausted. The perfect storm had been brewing all around us; in life and on the sea. I was delirious from the physical and mental stress, and I felt completely overwhelmed. The physical stress on our bodies came from rowing most of the night to combat an unexpected wind storm that was throwing waves against our boat and casting us around. We'd grown up on the Sea of Galilee, and we knew this body of water well, but tonight it was having its way with us.

The mental exhaustion that added to the storm came from the happenings of the last couple of days. We received word that John the Baptist was killed at the hands of Herod. Jesus wanted to get away to a solitary place and be alone. We withdrew by boat and crossed the sea. When we got to the quiet location where Jesus asked us to go, crowds of people were there waiting. I didn't know how He would respond because the purpose of this journey was to get away.

To my surprise, He had compassion for the people and began to heal the sick. Though He was fatigued and greatly saddened from losing His friend, Jesus continued until late into the evening.

I told Jesus that He should send the people back to their villages before nightfall, so they could buy food to eat. Jesus replied, "They do not need to go away. You give them something to eat."

I gathered up everything we had into a basket—a total of five loaves of bread and two fish. I looked at the meager fare and then at the mass of people. By now there must have been five thousand or more, and I realized that feeding everyone wasn't possible. Advising Jesus of our predicament, He told me to bring Him the bread and fish. Directing the people to sit on the grass, He looked up to Heaven, gave thanks, broke the bread, and gave it to us to hand out to the people. All five thousand ate, and there were twelve baskets of bread left over.

We were astonished to see another miracle of this magnitude performed by Jesus. Soon, however, He dismissed the crowd and told us to head back across the sea while He went up the mountainside to pray. As we started across the water, I reflected on the last two days. My heart felt heavy at the loss of our friend John. Yet at the same time I felt the awe of seeing Jesus heal the sick and feed five thousand people with just a small ration of food.

Am I, Peter, qualified to stand beside the Savior of the world? Is there anything He couldn't do?

As if trying to wrap my head around all of this wasn't enough, a storm—howling in the distance and beginning its death march toward us—was the final straw. Desperately we continued to row into the night, never thinking we'd see another miracle of Jesus that day. Exhausted now and with the storm fully upon us, we felt the weight of the world on our shoulders. Looking up, I saw something in the distance moving toward us as morning approached.

Shortly before dawn Jesus went out to them, walking on the lake. When the disciples saw him walking on the lake, they were terrified. "It's a ghost," they said, and cried out in fear.

But Jesus immediately said to them: "Take courage! It is I. Don't be afraid."

"Lord, if it's you," Peter replied, "tell me to come to you on the water."

"Come," he said.

Then Peter got down out of the boat, walked on the water, and came toward Jesus. But when he saw the wind, he was afraid and, beginning to sink, cried out, "Lord, save me!"

Immediately Jesus reached out his hand and caught him. "You of little faith," he said, "why did you doubt?" (Matthew 14:25–31)

Trembling, I held onto Jesus as we climbed back into the boat. As soon as we got into the boat, the wind died down, and the others in the boat worshiped Him, saying, "Truly you are the Son of God."

I looked around at all the humbled and inspired faces of the men around me and realized that when my faith in Him is strong, I can face any storm that comes into my life. But, without my focus on God, I will sink and perish.

My walk on the water that day was not dependent on me ignoring the wind and the waves, but upon focusing and trusting the One who called me out of my fear and complacency. I realized that day, you can have all the faith in the world, but when you step out of the boat and walk into what God has for you, it is important to keep your eyes fixed on Him.

Are you like Peter, taking your focus off Jesus when you should be creating a closer relationship with Him on your way toward your goals? Too often, we let unimportant "busy work" and tasks that don't serve us pull our focus away from God's true purpose for our lives. These tips will help you keep your eye on the prize.

STOP PROCRASTINATING

"I will hasten and not delay to obey your commands."

—PSALM 119:60 NIV

What is procrastination, really? It's putting off, stalling, and postponing work on your goals. It's doing everything *but the tasks* that will get you to the OolaLife.

Have you ever gone through your day, only to realize it's dinner time and you haven't completed a single thing? Do you ever complete menial tasks, then *add them* to your list, so you can have the pleasure of crossing them off? That's not Oola.

Why, then, do people procrastinate? The most common reason is simple overwhelm—their goals are unclear, too complicated, too much work, or too emotionally overpowering in scope. Sometimes people don't have the information or skills they need yet (perhaps this describes you). Or you simply don't know how to start.

One of the easiest ways to conquer procrastination caused by overwhelm is to use the OolaPlanner to break down large goals into bite-sized, achievable tasks* that will also help you gain confidence and achieve mastery as you work through them. Stay on track. Follow your plan. And keep moving forward in the direction of your goals.

ELIMINATE THE **TIME** BANDITS

"The temptation to give in to evil
comes from us and only us."

—JAMES 1:14 MSG

Just over one hundred years ago, when the sun went down, candles were lit, and Bibles were opened. Today, technology has changed

---

* Read more about the OolaPlanner at *www.oolalife.com/planner*.

the way we live. We have access to a world of information in an instant. It has allowed us to be more efficient and free to work from anywhere we want. But ironically, technology has also created a never-ending supply of ways to waste time. Between social media, news feeds, streaming, podcasts, Pinterest, Instagram, and that old-fashioned thing called email, our screen time lasts from the moment we wake up in the morning to the minute we fall asleep. Add these time bandits to the daily stuff we do—calls with our sister, a stop-off at the mall, running to the grocery store because we forgot bread—and our day could literally be *filled* with activities that don't get us closer to our goals.

Stop it. Identify the time bandits in your life. Spend a minute or two figuring out how to handle the routine tasks. Then move on with accomplishing things that really matter.

BE **CHOOSY** WITH YOUR TIME

"I am not trying to please people.
I want to please God."
—GALATIANS 1:10 CEV

God has given every one of us the same twenty-four hours in a day. And while it's nice to be asked to chair the school fundraiser, plan the family barbeque, or spearhead the lunch-and-learn program at work, wouldn't your time be used more effectively if you committed to less—and then only to those things that will move you forward in the direction of your dreams?

There is great power in the word *no*. And usually, you don't need to back up that response with an explanation other than, *I'm sorry, I have a conflict*. Simple, clear, and focused.

OOLAACCELERATORS

"Follow only what is good."

—3 JOHN 1:11 NLT

The next seven chapters dive into the OolaAccelerators. These are God's antidote to the fear, guilt, anger, self-sabotage, laziness, envy, and focus issues we learned about in the last section. This is where the real fun begins. In fact, not only are these the positive emotions and mind-set that the Lord has put on our heart but they'll fast-track our journey toward the ultimate OolaLife. He wants us to live these every day.

Over the next seven chapters, you'll learn daily practices and God-inspired behaviors like gratitude, discipline, integrity, and wisdom that will accelerate personal growth. You'll get tips to help you incorporate these behaviors into your life. And you'll discover insights from believers who relied on these Accelerators at different points on their journey.

CHAPTER 17

GRATITUDE

"Always giving thanks to God the
Father for everything."

—EPHESIANS 5:20a NIV

"**B**e grateful, Dave. And have faith," she said.

For what? I thought, as night after night I vented my problems over the phone to my sister Denette. I was at the lowest point of my life—going through a divorce, losing my business, and in the midst of bankruptcy. I would tuck the kids into bed and leave them with my soon-to-be ex in the dream house we had built together. I would hop in my mom's beat-up old Taurus (because my cool cars were just repossessed), and head to the bad side of town to the crappy motel room that was now my new home.

There was no light at the end of this tunnel, as far as I could see—and in my misery, Denette's encouraging advice about gratitude became almost irritating, instead of comforting. Yet night after night, she would lift me up in prayer until, at last, I began to slowly work my way up from rock bottom.

Be grateful, Dave. And have faith.

Eventually, my calls to her dwindled to a few times a week and then slowly, as things improved, just once a week to check in. When a few months later, an urgent call came through on my cell phone from Denette, I could hear the tears in her voice as she told me, "Jared has cancer."

Jared is her sixteen-year-old son. He is 6'2", shredded, charismatic, and a star football player with his eyes on a promising college career. Now, he was facing a diagnosis of a rare form of bone cancer where only 5 percent of people survive.

Not knowing how to respond to this tragic news, reflexively I replied, "Be grateful, Denette. And have faith."

While the words came out of my mouth, did I really believe them? All through Jared's chemotherapy, radiation, surgery, remission, and—tragically—succumbing to leukemia brought on by the years of chemotherapy, I tried to find the meaning of gratitude. *How could anyone be grateful for this?* I wondered. *Especially a mom who just lost her son.*

When we buried Jared and sadly returned to Denette's quiet farm-house after the funeral, Jared himself showed me the true meaning of gratitude in a letter that his brothers and sister found on his night-stand—a letter he had written just months before his death.

I'm grateful that God chose me for cancer and not my mom or dad.

The letter continued...

I'm grateful that God chose me for cancer, and not my sister or broth-ers. I'm grateful that God chose me for cancer, and not my cousins, aunts, or uncles. I'm grateful that God chose me for cancer, and not my friends. I'm grateful that God chose me for cancer, so I could teach others how to be strong—JJ Strong.

As I look back on that time, I realize that—no matter what God puts in our life—there's a reason to be grateful for it. While we may never know His intention, we can still be grateful *and have faith.*

DO YOU HAVE A NEGATIVE HISTORY WITH **GRATITUDE**?

If, like Dave, you, too, have struggled with gratitude, realize that our unbalanced world is in a constant state of complaining. Spend a few hours online and you'll meet people who are grumbling about their jobs, their spouses, their neighbors, the state of the economy, church, politics, and so much more. Listen closely and you'll hear people complaining of too much foam in their latte, weak Wi-Fi, and a package that took three days to arrive.

But think about the rest of the world. How many billions of people can't get enough to eat every day or don't have access to clean water?

How many don't have the chance to go to school, work a steady job, or live in a home of their own? The answer is billions, by the way. Do you really have that much to complain about? Maybe we can live with an improper foam/milk/espresso ratio in our latte.

Gratitude, on the other hand, is the opposite of complaining. In fact, those two beliefs cannot coexist in your brain at the same time. Try it. The next time you are goose bumps, tear-in-the-eye grateful, try to complain. It can't happen. Gratitude *in* pushes complaining *out*.

WHAT WOULD YOU WRITE IN YOUR GRATITUDE LETTER?

One of the ways that we recommend to help you stay in a state of gratitude is to write a few lines every night in a gratitude journal. Whether it's being grateful for your kids, spouse, and family, or gratitude for a new opportunity that showed up that day, or simply being grateful for the kindness of a stranger who held the door as you were running errands in town, God smiles when we're grateful.

Of course, the most difficult writing you'll do is finding gratitude on those days when everything seems to go wrong. But that's where the real power of gratitude lives. Being late for an early morning meeting, some new crisis deadline at work, getting an unexpected bill in the mail—all followed by a rushed and unappetizing dinner in front of the TV. *What's there to be grateful for in that?* you might wonder.

By taking some quiet time to think through your day and write down your thoughts, it's easier—not to mention uplifting—to find gratitude in even the smallest ways. Be grateful in *all things*.

◎ ◎ ◎ ◎

PENNIES FROM HEAVEN

by Laurie Libman-Wilson

normally find solace walking along the beach—listening to the waves of the ocean and feeling the sun on my face—or cuddled in a blanket in front of the crackling fireplace with my favorite sweats on and a cup of coffee. But on this particular day, I found my solace and a drop of inspiration, while surrounded by honking New York City taxi cabs, sirens, concrete, and skyscrapers.

Sitting on an iron bench in midtown Manhattan with a view of the Hudson River in front of me, buildings reaching toward the sky behind me, and with people all around me, I was done. Emotionally exhausted. I stopped, sat down, placed my head into the palms of my hands, and cried.

They say that the five stages of grieving are denial, anger, bargaining, depression, and then finally acceptance. They also say that this whole process generally lasts twelve months. Well, this is year two for me, and I have been stuck in depression for over a year. The crazy thing is that I didn't lose a grandparent or my mom or dad. I didn't lose a child or a husband. I didn't even lose a life-long friend. I lost a friend that I only knew for one year. *What is my problem?* I thought to myself over and over. *Why can't I shake this sadness? Why do I feel a calling to somehow turn his death into something meaningful that will have a positive impact on the lives of others?*

I had met Conrad three years earlier on a work trip. It was a gorgeous winter evening south of the border in San Miguel de Allende, Mexico. I walked along the centuries-old cobblestone streets and admired the artsy Spanish-inspired architecture on my way to the Limerick Pub. It was a local hangout where I would meet up with my friends whenever I was down there. It was a great place to meet as a group to relax, grab dinner, enjoy a glass of red wine, and catch up about the events of the day. My friends had invited a local guy to join us that evening. His name was Conrad. He was a good-looking, quiet, yet charismatic man in his mid-thirties. I felt an instant connection to him. Not in a romantic way, just an undeniable connection, like kindred spirits. But as I learned his story, I found out that we couldn't be more different.

I grew up in L.A. as a free-spirited, creative woman, thinking outside the box. I was passionate toward life and always saw the bigger picture in things. I was raised by entrepreneurial parents who didn't always encourage my world travel, but they didn't stop me, either. Conrad's life was filled with poverty, pushing the limits of the law and hanging out with the wrong kind of people. We had nothing in common, but I trusted him, liked him, and was intrigued. I was relaxed and transparent with him and found myself telling him stories of my life with more ease than ever before. Eventually, he opened up about his life and his struggles. He shared with me pieces of his past that he had never told anyone before. Then with tears in his eyes, he told me a story that made me feel numb.

He told me that he tragically lost two sons at ages eleven and thirteen. He carried immense guilt and wondered whether, if he had lived differently, this tragedy and pain could have been avoided. His life had been in a death spiral ever since. He wanted to change. He wanted to take this tragedy and create something to carry on their legacy—to spread light into the dark world in which he found himself. But, with each effort to move forward, the pain pulled him back, and he needed ways to numb what he was feeling. The vicious cycle of thinking about the past, feeling the pain, and then numbing life was his current day-to-day. Over the next year, we talked often. I tried to help him understand his loss and discover if there was a way some good could come from it. This was hard because I couldn't wrap my head around it myself. The more I got to know him, the more his pain became my own. I was scared for him. My ultimate goal was for him to find purpose for all of this, but most days I simply wanted him to be okay.

Time didn't heal his pain; it only made it grow deeper. The more pain, the more drastic were the measures to numb it.

I was living in Nicaragua when I got the news. Conrad had overdosed. He was unconscious and clinging to life. I left for San Miguel immediately. After a battle, he slipped into a coma and died. I was by his side during his final hours. I couldn't believe this was real. How could it happen? How could God allow the kids to be taken from Conrad, and now Conrad from me? What was God's purpose in this? After the pleading, screaming, and pretending that it didn't happen, I just felt nothing. I just felt empty and sad—for two years.

Sitting on that park bench in midtown with my sandals firmly on the ground and my summer dress floating in the breeze, I was broken. Fatigued from two years of questions, sadness, and pain, I completely surrendered and started to pray. "God, please tell me what to do! Talk to me like you've talked to others. Whisper if you have to; I am listening, God! Please show me a sign...something," but—nothing.

With heaviness, I stood up and started walking. I was swallowed up by the flow of people moving in every direction. I was like water flowing around rocks in a spring stream, when I saw a penny on the sidewalk. I've seen many pennies on the floor in my life, and I always pick them up as a sign of good luck, but this one felt different. I felt it throughout my entire body—*pick it up*! I was getting closer and closer to the penny, and with each step, I felt more energy to pick it up. I reached down, picked up the penny, and felt chills overtake me.

Months later, I discovered the poem, "Pennies from Heaven," that tied it all together for me. *Don't pass by that penny,* it goes. *It's one that an angel has tossed down to you.*

That simple copper coin on that sidewalk that day in New York let me know Conrad and his boys are okay. A message from an angel. It was at that moment the fog lifted, and I could move forward again.

This transformational moment inspired me to make the penny famous as a symbol of gratitude and mindful change. Not only did I see the penny as a message from Heaven, this coin is a world traveler that has traveled from person to person, connecting us to other humans seeking joy, positivity, and love. I felt God directed my purpose to inspire daily gratitude through creating mindfulness tools and products that help bring about self-awareness and empathy and cultivate gratitude that ripples around the world. I know that sounds a little crazy and far-fetched, but it didn't to me; to me it felt real.

Now, eight years later, when strolling midtown or the beaches of Del Mar, when I spot one of our penny creations around the neck of someone enjoying their day or a gratitude jar in a trendy restaurant in L.A., I smile, knowing that God is using me to inspire gratitude, one penny at a time.

Just like the pennies in the story above, your gratitude travels from person to person—affecting their attitude and outlook. In fact, being in a constant state of gratitude positively affects everyone around you. But what happens when the good times fade and the days turn dark?

As we'll see in the next story, it *is possible* to be grateful even then. As Jesus teaches us, our Father always hears our pleas. Now that's something to be grateful for.

◎   ◎   ◎   ◎

FATHER, I THANK YOU

"'Take away the stone,'
Jesus said."

—JOHN 11:39 BSB

Suddenly, the door swung open. Martha walked in, breathing hard. She'd run all the way through the streets of Bethany to tell me something important. My sister was always the calm one, but she approached me with uncharacteristic urgency. With a house full of guests, she grabbed my arm and dragged me into the other room for privacy. She said in a firm but shallow breathe, *Mary, the Teacher is here and wants to see you.* Anger, pain, and grief welled up inside of me as I heard her words.

Jesus was a friend. He said that He is the resurrection and the life, but my brother, Lazarus, was not alive. He had been dead for four days. As a friend, Jesus should have been here to heal him.

I ran out of my home, leaving behind our house guests and crying as I ran toward Jesus. Those who were there consoling me tried to catch up, but I wouldn't stop until I saw Him.

Through my tears, I could see Him just outside our little village of Bethany. *Why did He come now?* I kept thinking over and over. Why didn't He come to Bethany when He first found out that Lazarus was sick? He was in Jerusalem, only two miles away, and He chose not to come to my brother's aid. He healed so many others, most of whom He didn't know, but He chose not to heal my brother, and now Lazarus is dead.

When I came into His presence, I couldn't even look him in the eye. As tears streamed down my face, I fell to the ground sobbing, "Lord, if You had come when we sent word, my brother wouldn't have died." Jesus wasn't some stranger that I was reprimanding for letting me down, but He is the Man I trusted with everything.

Why didn't He come to save Lazarus? My mind seemed lost as I played over and over again the scenario I thought was supposed to happen. Jesus was supposed to come before it was too late. How many people did He heal that He didn't even know? How many people did He minister to and bless that were not even as good as my brother Lazarus? We trusted Him. We served Him. We let Him into our home and into our hearts, and He didn't come until it was too late. When Jesus saw our pain and the pain of the other mourners, He was deeply moved in spirit and troubled.

Jesus asked, "Where have you put him?" I pointed to the tomb.

> Jesus wept.
>
> Then the Jews said, "See how He loved him!"
>
> But some of them said, "Could not He who opened the eyes of the blind man have kept this man from dying?"
>
> Jesus, once more deeply moved, came to the tomb. It was a cave with a stone laid across the entrance. "Take away the stone," he said.
>
> "But, Lord," said Martha, the sister of the dead man, "by this time there is a bad odor, for he has been there four days."
>
> Then Jesus said, "Did I not tell you that if you believe, you will see the glory of God?"
>
> So they took away the stone. Then Jesus looked up and said, "Father, I thank You that You have heard me. I knew that You always hear Me, but I said this for the benefit of the people standing here, that they may believe that You sent Me."

When He had said this, Jesus called in a loud voice, "Lazarus, come out!" The dead man came out, his hands and feet wrapped with strips of linen, and a cloth around his face.

Jesus said to them, "Take off the grave clothes and let him go." (John 11:35–44)

I was taken aback by the first three words that Jesus spoke when the tomb was opened: "Father, I thank you." Jesus showed God gratitude that He had listened. I'd been living the last four days in pain, agony, and anger—far from gratitude. My heart wasn't grateful when Jesus showed up late; my heart was angered that He wasn't there when I wanted Him to be. Instead of having complete faith in Christ's timing, I wanted Him to do things on my time frame.

After Jesus raised Lazarus from the dead, I felt deep gratitude. I wanted to show everyone my grateful heart and invited them back to the house.

Here a dinner was given in Jesus's honor. Martha served, while Lazarus was among those reclining at the table with Him. Then Mary took about a pint of pure nard, an expensive perfume; she poured it on Jesus's feet and wiped His feet with her hair. And the house was filled with the fragrance of the perfume. (John 12:2–3)

The aroma blended with the gratitude and love that also filled the space. Jesus gave me back my brother, and He taught me a great lesson. He taught me to be grateful always and to have faith in God's timing and in His purpose. He sees the bigger picture for my life and the world, and I need to trust that truth.

Being grateful for God's gifts—and more importantly, His tim-ing—is difficult at best for most people. We want resolution, progress, opportunities, and problems solved instantly. But that isn't always God's plan for us. These tips will help you focus on being grateful until God reveals His purpose to you.

STAY IN A STATE OF
GRATEFUL ANTICIPATION

"Devote yourselves to prayer, being
watchful and thankful."

—COLOSSIANS 4:2 NIV

If you woke up every day and said, "Hey, today is going to be a great day. I feel like something amazing is going to happen," chances are good you'd be right. Chances are even better that God will send you something to be grateful for.

What kind of gratitude-inducing opportunities are we talking about? Ways to improve your finances, your career, and your lifestyle. New people to meet and new ways to grow your network. Chances to impact more people with your faith and to grow as a Christian. But there's a secret to finding these opportunities: you have to pro-actively seek them out. Prayer is awesome, but so is action. There is opportunity hidden in every day, but it will only be found by those who actively seek it. It's out there. Go get it.

EMBRACE THE TWO LAWS OF GRATITUDE

"Every good and perfect gift comes
down from the Father."

—JAMES 1:17 CEV

While often debated in Christian circles, the Law of Attraction is something we've seen at work. If you're not familiar with it, the Law of Attraction says that what you think about, talk about, believe strongly about, and feel intensely about, you will bring about. To us, this sounds like a chat with God, and even the Bible alludes to this when Jesus says:

> Truly I tell you that if anyone says to this mountain, "Be lifted up and thrown into the sea," and has no doubt in his heart but believes that it will happen, it will be done for him. Therefore, I tell you, whatever you ask in prayer, believe that you have received it, and it will be yours. (Mark 11:23–24)

Prayer, having good intentions, taking action on them, imagining the joy you'll experience when you finally have the opportunity that God puts in front of you—all these things work together to bring about good outcomes in your life. You've probably seen this yourself a time or two. When you're trying to attract something into your life, you probably pray about it, focus on it, and work toward it. That's the Law of Attraction at work in your life.

Interestingly, the most important aspect of the Law of Attraction is being grateful for everything that shows up in your life *before you even have it.*

The other principle we like is the *Law of Action.* When opportunity knocks, you have to take action. Having God drop things in our lap doesn't help us grow, but learning new skills, taking on bigger roles, and growing in confidence *does.* That small gig that requires you to take action might actually be the stepping stone to a much bigger goal that God has waiting in the wings for you.

STOP COMPLAINING

"Give thanks in all circumstances; for this is
the will of God in Christ Jesus for you."

—1 THESSALONIANS 5:18 ESV

There's so much to be grateful for. Why not focus on *those* things instead of complaining about what's not perfect about your life?

Complaining keeps you in a state of constant dissatisfaction. You won't see new opportunity that way. Plus, *blaming others* for what you don't like keeps you endlessly looking for what's wrong instead of seeing the good that God is putting in front of you.

Life isn't always easy. But you can stop complaining and be grateful for all of it. See whatever we get as a gift from God, and live in a state of gratitude for everything He does for us.

LOVE

"What a person desires is unfailing love."

—PROVERBS 19:22 NIV

R emember Heather Thomas, the inspiring pastor's daughter from the beginning of this book? When Heather was broken, dispirited, and publicly shamed after her divorce, she had to learn to *love herself again first* before she could show love to others. As she worked diligently to put her life back together, she wondered what she could do to practice self-care, be proud of the example she was showing her kids, and begin to pursue the missions work that God had put on her heart.

Some days she believed that no one but God actually loved her, and she questioned if she would ever get out of this funk. But slowly, she began the work of getting healthier, stabilizing her finances, earning the money to go to Nicaragua on a missions trip, and becoming a role model for her children.

By the time she finally landed in Managua with 10,000 Oola dream stickers in her luggage—ready to speak to groups of thousands of women—she had come to realize that love starts with *you*. As Jesus commanded, *loving yourself* goes hand-in-hand with showing love to others. And it's essential to getting love in return. In this moment, Heather lived just as Jesus instructed us to: *Love others as much as you love yourself.**

RANDOM ACTS OF **OOLA**

How do you show love? While you likely have a deep abiding love for your family, what about showing unconditional love to others as Jesus requires of us? While most Christians know about the Ten Commandments, Jesus gave us a new commandment: "You must love each other, just as I have loved you."†

---

* Mark 12:31 CEV.
† John 13:34.

For Oola readers around the world, that unconditional love for their neighbors has manifested into what we call *Random Acts of Oola*.

It's some pretty cool stuff.

On social media, we've seen people buying coffee for the people behind them in line, picking up the check at a restaurant, or dropping off flowers on a random doorstep. We've heard stories of people all over, discovering the value in a simple smile, eye contact, and kindness.

Whether it's Debbie in Nebraska—who sent Oola stickers to all her friends just to make them smile—or the attorney couple in California who volunteered their time to help make the world a better place, Oola readers are showing up in major ways. One reader in Texas even bought thousands of dollars' worth of OolaPalooza tickets to give anonymously to those most in need. One ticket went to a nurse who tended to the victims of the mass shooting in Las Vegas, another went to a woman who lost her home and all her belongings in the California wildfires, and two more tickets went to a couple on the brink of divorce. That's pretty Oola!

When we think about the greatest lessons Jesus has taught us, we know that kindness, compassion, gentleness, and encouragement are traits we like to practice and show to the world. How could you live and love like Jesus?

ADOPTION IS LOVE

by Hailey Aliff

My heart felt weak and my body heavy as I sunk into my familiar rust-colored mission chair and rested my legs on the matching ottoman. The room I was sitting in with my husband Jeremy was calm, painted a soft white with neutral accents of olive green and natural browns. Moonlight peeked though the sheer lace canopy as it draped the table next to me that held a simple terracotta pot with a lively green succulent. I knew every detail of this room because we have spent countless hours here on our knees, praying, crying, and hoping for a miracle. Most people would call this room a nursery, but Jeremy and I called it our "faith room." We called it our faith room because every time we walked into this room, our faith would be tested.

I gazed across the room at the empty crib that was holding nothing more than unanswered prayers, yesterday's tears, and shattered dreams. We got down on our knees, held hands, and like the countless times before, we started to pray. We prayed for a baby. We prayed that I would someday feel the kick of a baby in my tummy and hear the sound of a tiny heartbeat at the doctor's office. We prayed for sleepless nights, walking the hallway with our newborn. We prayed for 2 AM feedings and evening bath time. We prayed for soft kisses, gentle hugs, and early morning snuggles. We dreamed of a baby with Jeremy's sweet smile and my granny's kind eyes. We have been praying these prayers for over four years. We were strong, we remained faithful, but we were weary.

When Jeremy and I were dating, while other couples talked about travel and careers, all we would talk about was becoming parents. We loved kids and the idea of being parents. We loved everything about it. I grew up in a family of midwives and doulas and graduated from midwifery school myself when I was twenty-five. Seeing the miracle of birth firsthand only further fed my desire to bring a child into this world. I wanted nothing more than to be a mom and share that with someone I love.

Jeremy wasn't like most of the guys I knew growing up. He was just like me. When I asked Jeremy what he wanted to do after we got married, he said, "Become a dad." Although this pulled at my heartstrings for a moment, I was quietly concerned that he didn't talk about a career and money like all the other guys I knew. He was confident that a career would work out and we would make ends meet, but being a father was more important; it was his purpose as well.

After getting married, we took the first year being newlyweds: traveling, hanging with friends, getting to know each other better, building a business together, and planning a life together. Then it was time. It was time to settle down and start our long-awaited family. We were so excited. This is when we built our faith room. Like the rest of our family, we thought getting pregnant would happen quickly and naturally. But as months turned into years, and laughter and notebooks of baby names turned into tears and a planner full of doctor's appointments, it was still just the two of us. Our house started to feel more empty and quiet and less warm and welcoming. Our joy turned to worry and our excitement into fatigue.

It was one of these evenings in the faith room, where I had something heavy on my heart that I needed to talk to Jeremy about. After praying, and with uncertainty in my voice, I said, "What do you think of adoption?" He was quiet. Then he broke his silence and said that he had been having the same feelings recently, but his thoughts had always ended with concerns. He said that he was struggling with the fact that he didn't think he could love someone else's baby the way he could love his own. He knew that he could be a committed and dedicated dad but didn't think he would feel connected. Keeping it 100 percent real, in my heart I had the same feelings. Is it possible to love someone else's baby? We decided to pray to God for guidance.

Jeremy and I would meet in the faith room every night and pray. We asked family and friends to do the same. We shared our hopes, our fears, and our deepest insecurities. Would we be able to love? Would we be able to feel like this baby was our own? Over the next year, God started to soften our hearts and open our minds. One evening, in our faith room, we felt something new: an urgency to fill out the adoption paperwork and do it now. We acted on it.

Then, months later, we heard the story of a single mother of two who recently got pregnant and knew that she couldn't financially or emotionally raise another baby. She sought out abortion but, after a conversation with her mother and grandmother, decided to consider adoption. The day we met her, we were filled with anxiety and the lingering question about whether we could love this woman's baby as our own. The moment she walked into the room, a feeling came over me that to this day I can't describe. It was a feeling that I knew this woman from my past or from a dream. One glance at Jeremy and I knew he was feeling the exact same way. This was God's plan for our life. We were right where we were supposed to be at exactly the right moment.

We could see the mix of pain and joy in the birth mom's eyes. She made a difficult choice, but she knew it was right. After getting to know her, we wanted to honor her by allowing her to provide the middle name of our child. Without a blink, she said, "I would like her middle name to be Faith."

With that one word, it was as if God had winked at us and said, "Thank you for trusting Me."

Today, as I reflect on our journey and His master plan, Jeremy and I are holding Emerson Faith Aliff. I look over at the table and see a quote in a black frame that says, *"Adoption is when a baby grows in a mommy's heart instead of her tummy."* We've dreamt of, prayed for, cried for, and fought for this baby girl for years. And what a beautiful depiction of the Gospel she is. Adoption is love. Even though we don't deserve His favor He found a way for us to be adopted as sons and daughters of God.

We thank Jesus for trusting us to take care of His special gift.

Troy and his wife Kris adopted their daughter, Alea, too. From the earliest days of their marriage, they always knew that God was calling them to expand their family through international adoption. Kris considered it prayerfully, while Troy wondered privately whether he would love an adopted child the same as his three biological kids.

Time has answered that question. After being Alea's dad for sixteen years, all he sees is love—all he sees is family. Though their eyes have different shapes and their skin is a different tone, Troy and Kris only see Alea as their daughter.

Love is love. And that is the ultimate lesson of God's gift of His Son to us.

MY BELOVED SON

*"For God so loved the world, that He gave His
only begotten Son, that whosoever believeth in Him
should not perish, but have everlasting life."*

—JOHN 3:16 KJV

am the only one who can say I was there at the beginning and at
the end.

In the cold night sky, a bright star shined above. Distant
onlookers knew it was a sign that something magnificent was happening. It was as if the heavens opened and dropped a glorious chan-
delier through the darkness, to mark the significance of this moment.

Sweat dripped from my brow and hit the ground. This was the
hardest thing I have ever gone through, and nothing could prepare
me for this pain and anguish. I'd heard all the stories about childbirth
from others, but when you are the one giving birth, it is a whole new
adventure. I wasn't in comfortable surroundings with midwives and
warmth; I was in a humble stable with barn animals and my husband
Joseph.

Then I heard it, the sound I had been waiting for since the angel
Gabriel visited me months earlier. I heard the cry of our newborn
baby boy. This simple sound erased every memory of pain and
made my heart race. Every worry was laid aside. There was a shift in
the atmosphere that brought everything into focus on why He was

250

brought to us and into the world. I held His fragile body in my arms and looked at my beloved son with tears in my eyes. My son was given to me and to all of you. He has come to save us all, and this moment was the moment that all mankind would be shaken.

> *For God so loved the world that He gave His one and only Son, that whoever believes in Him shall not perish but have eternal life. For God did not send his Son into the world to condemn the world, but to save the world through Him. (John 3:16–17)*

In the cold night sky, darkness loomed as the clouds began to roar. Distant onlookers knew that this was a sign that something heart-breaking was happening. It was as if the heavens had opened, drop-ping down darkness over all, to mark the significance of this moment.

Blood dripped from his brow and hit the ground. This was the hardest thing I have ever gone through, and nothing could prepare me for this pain and anguish. I heard all the stories about losing a child, but to be the mother losing a child is a much deeper experience. I wasn't in a comfortable home, sitting at my bedside. I was on the side of a mountain with hard stone under my feet.

Then I heard it, the sound I had never wanted to hear; the sound I had spent my whole life dreading. I heard the child I bore cry out in agony, a sound that made my heart break for I loved Him dearly. Yet through His pain, everything was brought into focus: why He came to us and what He meant to the world. Through His agony, He said, "Father, forgive them for they know not what they do." John supported my fragile body in his arms as I looked up at my beloved son with tears in my eyes. My son was given back to God and to all of you. He has come to save us all and this moment was the moment that all mankind would be shaken.

> *Near the cross of Jesus stood his mother, his mother's sister, Mary the*

wife of Clopas, and Mary Magdalene. When Jesus saw his mother there, and the disciple whom he loved standing nearby, he said to her, "Woman, here is your son," and to the disciple, "Here is your mother." From that time on, this disciple took her into his home. Later, knowing that everything had now been finished, and so that Scripture would be fulfilled, Jesus said, "I am thirsty." A jar of wine vinegar was there, so they soaked a sponge in it, put the sponge on a stalk of the hyssop plant, and lifted it to Jesus's lips. When he had received the drink, Jesus said, "It is finished." With that, he bowed his head and gave up his spirit. (John 19:25–30)

I love my son Jesus. God loves His son Jesus. And Jesus so loved you that He gave His life for your sins to be forgiven.

I was there in the beginning. I was there in the end. He is there always. God is love.

There is no match for love. Just as Christ wants us to put love into practice, *His love for us* compelled him to willingly die on a cross as payment for our sins—even though none of us deserved such a profound sacrifice. So how can you amplify your walk with Christ *and* grow in love for yourself and others?

LOVE YOURSELF

"God is love."

—1 JOHN 4:16 GWT

Taking care of yourself, getting healthier, doing things to bring joy and fun into your life, and being a little less concerned with serving everyone else all the time is not only loving, it actually helps you eventually show up for others in a much bigger way once you're whole.

After all, if you don't take care of yourself, how will you take care of other people?

Jesus had to say "no" in order to focus on God's purpose in His life. And Heather began to say "no" to give herself the space she needed to heal. Over time, she came to enjoy being a mom more, being a friend more, enjoying her job more, and joyfully serving at church again— plus she was able to open her life to other possibilities.

Eventually, she recaptured her passion for ministry—planning her missions trip to Nicaragua. On the day she left, though some in her church questioned how a single mom could leave three small children with her parents and travel to a foreign country, Heather felt proud of her next step. She wanted to show her kids what a comeback (and living your best life) looks like—all because she loved herself first.

BE INTENTIONAL AND LOVE
UNCONDITIONALLY

"Love is patient. Love is kind. Love isn't jealous.
It doesn't sing its own praises. It isn't arrogant."
—1 CORINTHIANS 13:4 GWT

While unconditional love is often difficult to show to your ex, that bully at work, or the nasty neighbor who's impossible to deal with, what you *can do* is to be intentional about how you love. Showing up, being patient, practicing kindness, and supporting the people you interact with in achieving their goals and dreams—this is unconditional love of the highest order, the way God loves us unconditionally. It's timeless, unchanging, has no limitations, and doesn't include, *I'll love you if you do what I want.*

But loving unconditionally also means to act with love under all circumstances—even with those people you wish were miles away.

You can still be intentional about how you love them by practicing patience, understanding them, seeing the good, and hoping better things for them. You can intentionally change the way you interact with them. But most importantly, you can pray for them. Even the Bible tells us to *pray for those who despitefully use you.**

You can pray that they learn better coping skills than to bully others. You can pray that they find relief from their hatred. You can pray that they learn to love others—and themselves. Or you can simply pray that they grow closer to God. Sometimes, prayer is the only way to show love. But it's a good one. It's intentional. And it's a way to love without conditions.

DON'T CHANGE THE PEOPLE YOU LOVE. JUST LOVE THEM.

"Let all that you do be done in love."
—1 CORINTHIANS 16:14 ESV

So many times we try to change the people we love. While the wiser ones among us would say, *Good luck with that,* many of us still try to impose our own conditions as a prerequisite for loving them fully.

I'll love you more if you go to college, some say. *I'll love you more if you lose weight,* others suggest. *I'll love you more if you earn more money,* still others imply. While we may not use those exact words, what we mean is *my love has conditions.* Right?

Our goal should be to love fully—even if their goals and dreams are different from ours or they're not following the path that we want. That's the definition of love that we want to provide our loved ones—and especially our kids.

* LUKE 6:28b (Jubilee Bible 2000).

DISCIPLINE

"*Whoever disregards discipline comes
to poverty and shame.*"

—PROVERBS 13:18 NIV

W hile we've talked a lot about taking steps to reach your goals, this next bit of news will still come as a surprise to some Christians: having Jesus in your corner is not a hall pass to success. It's not an automatic ticket to the Big Leagues. You can't say, *I'm going to give my life to Jesus, read this* Oola *book, and suddenly, everything I want will be mine.*

You can do everything right—you can plan well in advance—but life will still be filled with tests, trials, and hardship. Life is not supposed to be easy. In fact, challenges are God's way of nudging us into a closer relationship with Him. It's His way of saying, *Lean on Me when the going gets tough.* Challenges not only help us grow in faith, but they also help us grow in skills, wisdom, and maturity.

Is there a way to get past challenges? Of course.

Discipline is the thing that will see you through.

WHAT THE LAZY WANT, THE DISCIPLINED GET

Abraham Lincoln once said, "Things may come to those who wait, but only the things left by those who hustle."

Discipline is all about the hustle.

If there's something you've identified that you want in your life—a new job, a beautiful house, vibrant good health, financial independence—realize that steadily achieving smaller objectives on the way to your goal is the *only* way to get it. Hope is not a strategy.

Luckily, two things will help you be more disciplined: a list of daily tasks you *must* do and a sense of urgency about the goals that you're pursuing. For instance, when we decided to write the very first *Oola* book and take the message of the 7 F's out on the road, we wrote twenty-five chapters in just three days.

We *know* there's not an infinite amount of time.

◎ ◎ ◎ ◎

SHIRTLESS FIREMEN IN PINK SUSPENDERS

by Karen Hodges

The contemporary pink-and-gray chair comforted me, and the warm honey oak armrests gave my nervous fingers something to tap as I sat in the university hospital waiting room. I was thirty-nine and holding. I knew that I had let my health go over the last decade. I also knew that I had to lose weight and take control of my health because my family has a strong history of heart disease and stroke. I was overweight and on the fast track to living out my family legacy. Looking around the room, I noticed a bulletin board with posters and fliers dangling in the distance. I couldn't read the small font, but I could make out the word on the poster in the center. It said *Sugarhouse. Hey, that's where I live,* I thought to myself. I decided to walk over and check it out.

As I got closer, I felt the deep red poster pulling me toward it like the TV and the little girl in *Poltergeist.* As I read it, it spoke to me. It was promoting a one and a half mile Heart and Stroke walk (not a run, thank goodness) through Sugarhouse Park. It was right in my neighborhood, and it was to benefit the American Heart Association. Everything on the poster spoke to me. *Could I do this?* I wondered. Without giving myself time to think of excuses or letting fear get in the way, I signed up.

Before I knew it, it was race day. Or "walk day" as I like to call it. The event started on a crisp fall morning. The skies were bright blue and the Wasatch Mountains were painted with fall colors, framing the horizon. The release of a dozen white doves signified the start of the race. I looked down and told my feet, which were wrapped in purple Brooks Ghost sneakers, to move forward. I looked up and was inspired by the contrast of the white doves against the blue skies as they flew off into the distance. The next thirty-nine minutes and twenty-four seconds consisted of conflicting thoughts going back and forth in my mind: *One foot in front of the other. Just keep going!* was followed quickly by *God, why did I decide to do this?*

After the race, I reflected back. I remembered that off to my right and off to my left, I felt the breeze of people running past me. I think it's called being lapped. At the time, I was so focused that it didn't matter, but it planted a seed in my mind. What if I could someday run a race? Even if it was just part of a race? With no past running experience or coaches to guide me, I picked a 5K race six months down the road. It was called the Pink Series 5K, and they mentioned something about a surprise at the end of the race. I love pink, and I love surprises. I signed up.

Let the training begin.

I looked at the road in front of me and ran through a mental checklist as if my first attempt at running was a NASA shuttle launch. Blue spandex running pants with hot pink flames: check. Black running shirt with hot pink "TOUGH GIRL" written on the front: check. Purple Brookes Ghost sneakers and perfectly tied purple laces: check. Pink Oola hat to keep the sun out of my eyes: check. Houston, we are a go for launch—and off I went.

As I moved from a fast walk to a run, I felt an awkward mix of freedom and stiffness that I have never felt before. But I just kept running—slowly but surely, one foot in front of the other.

Over time, the task of getting out the door and getting moving became easier. With each training session, I tried to run a little more and walk a little less. Over the next six months, I would work through knee pain and hip problems. I would overcome morning stiffness and end-of-day fatigue. I would battle my body telling me to stop and my brain constantly telling me I wasn't a runner. "One foot in front of the other—one foot in front of the other," I kept telling myself.

After six months of training, I pulled up to the race in my brown VW Jetta and sat in my car. I looked at all the other racers walking to the starting line. I felt stress and pressure build up in my chest and started to question why I was here. The distant echo of the announcer on his megaphone forced me to get out of the car to be able to hear his instructions. With shaky hands and nervous knees, I walked through the crowd of other runners toward the starting line. There were so many runners that I felt like I was being swallowed up in a sea of DriFit gear and ponytails. To overcome my anxiety, I had to look back at all the training and the hard work that I'd put in to realize that I am worth it, and like every other runner here, I deserve to be here.

"5-4-3-2-1 Go," and the race began. No white doves. No crisp blue skies and fall colors in the mountains. Just me, my thoughts, and the sea of runners around me. I started off running and didn't walk until I passed the one-mile mark. A mix of running and walking completed the next 2.1 miles, all with a smile. I was so proud of myself as I crossed the finish line. I felt like a new person, and I instantly thought, *Which race is next?* But wait, what's the surprise they promised at the end of the race? The promotional materials promised a surprise. As I walked toward the awards stand, I saw it. A rhinestone-studded, bling-bling pink medal was waiting for me, and soon it was placed around my neck by two of the hottest shirtless firefighters in pink suspenders that I have ever seen. This made every minute of training and all the pain worth it. I've heard of the "runners high." Maybe this was it. I was hooked.

Since then, I have run twelve 5Ks, six 10Ks, one 15K, nineteen half marathons, four sprint triathlons, and four relay races, all by simply putting one foot in front of the other. I lost over ninety pounds, and in the process, I found myself. I am registered and got accepted into the New York City Marathon and signed up for my first Ironman. Who knows where this will take me, but I am hoping it leads me to the shirtless firemen in pink suspenders once again.

Where could discipline take you? Whether it's a more focused faith walk or better health or better finances, steady disciplined steps can get you there.

But what if God chooses you for a completely different career—and a much bigger role in His Kingdom? Would you have the discipline to live up to God's plan for your life? Saul of Tarsus did and became one of the greatest influences on the growth of the early Christian church. Check out this next story and get some inspiration for your disciplined life.

MY NEW DISCIPLINE

"'I am Jesus, whom you are persecuting,' He replied."

—ACTS 9:5b

S
ome might look at my current predicament as being imprisoned, and well, technically it is, but my current state of confinement does not compare to the spiritual prison in which I once lived. I was born at the turn of the first century with a silver spoon in my mouth and the world in the palm of my hands. Some might say I was privileged to be born with the purest Jewish blood and that I was granted Roman citizenship. I had the best teachers, and I was a zealous student, so I quickly rose in the religious ranks. Although I started out with an advantage, my accomplishments were not handed to me. My sheer discipline and determination created my early successes.

By age thirty, I was hitting the pinnacle of my career—my path was set on destroying the followers of Christ. My Hebrew name, Saul of Tarsus, became synonymous with intensely persecuting anyone who would preach or believe in the man they called Jesus. I stood there with pride in my eyes, holding the men's coats while they stoned to death Stephen, one of Jesus's devoted followers. As he cried out, "Lord Jesus, receive my spirit," I felt a sense of accomplishment and happiness.

Jesus's movement had begun to grow, and I thought I had found my path to success and my purpose in life. While breathing out murderous threats against Jesus's disciples, I went to the high priest and asked for letters to the synagogues in Damascus—letters that would allow me to take any man or woman who followed Jesus as a prisoner and bring them to Jerusalem for questioning and possible execution. My request was approved, and I received permission to speak in any synagogue for my cause against Christ.

I prepared for my 150-mile journey to Damascus and left Jerusalem with a mission. Only divine intervention could have stopped me.

> As he neared Damascus on his journey, suddenly a light from heaven flashed around him. He fell to the ground and heard a voice say to him, "Saul, Saul, why do you persecute me?"
>
> "Who are you, Lord?" Saul asked.
>
> "I am Jesus, whom you are persecuting," he replied. "Now get up and go into the city, and you will be told what you must do."
>
> The men traveling with Saul stood there speechless; they heard the sound but did not see anyone. Saul got up from the ground, but when he opened his eyes he could see nothing. So they led him by the hand into Damascus. For three days he was blind, and did not eat or drink anything. (Acts 9:3–9)

In Damascus, the men took me to the house of Judas on Straight Street. I secluded myself and began to pray and fast. Yet after three days of fasting and praying, I still remained blind and confused. There was a knock on the door, and someone walked in and came over to me. This man seemed nervous as he placed his hands on me and said, "Brother Saul, the Lord Jesus, who appeared to you on the road as you were coming here, has sent me so that you may see again and be filled with the Holy Spirit." Immediately, I regained my vision and could see clearly.

This man introduced himself as Ananias and went on to say that

Jesus had appeared to him in a vision, telling Ananias to come and heal me. There were reports, he said, of the harm that I'd done to the holy people, and—knowing that I came to Damascus with authority from the chief priests to arrest followers of Christ—he admitted that he was concerned about tending to me. But the Lord had plans for me.

"You are the chosen instrument to proclaim the name of Jesus," Ananias had said. The Lord himself had revealed this to him.

In that moment, everything I ever knew was uprooted. The change that came over me was startling, sudden and unforeseen. Due to the all-powerful grace of God, I began to comprehend the grim destruction I had brought upon the followers of Christ. Yet now, I knew I had to tell people the truth.

It was not some random change of career path that overtook me, but a change of heart and a new way of life. Instead of persecuting those who followed Christ, I began to preach that Jesus of Nazareth is the Jewish Messiah and the Son of God.

My renewed message of hope in Christ was not well received by everyone. I reaped the harvest of hate that I had once sown. Yet, the more they pushed against me, the more I pushed back and proved that Jesus was the Christ. I couldn't let the plans of God for my life die on the platform of man's opinion. I stayed disciplined. I was pressed but not crushed. Now, I was being persecuted by people for preaching the good word—but I am not abandoned by God.

In my newfound discipline to fervently preach the news of Jesus, I have found myself shipwrecked on the island of Malta and then bitten by a snake. I have been whipped five times where I received thirty-nine lashes. Three times I was beaten with rods, and once I was stoned. Through weariness and toil, through regular sleeplessness, through severe hunger and thirst and in fasting, in cold, and in nakedness, and through the perils in the wilderness, I followed God's plan for my life. Regardless of the obstacles, I spend my time, even my time in prison, to enhance the Kingdom of God. I know that the things I have faced pale in comparison to what my Savior endured on the cross. Sitting in this Roman prison, it is obvious that they can imprison my body, but my soul will always belong to Christ.

What discipline could you find within yourself if God gave you a magnificent new career? Would you work steadily and be diligent? If your hustle could use some practical strategies for showing up in a bigger way in God's Kingdom, these tips will help.

BE **REALISTIC**

"Whoever loves discipline loves knowledge."
—PROVERBS 12:1a ESV

The reality is, on the road to the OolaLife, you will have bad days, and you will be challenged. But it doesn't serve God's ultimate purpose for your life if you give up when the going gets tough.

The biggest dreams start with the smallest steps. It is more about consistency than magnitude of your action. Small action steps every day over time make the biggest transformations in life.

Start small. Set mini-goals that are easily attained to help you gain momentum and a growing belief in yourself. As confidence builds, move faster. A realistic view of progress and an honest understanding of the challenges you will face will help fuel the discipline you will require to achieve your dreams.

DIAL IT **IN**

"Put into practice what you learned and received from me,
both from my words and from my actions. And the
God who gives us peace will be with you."

—PHILIPPIANS 4:9 GNT

The bad days and challenges are why it's important not only to be realistic about your progress, but also to dial in your discipline. Decide what your goals are—whether fitness, finance, faith, or some other area—then plan ahead for the discipline you'll need. Bring in the supplies, schedule the time, recruit the support to dial in your discipline.

For instance, if your goal is to lose thirty pounds and drop a few sizes, can you clean out the temptation in your fridge, join a gym, create a special drawer for your workout gear, and set a daily alarm to get up an hour earlier? If your goal is to grow in your faith, can you sign up for a Bible class, download a Christian meditation app, and begin a nightly devotional study?

As you're planning the necessary support structure for maintaining your discipline, also plan ahead for what you'll do when you encounter a *lack of discipline.* How will you renew your efforts and push through that challenge? It could be an accountability partner who prays with you, or a reward you promise yourself for getting back on track and reaching a major milestone, or a simple serving of grace to yourself that you are not perfect, but you are making progress.

DON'T LET SOCIETY DEFEAT
YOUR DISCIPLINE

"Discipline yourself for the purpose of godliness."

—1 TIMOTHY 4:7b NASB

Discipline isn't just for achieving physical rewards. It takes discipline to be a Christian, too, *especially* in our modern-day culture. In fact, when it comes to staying on track with your faith, society's morals and values can easily get in the way. There are so many things to distract and tempt you, it's easy for others to gain control over your focus.

So what can you do?

Stay disciplined in the daily habits that bring you closer to God. Keep your Bible nearby. Set evening alerts on your smartphone to read the Word or a devotional or meditation, and you can even partner up with a mentor or friend to attend Sunday services together, go on missions trips, or participate in an ongoing activity at church.

CHAPTER
20

INTEGRITY

"In all your ways submit to him, and he will
make your paths straight."

—PROVERBS 3:6 NIV

ntegrity is who we are when *no one else can see* what we're doing. As Christians, we're told to have integrity in every area of our lives, whether it's our truthfulness, our thoughts, or (most importantly) our relationship with God. When we practice integrity, it allows for people to trust us. It also lets God know that He, too, can trust us with more duty and responsibility within His Kingdom.

KEEPING YOUR WORD WITH OTHERS

In today's culture, following through on one's commitments seems to be a casual thing. We'll deliver on time if it's not inconvenient. We'll be there for sure unless something better comes up.

But being a Christian means we need to hold ourselves to a higher standard. We need to adhere to what's right and have the difficult conversations early on when things don't go as planned.

Living in integrity also means acting maturely. When people see you as trustworthy, honest, transparent, and forthright about mistakes and setbacks, it creates a vibe and momentum around you that's compelling. People *want to be associated* with those who actually do what they say they'll do. Your integrity instills confidence. You become reliable, consistent, and bankable.

KEEPING YOUR WORD WITH YOURSELF

To further the point, the most valuable kind of integrity is keeping your word to yourself. If you've read this far in the book and you're now committed to change and finding out what God has planned for you, the biggest agreement you'll make on your journey is the commitment you keep *with yourself* to do the work, get past your Blockers, and begin the process of moving toward your goals. It's inking your daily to-do list, doing the worst first, and focusing on things that truly matter.

The bottom line is, if you're going to commit to a goal, honor it—just as you would honor your word to someone else.

One way to stay in integrity with yourself—and not bum yourself out for not making progress—is *don't overset goals.* Break down your biggest dreams into those baby steps you can handle right now. Get started and see some success. Mini-wins are energizing. They will build momentum and a belief in you that *anything is possible.* Stretch yourself as you accomplish more and more, but don't fall out of integrity with yourself because you didn't hit unrealistic goals—like losing twenty-five pounds in the first thirty days or paying off your $300,000 mortgage in the first year. Build momentum and begin trusting yourself again by setting smaller interim goals and achieving them.

HEALING CRYSTAL

by Verick Burchfield

We met on a sunny Friday afternoon. I was a simple college kid with big dreams and an empty wallet. I was riding shotgun in my buddy's 1984 white Camaro as we pulled into a Chevron gas station on McFarland Boulevard in Tuscaloosa, Alabama. I opened the passenger door and stepped out into the crisp air, wearing a black-and-white Nike athletic suit, Birkenstocks, and coke-bottle glasses. My high-and-tight haircut rounded out my look in an attempt to draw attention away from my shy nature. While leaning against the Camaro, I faced the orange-and-blue horizon to soak up the last few minutes of winter sun. I couldn't help but notice a cute blonde girl wearing a teal shirt, denim overalls, and Timberland boots moving quickly toward me. Before I knew it, she was standing right in front of me. She looked up at me and said, "You have the most beautiful eyes I have ever seen!" I justified this compliment with the rationale that maybe she could see my eyes from across the parking lot because they were magnified by my thick lenses. My mind started to pull from movies like *Top Gun* and James Bond as I searched for a clever response, but after what felt like an hour, I simply said, "And your name is?" She said, "My name is Crystal." We spent the rest of the weekend hanging out, talking, and getting to know each other. I called home after that weekend and told my parents that I met my future wife, and fourteen months later, that statement became a reality.

During the next four years, we learned each other's favorite colors, little quirks, taste in music, and favorite foods and fell deeper in love as we navigated jobs, paid bills, and had babies. We lived on love and not money, as we finished degrees and applied for jobs. Life was going as planned. But with the birth of our second child, Crystal seemed to recover less quickly and found herself tired—not the normal fatigue of a multitasking mom, but daily fatigue that seemed to be worsening over time. We had no idea what was wrong but, committed "in sickness and in health," we pushed on. We relied on the advice from our doctors and the strength of our prayers and continued our journey together.

Our sixth year of marriage brought our third child, a son, into our life. We were so thankful for him, but Crystal didn't bounce back; in fact she got worse. After months of bed rest, doctors started rounds of antibiotics, which eventually led to surgeries. The surgeries led to more medications and more problems. After two years of treatments and only limited progress, Crystal moved to be near a specialized clinic 700 miles away in search for answers. I was home raising three children under five, and "When is Mom going to be home?" was the common question that broke the silence at our dinner table. I would look up from the evening bowl of mac and cheese at a table full of little sad eyes and answer, "I don't know." We had lost hope in the system but maintained hope in God. We trusted that through Him, she could be healed.

The circumstances around her illness had also put us $250,000 in debt. We moved to be near where Crystal was receiving treatment into a downsized rental; half the size of our previous home. I had gained thirty-five pounds from the single-dad, mac-and-cheese life. I felt like a complete failure. I was a nurse practitioner by profession and took care of patients all day, but I couldn't figure out how to help my own wife. I felt defeated. I felt desperate.

On New Year's Day, frustrated and fatigued, we talked about what our dreams and goals would be for the coming year. We both knew that healing Crystal was all that really mattered.

In that moment, I heard loud and clear that I should fast and pray for twenty-one days. I had no idea how or why, but I felt very strongly that I needed to do this. So I started the next day. Every time I felt hungry, I would pray for Crystal's healing. Day in and day out of fasting led to many moments in prayer and lots of cumulative minutes with God.

Day Five into the fast, I got a text from Crystal. She was desperate, having arrived late at the clinic, and felt terrible and stressed. Her doctor told her she needed a bone marrow biopsy to see if she had bone marrow failure. She was at her wit's end and texted me that she was "running to Papa to pray." I said a prayer to give her guidance, and I had no choice but to get back to taking care of my patients. When I had a break, I grabbed my phone and noticed I had an unusual amount of missed texts and calls from Crystal.

> Text 1: The song from 10th Ave North came on the radio on my way to pray. Where will you run, child? Where will you go, child? I'll be by your side. This song always brings me peace... I really need to be healed. Love you!

> Missed phone call 1

> Missed phone call 2

> Missed phone call 3

Text 2: Verick, I am healed! I felt a heat throughout my whole body while I was praying. I know it sounds crazy, but I know that I am healed.

The human in me wanted to doubt her, but I didn't. The man in me wanted to be angry that it took this long, but I wasn't. I felt peace for the first time in years, and I knew with my whole heart that she was healed.

The next day, lab results revealed that all of Crystal's blood levels were in the normal range. The doctor said he had no explanation. They had never seen anything like this before, and it was simply a miracle.

Six years after Crystal's healing, we took our family to a favorite vacation spot: Blue Mountain Beach, Florida. We were eating dinner filled with great food and laughter that seemed to harmonize with the gentle waves of the Gulf of Mexico. After dinner, Crystal leaned over and whispered in my ear that she felt sick. She thought it was something in the food, but I instantly felt that it was something worse. The anxiety made my chest tight as I helped her to the car.

On the drive back, Crystal started passing out, and her heart rate was pounding at a rate of 160 beats per minute. I called 911 and the ambulance met us. They rushed Crystal into the ambulance, and then we followed her to the hospital. In the rearview mirror, I could see the terror in the eyes of our children. I remember their tears appearing red from the reflection off the ambulance in front of us. After two hours in the hospital, the doctors came in with blood tests, and it showed that Crystal's illness had returned.

I felt sad for Crystal and our children. I felt disappointed in God for letting us down. I was scared of what this all meant for our family, and I started to pray. As I sat in the chaos of what this all meant, I recalled a story and a Bible verse that I had learned in the fifth grade. The story was about King David begging God to let him stay close to God in spite of what he had done. He prayed to God in this way:

> *Create in me a clean heart, O God; and renew a right spirit within me. Cast me not away from thy presence; and take not thy Holy Spirit from me. Restore unto me the joy of thy salvation; and uphold me with the willing spirit. (Psalm 51:10–12)*

I wanted to flee. I wanted to run from Him the very moment I needed him the most—but I chose to stay.

The future is still unknown. I know that my faith will be continually challenged. Life will deliver moments of pain and despair, joy and peace, and I commit to going through them with Christ. I will remain faithful in prayer for Him to heal Crystal and continually pray for the presence of God in my life and in our family, knowing we would rather have Him and His presence over anything.

Is there something in your life that can't be explained, but continually causes you to trust God and lean into Him? Maybe this is your "integrity moment." You can decide to run, or you can stick with God and His plan for your life. It's always your choice.

The man in our next story chose to go all in for Jesus. How about you?

THE NEW GUY

"Must you forever resist the Holy Spirit?"

—ACTS 7:51 NLT

S ince the death of Jesus, the movement had grown greater and greater as more people realized He was truly the risen Messiah. The apostles, once known as the twelve disciples, now had to cover more territory and minister to more people to meet the demand. It was obvious they needed to grow the team to continue sharing the Good Word. I wanted to be on that team.

Today was the big day. The apostles were looking to appoint more people to help them. I was hopeful. I sat in the heat, awaiting their decision, daydreaming of all the things I could be doing for Jesus's ministry—the messages I would give, the souls I would help save.

Next to me I counted six other candidates. I knew these men. They were all great men who were full of spirit and wisdom. They were anxiously waiting with me while the apostles decided which of us they would bring into the inner circle.

They summoned us forward. I was ready to do whatever they asked of me. I wanted to change the world. My wait was over. They told me they had a job for me. They were commissioning me to help in the local community outreach program. *Come again?* I thought, baffled. *So, I am not going to be a disciple traveling the world, spreading the good news? I'm going to feed people?*

275

The apostles had been made aware that widows of the town were being discriminated against in the daily distribution of food. With all that Jesus had entrusted them to do, the apostles realized they didn't have the time to tackle the situation, so they thought it was the perfect job for the new guy. Truth be told, the new job description was more like waiting tables on the angry women at the local food bank than spreading the word of Christ, but I was there to serve and was happy to do it.

After giving us the news, the apostles prayed over us, and sent us on our way.

Looking at the task before me, some people might have been tempted to abandon ship because they didn't get the job they wanted. The reality was, I didn't care if I didn't get the fancy official title. I simply believed, and I wanted to serve. Whether I was distributing food or praying for the sick, I was still being a disciple of Jesus. And didn't our Lord say that it was better to serve than to be served?

I knew that if I kept my heart pure and my focus on Him, I could make a difference. I was confident that miracles would happen as I served tables.

But as the believers grew, so did the haters. The fact that Jesus was dead, yet his following was growing, bothered those of the synagogue. Still, I continued my duty and never backed down on speaking the truth of Jesus's word. In fact, I stayed true to His teachings to the point that the religious leaders urged the townspeople to accuse me of blasphemy.

I was arrested and brought before the council.

When they asked me for the truth, I could have denied Jesus like others had, but I was His follower, and nothing could change that. I stayed true. I didn't back down.

Integrity isn't something you can try on and take off like a garment when it's convenient; it must be the moral fiber that weaves you together and makes you *who you are* at your core. Incorruptible, stable, consistent, and steadfast is how I wanted people to see me—just like the One I followed.

The next few minutes before the council, I gave the speech of my life. I chose to stand up for what was right even if it cost me my life. The council would hear the truth, and the truth is what sets us free. As I neared the end of pleading my case, I felt a newfound power that needed to be released. It must be said. I knew what Jesus would do, and it was my responsibility to live like Him. It's better to die for the truth then live for a lie. I continued:

> *"You stubborn people! You are heathen at heart and deaf to the truth. Must you forever resist the Holy Spirit? That's what your ancestors did, and so do you!*
>
> *"Name one prophet your ancestors didn't persecute! They even killed the ones who predicted the coming of the Righteous One—the Messiah whom you betrayed and murdered.*
>
> *"You deliberately disobeyed God's law, even though you received it from the hands of angels."*
>
> *The Jewish leaders were infuriated by Stephen's accusation, and they shook their fists at him in rage.*
>
> *But Stephen, full of the Holy Spirit, gazed steadily into heaven and saw the glory of God, and he saw Jesus standing in the place of honor at God's right hand.*
>
> *And he told them, "Look, I see the heavens opened and the Son of Man standing in the place of honor at God's right hand!"*
>
> *Then they put their hands over their ears and began shouting. They rushed at him and dragged him out of the city and began to stone him. His accusers took off their coats and laid them at the feet of a young man named Saul.*
>
> *As they stoned him, Stephen prayed, "Lord Jesus, receive my spirit."*

He fell to his knees, shouting, "Lord, don't charge them with this sin!"
And with that, he died. (Acts 7:51–60)

That day, I lived in my truth and would die in my truth. Even as the stones flew, I remained unwavering in my willingness to serve and to live in unrelenting integrity.

That day, Stephen learned that obeying God's law and standing up for Jesus is one way to show integrity in your relationship with Him. But God also commands us to always be in integrity with others—*and with ourselves.* Here are some tips that will help you stay on track.

KEEP YOUR WORD WITH GOD

"Because of my integrity you uphold me and
set me in your presence forever."

—PSALM 41:12 NIV

How many times have you said, *God, if you get me through this, I'll never sin again. If you bring me the relationship I want, I'll never ask you for another thing. If you help me get past these bills, I promise I'll start tithing every week.*

You'll go to church, pray every day, read the Bible—are we right?

Then, when God actually gets you through the drama, you collapse in relief, and think, *Yeah, I'm good. Thanks for forgiving me—*only to promptly forget what you promised. While it sounds funny in print, how many times have you made promises to God, then fallen out of integrity in your faith walk? While it's true that we have a loving God who forgives us, why not strive *instead* to show up fully and grow your relationship with Him into a relationship where you always keep your word? Try it and find out how much more God will show up in your future, now that you're trustworthy.

START SMALL

> *"One who is faithful in a very little*
> *is also faithful in much."*
>
> —LUKE 16:10a ESV

One way to keep your word with yourself is to recognize that starting small is better than quitting big. If you want to start praying for ten minutes a day, cut it in half and see how things go at five minutes. If you're going to commit to doing cardio five days a week, start with two. The key is to consistently follow through on the commitment you made to yourself instead of quitting after a few weeks because the new habit was too hard or took too much time. Dream big, but make the action steps toward your dreams realistic and sustainable.

KEEP YOUR INTEGRITY WITH YOUR NEIGHBOR

> *"Keep your thoughts on whatever is right or deserves praise:*
> *things that are true, honorable, fair, pure,*
> *acceptable, or commendable."*
>
> —PHILIPPIANS 4:8b GWT

While dishonesty and broken promises aren't supposed to be an issue for Christians, you'd be surprised at how much justification goes on when we decide to ignore our commitments. Gray areas, wink-wink morality, fuzzy math, and "acceptable excuses" seem to make it okay. But it's not. While you may be well-meaning, your integrity level drops when you don't honor your word, even in the smallest of promises.

Instead, our advice is to always act decently. The right thing is always the right thing. Over deliver. Arrive early to the meeting, pay the bill before the due date, and show up to the commitment. Honoring your word to others will make more opportunities show up for you. You'll establish a reputation as someone who's trustworthy and reliable with bigger projects and more important duties. Not only that, but honoring your word makes God smile.

PASSION

"I will guide you in the way of wisdom;
I will lead you on straight paths.
When you walk, your steps will not be impeded;
when you run, you will not stumble."

—PROVERBS 4:11–12 BSB

A s we circled Rockefeller Center for the fifteenth time, flashing blue lights appeared in our rearview mirror. The OolaBus, it seemed, was being nabbed by New York's Finest.

For several days prior to that, we'd been in upstate New York collecting dreams, doing book signings, and streaming on Facebook Live. But on our last night there, Troy decided to get the OolaBus on the *Today* show.

"Think of all the potential lives that would be changed if people saw the OolaBus, googled the word, and realized that they don't have to settle for an overwhelmed, stressed-out life," he said.

Undeterred by the fact that a major gig like this is usually booked months in advance by top agents and publicists, the OolaGuru grabbed a dream sticker, wrote out his goal, and slapped it on our trusty Surf Bus.

He'd come up with the idea that, if we started out early enough and drove around the block enough times, we might actually be in the right place when the cameraman took a long shot of the street outside the studio during a bumper segment for the show's next guest. As Dave got more and more frustrated, and traffic got more and more congested, the cop's siren blurted out short bursts of warning—prompting Troy to pull neatly to the curb.

"We're on high alert and you're drawing a lot of attention," the cop said, as Dave bolted out the passenger door to a nearby coffee shop, leaving the scene as if he'd done that before. Excitedly Troy replied, "That's the point," and without taking a breath began passionately involving the cop in a discussion of the principles of Oola. Troy somehow managed to talk his way out of a citation (like he'd done it before), gave the officer an Oola book, and was back on the street doing laps around NBC Studios again. Nearly out of time now—with his left leg numb from navigating the clutch of a 1970 VW Bus, and bleary-eyed from the 4:00 AM start—he turned the corner just in time for the OolaBus to be captured as the background image for Natalie Morales's segment, appropriately entitled "Seventh Heaven."

There it was. We hit our goal: "Get Oola on the *Today* show," albeit only technically.

Was it a God thing? Or luck? Or simply persistence?

No, it was passion.

WHAT ARE YOU SO **PASSIONATE** ABOUT THAT YOU'D DEDICATE EVERY WAKING MOMENT TO ACHIEVING IT?

For us, spreading the message that you were designed by God for greatness is something we live and breathe every day. We are passionate about letting the world know that they don't have to settle for an ordinary life when extraordinary is within them.

We don't know why God calls us to do the things we do—we just have to trust that and be passionate. It keeps us up late, wakes us up early, fills our social media pages, inspires us to get into new business relationships, and takes us to countless cities each year. There's no stopping our passion for Oola.

But what about you?

What's the goal, topic, vision, mission, ministry, or future that you are equally passionate about? If it makes you lose track of time, puts a spark in your eye, and occupies most of your waking hours, yeah, that's your passion. Unfortunately, too many people we meet can't immediately tell us what they're passionate about. Unclear, they hang out at the OolaBus for a while before finally choosing a sticker and writing a goal. Sometimes they think their passion is not allowed, like the guy we met in California who loved restoring his vintage Camaro, or they think if it's not useful or lucrative, it's not worth pursuing.

But the people who our hearts go out to are those who first have to determine what's holding them back. They have to peel away years of relationship stuff, guilt, self-sabotage, disappointment, and missed opportunities so that they're not so focused on what's broken.

When they finally do, their passion and purpose is hiding just underneath.

So whatever happened to the OolaBus that day in Manhattan?

The heartwarming end of the Rockefeller Center story is that someone captured an image of the OolaBus's major "media moment" and posted it on Twitter. We shared it on our social media and, within minutes, people began to walk over to 30 Rock to catch a glimpse of the OolaBus or give us virtual high-fives online. It reminded us that passion isn't something you do alone. Having passion for God's purpose in your life *also* engages other people you may not even know and may never meet in person.

Now that's Oola.

THE FEMALE CHRISTIAN
MOTIVATIONAL JIMMY FALLON

by Kelsey Humphreys

"Terrific!" I passionately exclaim as people keep asking about the big move to Los Angeles to pursue entertainment. It's been terrific. Yes, *terrific* means wonderful. But look it up in the dictionary, and you'll find that word also means *massive, enormous*, and you know, *"to cause terror."*

When you hear about someone moving to L.A. to pursue a career in entertainment, you most likely envision a single, twenty-something with bright eyes, a couple of suitcases, and a fast metabolism.

Think again.

I'm an early-thirty-something wife and mom. I've survived giving birth, nursing, teething, and potty training; my eyes haven't been bright in years. My cross-country move wasn't in a red convertible sports car with my hair blowing in the wind; it included a U-Haul, two mom cars, two dogs, my daughter, my high school sweetheart husband, two grandparents, and 556 bathroom stops.

I left behind my husband's entire family and my best friends. I left behind a successful advertising career. We left a church family. We left behind comfort, ease, and what's known as the good life. We left it all for one reason: so that I can become the "Female Christian Motivational Jimmy Fallon."

Yup. Terror. I may be a little bit coo-coo-ca-choo, Mrs. Robinson, but that's what feeling passionate toward your purpose will do.

I had wanted to sing and act and make people laugh before I could spell. It was my God-given purpose, but then life happened. Four years spent on a "fall-back" degree. A few failed attempts at my dream. Marriage. Bills. Disappointment. And before I knew it, I shoved my purpose down, lost my passion, and drank to keep it down.

But God is good and patient—and, luckily, extremely persistent. At my low point, He gave me a breathtaking vision of a motivational talk show. He also told me very clearly one day that if I didn't get sober, He wouldn't bless that vision. It was almost audible; I'll never forget it. Again, I sound cuckoo for Cocoa Puffs, but this is what led to my move and this story.

Without the numbness of chardonnay, all my passions came up and out, refusing to stay down and stuffed away. I started showing up every day. I acted on the loving nudge into entrepreneurship, then into writing a bestselling book. I wrote and researched, I shot and edited videos, I pitched to guests. Doors started to open, I kept showing up. My husband, Christopher, and I started to pray and invest in this little talk-show dream.

Within eighteen months, I was flying to New York City to interview Tony Robbins. I've interviewed amazing people like Dave Ramsey, Candace Cameron Bure, Larry King, and Rachael Ray. I even got to interview these two guys who created an international movement called Oola. I started to get checks from YouTube. I kept trying, traveling, interviewing, and uploading. I was able to do a lot from my checked bags and my tiny home studio in Oklahoma City. But there is a city considered the entertainment capital of the world—and it is not OKC.

On a work trip to Hollywood, I felt another one of the Lord's loving shoves, er, I mean nudges. *"Quit settling for the smallest version of*

your dream, just because it's comfortable. Commit to the vision. Get in
the game. Go where the game is played."

"But, Lord…," I began (as if He doesn't get just how real this
human struggle is), "I am not a size zero, twenty-year-old who has
been in 'the industry' since infancy. I cannot move in with four room-
mates and survive on ramen! I have no real credits outside of You-
Tube! We have a child and a mortgage, Father. *A mortgage.*"

I envision that the more excuses I had, the more He laughed and
told Jesus, "Watch this."

In the fall, Christopher and I started praying about L.A. In December, he found a job description that was seemingly written for him.
He started the trillion-step interview process. In late January, without
having visited in person, my husband was offered the job and officially accepted. Then, because the tech world can be cray-cray, they
asked him to start in four weeks. We told our families. It was almost a
weeping and gnashing of teeth situation. But a door had been opened
to us, and we were going to show up.

LORD. You playin'? What about saving, planning? Do you know
how much stuff is in the attic? You remember you blessed us with a kid,
right? What are you doing?!

More laughter from above.

In February, we took a two-day trip to L.A. We set a fifteen-minute
commute radius around Christopher's new office and a budget. Day
One, nada. Hashtag anxiety. On Day Two, we found a renovated, dog-
friendly home in a great school district within walking distance of a
wonderful preschool, with a fenced yard, garage, and private driveway. We didn't know it, but a church we would love was also within
walking distance. Oh, and we found that listing accidentally because
it had just been posted *that morning.*

If that wasn't enough, I posted photos of our furniture on Facebook, and we sold almost everything in *one day.* After many donations,

we were able to make the move with just one fifteen-foot rental truck. Anyone with a small child and a marriage of ten years should be clapping. You understand. Over the next two weeks, we coordinated a handyman, cleaning service, and photographer to get our OKC house listed. We decided to try listing it "For Sale by Owner."

Are you sitting down? Our house was on the market for three days. That's it. I feel like at this point Jesus turned to God, hands up, nodding, and admitted he was impressed. But God wasn't done.

At the time of this writing, we haven't been here six months, yet:

We have a small group at church that we love.

My daughter has two best friends.

I have already secured an agent, manager, and some of my biggest celebrity guests yet.

I've started auditioning and landed a commercial role.

I got accepted into the Groundlings Comedy School, whose alumni include Melissa McCarthy, Kristen Wiig, and although he didn't officially graduate, my man Jimmy Fallon.

I've learned that God is passionate about our passions. He wants us to show up and engage, not coast on autopilot. A passion-filled, purpose-driven life forces us to grow and change. It's risky and scary. Trust me, it causes terror. But Webster defines "terror" as sensational, marvelous, outstanding, and—wait for it—out of this world!

Yeah, God gets it about your passion. When you show up fully to pursue something that's in your heart, you can rest assured that God has put it there. Whether it's some great thing you're supposed to do or something just for fun after decades of hard work in your career, God's plan is super cool and divinely perfect for you.

LOAVES AND FISHES

"The people realized that God was at work among them in what Jesus had just done."

—JOHN 6:14 MSG

saw people leaving the village by the masses, all moving in the same direction. The cobblestone streets were coming alive, and I wanted to know where they were going. The young-boy curiosity in me pulled me out the door, but the wisdom in me had me grabbing five barley loaves of bread and two fish before I left. I saw this in one of two ways: it would be a great way to sell some food to the masses and make a little extra money or, hey, if where they were heading was cool, I'd have some food to keep me full during the festivities.

As I walked up the hill, I looked around and saw more people than I'd seen gathered in one place before. Tomorrow is Passover, but I don't think this was why everyone was here. As I scanned the crowd, I noticed they were all looking in the same direction. They were all looking at Jesus and His disciples.

Jesus was becoming very well known. He worked when others were resting. His fame was becoming widespread because His love and message didn't discriminate by gender, religion, or lineage. His messages and gatherings were growing and inspired thousands. He also managed to enrage a few people while He was at it. It was apparent that the religious leaders were becoming serious haters of Jesus because they didn't understand his drive to work every day of the week and serve all who needed it.

Today, though, He wasn't supposed to be leading a gathering of people. In fact, it seemed like Jesus and the team were just needing some rest. They looked like they'd had a hard couple of days. I noticed fatigue with the disciples. But with a message of genuine love, healing, and restoration of lives, there was little time to rest. People were naturally attracted to Jesus's authenticity; He was the real deal.

As I began to sweat in the daytime sun, people from every nearby village started filling every inch of space to hear this man. The crowd swelled to five thousand men, not counting the women and children who came with high excitement. Hour upon hour, Jesus poured out His soul to the people who were thirsty for His words and for a better way of life.

Evening approached, and the people were starting to get hungry.

Wasn't Jesus tired yet? Wasn't He hungry, too? He kept sharing powerful wisdom and bringing healing to those who sought Him out. His passion for people overrode His own need to rest. He looked at the crowd and could see the many who seemed lost and searching. Like sheep who needed a shepherd, He didn't want to just send them home without getting what they yearned for.

Oblivious to His own hunger or fatigue, His compassion kept Him going.

His team, on the other hand, were starting to panic. They finally interrupted his teaching with great urgency—worried that even eight months' worth of salary wouldn't be enough to feed the people. It seemed obvious to everyone but Jesus, who simply told the disciples, "You give them something to eat."

Didn't He see there was a huge demand and not enough supply?

The situation spurred me into action. I knew that I was holding only five loaves of bread and two fish, but this was an opportunity to sell what was in my basket. More than that, however, I felt passionate to help Jesus if I could. The disciples brought me to Him. It didn't look like what I had was enough to make a difference, but with an open heart, I gave Him all I had, hoping to help in some small way.

> Jesus said, "Make the people sit down." There was a nice carpet of green grass in this place. They sat down, about five thousand of them. Then Jesus took the bread and, having given thanks, gave it to those who were seated. He did the same with the fish. All ate as much as they wanted.
>
> When the people had eaten their fill, he said to his disciples, "Gather the leftovers so nothing is wasted." They went to work and filled twelve large baskets with leftovers from the five barley loaves.
>
> The people realized that God was at work among them in what Jesus had just done. They said, "This is the Prophet for sure, God's Prophet right here in Galilee!" (John 6:11–15)

What I saw today was a miracle. But also I learned so much from Jesus. In the midst of chaos, He used an obstacle as an opportunity. His most passionate focus—something He never lost sight of—was people! Though His team didn't see the big picture, Jesus did. Today I learned from the hardest working man in town that little can become much when you put it in the right hands.

Watching Jesus that day inspired me and helped me see that we were not meant to live ordinary lives. Changing the world, as He did, means you have to do what others aren't willing to do. He believed in His purpose and the impact He would make. Living your purpose isn't for the faint of heart, as I saw that day. I also realized that although I had started off the day with a plan, I would rather play a small part in God's big plan than a big part in my own.

◎ ◎ ◎ ◎

What's your part in God's Kingdom? If a young boy can be the spark behind a miracle that feeds five thousand of Jesus's followers, imagine what you could do—once you call upon the power and wisdom of the Lord. How can you get started?

REDISCOVER YOUR **TRUE** PASSION, NOT SOMEONE ELSE'S PLAN FOR YOU

"We have everything we need to live a life that pleases God."

—2 PETER 1:3 CEV

When we keep our relationship with God as our main passion in life, there's no limit as to where He can take us. But the key is to listen to God instead of the people in your life, who are critical of you, who tear down your passion, or who have a reason to rain on your parade.

The only agenda that matters is God's plan for you. The rest is just noise.

Gary Vaynerchuk is the forthright and brash serial entrepreneur who's invested in more than fifty start-ups including Twitter, Tumblr, and Uber. His caution is that most people live their lives based on other people's opinions—their parents, spouse, older siblings, or neighbor.

But "living your life under the judgment of somebody else," Gary says, "is the great weakness of human beings." We agree. Listen to God—and do you.

MIND THE **MARBLES**

"Job answered God: 'I'm convinced: You can do anything and
everything. Nothing and no one can upset your plans.'"

—JOB 42:1–2 MSG

To help remind him that time is short and he *must* pursue his
passion and purpose every day, Troy keeps two jars of marbles on his
desk: one with marbles that represent the years he's already lived, and
the other representing the years he has left. As every year he moves
one marble over and the level in the "years left" jar drops again, Troy
puts more and more energy into his hustle.

If you've been thinking that you're getting too old to make a start
on your passion project or your skills aren't quite what they used to
be, realize there are countless stories of people over fifty who started
successful companies, launched cool humanitarian projects, and
developed unique scientific breakthroughs that have literally changed
the world. It's never too late to pursue your passion. God is waiting to
be your active partner in this. Don't disappoint Him.[*]

YOU'RE GOING TO DIE.
DON'T WAIT TO **FOLLOW** YOUR PASSION.

"To everything there is a season, and a time
for every purpose under heaven."

—ECCLESIASTES 3:1 BSB

One of the coolest things about passion is that it trumps every
other Blocker including fear, guilt, self-sabotage, and more. If you've

---

[*] Age doesn't matter. The prophet Job lived 140 years and saw his children and their children "to the fourth generation." (Job 42:16).

spent a lifetime *not* pursuing your passion because of Blockers that you've put in the way, realize that we're all going to die. Your time here is determined by God, and there is no time to waste. Use the understanding that your days are numbered to get you moving.

Quit overthinking your purpose and questioning if it's possible. You are losing valuable time. Do the work of overcoming your Blockers. Then passionately get after the unique calling He has put in your heart—sooner, rather than later.

HUMILITY

"Pride leads to disgrace, but with
humility comes wisdom."

—PROVERBS 11:2 NLT[*]

---

[*] New Living Translation

'm strong, but I'm tired, you might be thinking—especially if you're beating your way back from brokenness, hardship, or failure to a stable job, a drama-free household, and the simple normalcy we all need to move forward and pursue our calling. Whatever happened in your life, you may feel discouraged, ashamed, even abandoned by God. But more than anything, you probably feel *humble.*

The reality is—as humans—we all go through dark seasons and challenges. Sometimes these downfalls are brought about by our own arrogance. When Dave was at the peak of his success, his humility level was at its lowest: *Hey, God, I got this. Go help the people who really need You.*

At other times, there's a lesson God wants us to learn. But all too often, an epic failure is the only way that God can get our attention. It's His way of humbling us, so we understand we can only do this life with Him. The moment we think we've "arrived," He steps in and says, *You might think you have it all, but you need Me in this.*

When the unthinkable happens and your world falls apart, recognize it for what it is—and let your drama drive you to back God.

PEBBLE, ROCK, **BRICK**

If you haven't experienced humility early in your life, you must learn it by the experiences of others, or you will be taught it in your own life. If you're wondering, option A is much less painful.

When things are good, it's easy to take the credit and believe we don't need God. To wake us up, He'll toss a pebble into our life—a romantic break up, a cash crunch, or something easy to fix. While that's a great time to look to God for answers, many of us stumble blindly on, ignoring the pebble and working hard to stay in control.

If the pebble doesn't get our attention, God throws a rock at our life—whether it's a worsening situation, a pop-up crisis, or some major disaster that makes us take a hard look at our faith walk. And if we still don't listen, you guessed it, we get a brick to the head—a life-changing, life-threatening, overhaul-requiring tsunami of a problem.

NEVER GOING IT ALONE

by Adam Sculnick

The winter came, and I felt like I was at the bottom of a river of shame, drowning in a powerful torrent of guilt and helplessness as flowing water pinned me down. I had found rock bottom.

All the money I made, gone. There was no savings, no reserve, and no backup plan. I'd been buried under the weight of my own debt, my own failing business, and my own bad decisions for so long that the only relief I knew was to swallow my pride and ask for help.

I needed a car. I needed something that I could drive to work, something I could drive to pick up my kids from school, and something so I could carry groceries. Nothing fancy, just not a motorcycle for a family of five. My car and my back had been destroyed in an accident and my bank account depleted, leaving me with my 2005 Yamaha as my sole means of transportation. So, with everything I had left in my spirit and nowhere else to turn, I asked my mom for money to buy a car.

Like a homeless child holding a sign, intentionally guilting passersby into helping, I came to her at thirty-one years of age, as close to being on my knees as I'd ever been.

The truth was, she couldn't afford it, either. I knew it was wrong, and she knew it was wrong. But her mom instinct could tell my pain and desperation were real. She maxed out her credit cards for $3,000,

298

so I could own a used car. It was as if someone tossed me a lifesaving ring and I was able to pull myself up for a gasp of air.

However, after a single breath of relief, just days later, Christmas pulled me under yet again. I had to choose: rent or Christmas presents for the kids. Sick of seeing my kids go without, I skipped rent. My wife? The woman I pledged to spend my life taking care of was about to get nothing more than an "I love you" and a "Merry Christmas" as gifts this year. I couldn't look her in the eyes. I was ashamed. I failed her as a husband, as a father, and as a man. I was depressed; I was broken. I felt like the dirt beneath me.

As we traveled south on the familiar road to visit my grandmother for Christmas, my mind wandered to the disappointment I must be— to my mistakes, my misfortune, and my wrong doings. Just then, a loud *pop* snapped me back in the moment. Our old tire on our old car had exploded at highway speed. That car I bought to ease our anxiety just kicked that anxiety into high gear with the realization that I'd just put my family in danger. No one was hurt, but we discovered the car was not safe, and it would take twice what I paid for it to get it safely back on the road.

With no money, the glimmer of hope was gone. The free fall was fast, dark, and horrific. It was earth-shattering. Every insecurity I had ever felt was magnified. It was the last straw. As a man, a husband, a father, a business owner, and even as a human being, I felt now like nothing more than a carcass—beaten, torn to shreds, ripped asunder by the life I couldn't seem to get ahead of.

As a teen, I had been extremely self-destructive. I felt I had grown past this darker season of my life and left it behind me. However, in this moment, I was at seventeen again. I wanted to cut myself. I wanted to bleed all over this life I'd been trying desperately (but failing miserably) to build. I wanted to let it all go. I wanted to drink so much booze that I'd forget not only my struggles but myself. I wanted to black out my life completely. I wanted to wake up a different person, in a new place, in a new time, and realize it was all just a bad dream. My wife would be next to me smiling in the early morning light through the window. My kids would be safe in their beds without a care in the world.

I needed help again, and this time it would take more than $3,000 for a car. It would take more than my mom.

It was in that moment that I found faith. I knew I needed to change. Glancing at a stack of books on my nightstand, the word *balance* on the cover of the original *Oola* book spoke to me. If my world were to be described in a single word at this moment, "unbalanced" would be the word I'd choose. I began reading. Chapter by chapter, I saw more than words, concepts, philosophies, and stories. I could see God at work.

Instead of stressing, worrying, and fixing, I started praying. I started reading the Bible. I started exploring what it meant to know God. I started teaching my sons to understand and to live the way Jesus lived instead of trying desperately and unsuccessfully to use my own words to explain how to best live life.

And an incredible thing happened: life changed. It all changed. I was getting more of my to-do list done. I was able to save money and still pay the bills. I was gaining new clients left and right at work. My boys were behaving better. My daughter couldn't stop smiling. My wife and I went on our first date since my daughter was born almost five years ago.

And my stress? Gone. Totally gone. Not because I took new meds. Not because I found a coping mechanism. Certainly not because I was rolling in cash. We still had the struggles we'd always had. Everything was the same. But at the same time, everything was entirely different.

I had heard of God. I had been introduced to God, but now I had Him. He was with me. I knew it because I could feel it.

Now, instead of fighting and losing the battle of life on my own, I was supported by something bigger than my problems, bigger than anything I could ever encounter. I had help, and it felt good.

Help is a funny thing. As a man, I was taught that it's a sign of weakness to get help, to need others. Now, I see it differently. Help to me is not a sign of weakness, but a sign of strength. It takes strength to see the times in life when you can't go it alone. With God, I will never go it alone again.

If your world has spun out of balance, prayer is the first step in asking God for help. While we can't always dig ourselves out of the mess right away, God can do the heavy lifting we need to beat our way back to balance. Of course, sometimes our lack of humility gets God's attention. In this next story, Jesus changes the heart of one of Jericho's most arrogant men simply by bestowing grace.

THE REAL DEAL

*"Today salvation has come
to this house."*

—LUKE 19:9b NIV

was short of breath and could feel my heart pounding as I scurried ahead of the crowd. I had to get there before everyone saw what I was attempting. Although awkward and slow, in my mind I felt like a stealth warrior as I began to scale the sycamore tree in front of me. The leaves shook along with my little legs. *One foot in front of the other*, I thought. *Just don't let go.* The patchy bark broke away from my foothold as I reached for the sturdiest branch I could find. The higher I got, the more nervous I became. The greasy palms that I have been accused of having felt more like sweaty ones as I continued to climb. It was obvious my petite stature was not meant for climbing as I continued to scale upward.

I was hoping that no one would see me up in this tree. How embarrassing would it be for a public figure such as myself to be discovered sitting in a tree? Even though I was physically short, my status as the chief tax collector had gotten me noticed around Jericho. The city in which I worked was rich in balsam. Because of our booming economy, the taxes on people were pretty hefty, especially after I collected my share. I was despised as a traitor and known as being corrupt as I collected taxes from the Jewish community for the

302

Roman Empire. But this title also gave me a lot of power amongst the people of Jericho.

Even with my busy schedule, I had to see what everyone was talking about. A man named Jesus was in town, and something drew me to Him. Even though His popularity had gotten Him more than ten thousand followers, it was His message that tugged on my heart and compelled me to climb. I saw the parade of people moving toward me, and I could see Him coming closer. I prayed the leaves and branches would camouflage not only my body from Jesus, but also my indiscretions. When He stopped and looked up at me, my eyes widened. I almost lost my grip.

"Zacchaeus," He said, "come down immediately. I must stay at your house today."

Stunned, I glanced around. Was He really talking to me? He knew my name! And if He knew my name, He must have known everything else about me, too. Yet, despite what He saw—the years of dishonest behavior and sins on my heart—He had still asked to stay at my house. While I was wealthy and had plenty of room, a man like Him didn't come to the house of a man like me. He was holy. By staying at the house of a man who did disreputable things...why, He was risking His ministry to know me.

Yet as my two feet landed safely on the ground, I looked up at Jesus and welcomed Him gladly.

As He looked right at me, I realized that He was the real deal. He didn't look down on me. I felt an instant connection to Him, and I felt my heart begin to change.

I thought back to all the people I'd wronged and the money I'd taken from their families. I have lived a life that's all about me—and not for others or for the Kingdom of God. Jesus came into my life and all this changed. I looked up at Him and said, "Look, Lord! Here and now I give half of my possessions to the poor, and if I have cheated anybody out of anything, I will pay back four times the amount."

I didn't have to think about it. I knew it was the right thing to do.

"Today salvation has come to this house," Jesus told the angry crowd around me, many upon whom I'd imposed harsh taxes, "because this man, too, is a son of Abraham. For the Son of Man came to seek and to save the lost."

It is said that either you have humility, or you will be humbled.

While you can be humbled by going through hardship, I found humility and a change of heart by experiencing Jesus's love and acceptance firsthand. When He openly and publicly accepted me at the risk of what others thought, it made me want to be a better person. I saw a bigger picture for my life. The day I climbed the sycamore tree to be above others and see Jesus became the day where I learned to put others above myself so I could really see Jesus.

Putting others above yourself is the easiest and surest way to practice humility. So is simple kindness. But perhaps the biggest lesson we learn in life about humility is when things go bad—and we need to turn to God for help and grace.

DON'T WAIT FOR THE BRICK

*"The day of judgment is coming, burning like a furnace.
On that day the arrogant and the wicked
will be burned up like straw."*

—MALACHI 4:1 NLT

Before God runs the pebble-rock-brick sequence on your life, take stock of what you're doing that may be unkind, arrogant, and disrespectful. It might be the way you talk to people or strive to be first in line or brag about your success. If you're less humble than God wants you to be, don't wait for the brick. Change your heart and mind now to be more respectful and kind.

ALWAYS STAY HUMBLE AND KIND

*"Clothe yourselves with compassion, kindness,
humility, gentleness, and patience."*

—COLOSSIANS 3:12b BSB

If you're a country music fan, we probably just dropped Tim McGraw's song into your brain. And we're not going to apologize. Humility in your brain is a good thing. Humility is a virtue, but it's also a way of life. And one of the best ways to show humility is by practicing kindness. God smiles when we're kind to others. There's no payoff in it. It's just something that Christians like to do. Kindness also takes the focus off ourselves. While a big part of Oola is working on yourself, hitting your goals, and growing in the 7 F's, *humility* reminds us that it's not all about you.

God has designed you for greatness, so use your time and talents to help others and make the world a better place. Where can you be kind, with no expectation of anything in return? We're here—all of us—for such a short period of time. Humbly being of service will add a sense of kindness to your day and move your life in a positive direction as it helps make the planet a better place.

YOUR HEART **KNOWS**— AND SO DOES GOD

"For everyone who exalts himself will be humbled, and he who humbles himself will be exalted."

—LUKE 14:11 ESV

Only your heart knows the difference between *true humility* and *humblebragging*.

The *humblebrag* is that narcissistic tactic of making a modest comment about yourself that's actually meant to draw attention to your own achievements or impressive qualities.

It alerts people that you're using fake humility to serve some private agenda. When you're inclined to be insincere in your humility, step back, consider what Jesus would do, and leave the comment unspoken. You can't delete the bad vibe that lingers afterward if you humblebrag. That goes for online interaction, too.

God asks for *true humility*. The selfless act of putting others ahead of you with no secondary gain, attention, or recognition.

Not only does your heart know if you are doing things for the right reasons, but so does God. Being generous for others is awesome, but true humility is pleasing to Him.

WISDOM

"Get wisdom. Though it cost all you have,
get understanding."

—PROVERBS 4:7 NIV

D uring His ministry in Galilee, Jesus embodied all the wisdom of the ages. His advice, judgment, and intelligence not only created a record of wisdom that we can look to for advice, but it also revealed to us the goodness of God's love and the excitement of God's hopes and aspirations for us.

But Christ's gift of wisdom didn't stop with His ministry. The resurrection actually made His wisdom permanently accessible to everyone. Colossians 2:2–3 tells us that God's greatest secret is Christ himself. *He is the key* that opens all the hidden treasures of God's wisdom and knowledge to us. How cool is it that, as Christians, we've got a profound source of advice, which we can access—from Jesus—through prayer.

WISDOM ALSO COMES
FROM **EXPERIENCE**

While we can gain tons of wisdom from reading the Gospel and studying Jesus's life, we can also gain wisdom just by living our lives. In fact, there are two other ways wisdom comes to us: from our own experiences and through mentors we seek out.

When we're in action, learning new skills and taking risks, some of the best lessons we'll learn are from our losses. When we push past the loss—and learn from the experience—we achieve true wisdom. We realize that loss doesn't define us; it is just part of the journey.

But we can also gain wisdom from the fun times in life. If we want to know how authentic Cuban food tastes, we can go to Cuba and find out. If we want to check out firsthand how amazing the culture of France is, we don't have to read about it in a book; we can go to France and explore it for ourselves.

It's very Oola to gain wisdom through experiences.

FIND A **MENTOR**, BE A MENTOR

The other way to gain wisdom is by working with mentors who are wise in any area you're working on. Adding mentors to your inner circle and nurturing those relationships is a life hack that will get you to greater wisdom by living vicariously through their experiences and expertise.

Of course, the sweet spot of Oola is to not only seek proper mentors, but to be a mentor yourself and help others grow. You may not be an expert in everything, but you at least have knowledge in things that will benefit others who are trying to learn. Maybe you're good with money, great at gardening, healthy cooking, making jewelry, running a small business, or you know what it takes to hold a marriage together for twenty-plus years. Your knowledge is valuable. Use it to empower others.

Oola itself started in the 1990s as a small group of guys who met once a year at the Hard Rock in Las Vegas to set goals. Dave, Troy, and a few buddies met annually to challenge each other to do more and to be more. They worked together to map out plans and make their goals become a reality.

If you think mentoring might be a unique ministry for you, start by checking in at your church to see if they have mentoring teams for men, moms, teens, Christians in recovery, and others. Big Brothers Big Sisters is a well-established mentoring organization that pairs experienced adults with at-risk teens who need guidance and accountability. And if you want to share the Oola lifestyle and mentor others, you can even teach an Oola class using our handy curriculum.*

---

* Find out more at *oolalife.com/find-balance-class*

MY THREE FATHERS

by Jan McKee

I t was Saturday night, and I finally found some time to just sit and relax after a long week. I was mindlessly scrolling Facebook and stumbled upon some old family photos. I stopped on one that was precious to me. It was of my dad and me when I was just two months old. He was holding me tight to his chest. I could feel the security he provided simply by seeing this old photo. Those were happy times. I loved my dad. He was my protector. He was not only that way with me, but for my three older siblings, too, especially during that time of turmoil. You see, around the time this picture was taken, my mom left him for another man—when I was just six weeks old.

Having stirred up old but familiar uneasy feelings, I needed to scroll on. I then came across a friend's random post, you know the kind, designed to be fun, like "If you were an animal or a Disney character, which one would you be?" Only this one asked, "If you were the opposite sex, what would you look like?" Sounded fun. I uploaded a recent picture of me, clicked submit, and anxiously awaited for the male version of me to appear. I wasn't prepared for what happened next.

With that one click, my life became a lie.

As the Facebook-generated image appeared, I felt a gut punch so hard it literally took my breath away. Before me was a split screen: me as I look today on the left, and on the right, what I would look like as a fifty-year-old male. But I didn't see myself in that male picture. All I could see was my stepdad—the man my mom left her marriage for, and the guy who sexually and physically abused me as a child. It was the face that I have spent a lifetime trying to erase from the depths of my mind. All the pain of my past came rushing back into my present with a tsunami-like force. But how could this be? How could this computer-generated image of a fifty-year-old male version of me be the spitting image of my stepdad, my childhood abuser—the man I have spent a lifetime trying to erase from my mind?

In seeing the undeniable physical resemblance, it was in this moment that I realized my childhood abuser was actually my biological father. He wasn't my stepdad like my mom had told me. He was my biological father, and everything I believed up until then about my family—and who and what a father should be—was a lie. I sat there with a blank stare into the abyss of my computer screen and started to recollect the shattered memories of my childhood, grasping for clarity. This Facebook image smashed the puzzle of what I thought was my life. I was left with only scattered pieces and the painful task of putting them all back together piece by piece, memory by memory, and year by year.

My most pressing question was, *Who is my father?*

My fifty-year journey to this moment began before I was born. My mom and dad had already been married for fifteen years when Mom started having an affair with a police officer. I was six weeks old when she left my loving and caring dad for this other man. The two quickly married, and the abuse began immediately. The next seven years were a mind-numbing blur of the sexual, mental, and verbal abuse I endured from my stepdad at a time in my life when I should have been learning to walk, read, and write. I've blocked most of it, but doctors have since confirmed my nose had been broken, and my older sister recalls coming home to visit and seeing me covered in bruises. Times were different. People didn't want to see what was right in front of them.

Eventually, Mom got tired of the beatings and left him when I was in the second grade. Of course, the nightmares stemming from the sexual, mental, and verbal abuse haunted me for years.

This father had abused me.

And although my mom had ended her first marriage and forced my loving dad out of the house when I was just six weeks old, the man holding me in the picture never left me. He loved me. He let me know it, and he worked hard to be in my life. He paid child support for eighteen years. He taught me how to change the oil in my car and how to grow into a strong, independent women. He walked me down the aisle. Even in death, he willed me a portion of the family farm. But he knew the dark family secret, that I wasn't his daughter, and kept it from me.

This father loved me but lied to me.

Now my new reality has turned my eyes to my one true Father—my heavenly Father. Tears roll down my face as I reflect and realize that I had been living a lie, but in Him there is truth. He has never hurt me. He has never lied to me. He has never abandoned me. He has shown up in my life through the birth of my children and the loss of my husband. He helped me to let go of the pain of my childhood and take risks to live more freely. And I know He will forever be by my side. I pray daily, thanking Him for being my Rock and my Redeemer.

This Father never fails me.

Even today, months later, I continue to put back together the pieces of my life that were shattered that Saturday evening. I try to find gratitude and purpose for all three fathers in my life. Some days it is easy, and other days are filled with pain. Some days I feel love, and some days I feel anger. Some days it makes sense, and some days it makes no sense at all. But the days that I put all my faith and happiness in my heavenly Father, I feel peace. I feel grace. I feel happiness. I feel complete. I feel whole.

Our Father, who is in Heaven, is the ultimate source of wisdom. He's someone we can rely on, no matter what our earthly circumstances are. He is unwavering in His loyalty to us and trustworthy with our deepest thoughts and fears. He understands our human frailties, and He gets it when we don't understand what is happening to us.

He loved us so much that He sent His Son Jesus, not just to fulfill a promise to us, but to make sure we get it about how much He cares.

THE TRUTH IN FRONT OF US

"Suddenly, their eyes were opened,
and they recognized him."

—LUKE 24:31 NLT

W e packed our things and headed out for the long walk from Jerusalem to the village of Emmaus. We were sad and heartbroken as we started. Much of our seven-mile journey was spent in shock and disbelief of our new reality. It felt as if we not only left a city we had learned to love, but we left behind our dreams and turned our back on the hopes and plans that we had held onto for many years. Everything we believed in had disappeared in a matter of days—with years of work lost and our purpose and vision evaporated into thin air.

The road ahead of us was rocky, mountainous, and not an easy trail to navigate, but it was nothing compared to how difficult life was going to be from this point forward. I was struggling to process what had happened.

Our sandals stirred up the dust as we continued walking and dwelling on our pain and our loss. Suddenly I could sense someone over my right shoulder walking right behind me. *Where did this guy come from?* I thought. He walked right beside us and then asked, "What are you discussing so intently as you walk along?"

I was so upset I couldn't even look at him. Cleopas responded back quickly saying, "Are you the only visitor to Jerusalem who does not know the things that have happened there in recent days?"

I figured that this man must not be from Jerusalem and must have not been in contact with anyone for days because the sadness we carried was the talk of the town.

The stranger didn't answer of his whereabouts. He only said, "What things?"

Annoyed, I chimed in and exclaimed with passion, "About Jesus of Nazareth! I am sure you heard of this man. He had a powerful ministry that helped so many. He healed the sick, cast out demons, and was the Son of God. Did you not hear that the chief priests and rulers were so afraid and envious of Him that they had Him executed by crucifixion? We were some of his most loyal followers, and we believed that He had come to redeem all of Israel."

I exhaled deeply in an attempt to calm myself, then looked down and continued on our journey. The nerve of people. Jesus literally died just three days ago, and we didn't even have time to fully mourn Him. And now all the talk. There are even stories of His body missing from the tomb. Haven't we been through enough?

The rumor was that a group of women went to his tomb, and there was no body. They reported an angel appeared to them and said Jesus was alive. Then some of His other followers went out to investigate and reported that they couldn't find Jesus, either. This whole thing is so upsetting. Where had He gone? Who would take His body? Nothing added up.

The stranger on the trail looked at us intensely and asked, "How foolish you are, and how slow to believe all that the prophets have spoken! Wasn't it clearly predicted that the Messiah would have to suffer all these things before entering His glory?"

I continued to walk and thought back to the prophecy that said all of this would happen. It said that Jesus would die and rise again for the glory of God. From the time of Moses, everyone had known of this truth. But the stranger beside us opened the Scriptures to us, and our eyes were opened to the possibilities.

In that moment, we started to feel hope. Maybe this was all part of Jesus's bigger plan and larger purpose. We felt that familiar passion flow through our veins again, giving us a second wind as we continued our long and treacherous journey.

We continued our conversation with the stranger as we entered the village of Emmaus. The man was going to continue on his journey, but it was late, he was alone, and the journey we just completed was long, so we asked him to stay with us in our home and at least have dinner. He agreed. We put away our belongings and started to prepare a meal for the three of us. With the table set, we sat down.

> When he was at the table with them, he took bread, gave thanks, broke it and began to give it to them. Then their eyes were opened and they recognized him, and he disappeared from their sight. They asked each other, "Were not our hearts burning within us while he talked with us on the road and opened the Scriptures to us?"
>
> They got up and returned at once to Jerusalem. There they found the Eleven and those with them, assembled together and saying, "It is true! The Lord has risen and has appeared to Simon." Then the two told what had happened on the way, and how Jesus was recognized by them when he broke the bread. (Luke 24:30)

I still can't believe it! Jesus was with us the whole time. He never left our sides. We were so focused on ourselves, our grief, our disappointments, and our troubles that we couldn't see the truth that was right in front of us. This stranger with whom we broke bread was Jesus.

We couldn't wait to get back to Jerusalem and share what had happened. While sharing our story with the disciples, I realized that our minds had been opened to the understanding of the prophesies and the possibilities. This journey started in dismay and disbelief, and by opening our eyes, hearts, and minds to Jesus, we opened up unlimited possibilities for our lives.

Are you also so focused on your own troubles and disappointments that you can't see the truth of Jesus right in front of you? To be in a relationship with Him is the ideal way to gain wisdom as you work on creating your future.

HAVE THE WISDOM TO PRAY FOR WHAT YOU **COULD** BECOME

"My future is in your hands."

—PSALM 31:15a NLT

While many Christians pray routinely for problem-solving or stuff they want, we think God would be thrilled to respond when you seek His wisdom and ask: *Who do You want me to become?*

You don't have to wait for a midlife crisis to ask: *Am I in the right place? Is there something more important for me to do? Where would You put me if I were ready?*

Don't forget to also ask: *What do You need me to do to get ready for a bigger role in Your Kingdom?*

ASK GOD, **NOT** YOUR FRIENDS

"If any of you need wisdom,
you should ask God."

—JAMES 1:5a CEV

When faced with indecision, who do you turn to? If you're like us, we usually text or phone a friend in search of the answer. But do you listen or do you hop friend-to-friend for advice until you hear the answer you want? Friends and mentors are great, but there is a better way. Why go to your friends for wisdom on the bigger questions of your life, when God has the 50,000-foot view of your world—and has the added benefit of knowing what's ahead?

Go to God in prayer, then share your exciting new plans with your friends when you're ready.

CUT YOURSELF SOME **SLACK**

"Don't let your heart be troubled.
Believe in God; believe also in Me."

—JOHN 14:1 CSB

If you're a Christian who has doubt around what you believe, give yourself a break. Part of working on wisdom as an OolaAccelerator is to gain information and experience to back up what you've heard or been taught. Even the twelve apostles—who were with Jesus every day—doubted His existence after the Resurrection. Doubt is okay. All we're challenging you to do is work on it.

3 SIMPLE STEPS TO THE **OOLA**LIFE

> "Commit to the Lord whatever you do,
> and he will establish your plans."
>
> —PROVERBS 16:3 NIV

Getting to your OolaLife takes action. Over the past twenty-three chapters, our intent has been to educate you about the seven F's—and inspire you to overcome OolaBlockers and fully utilize the OolaAccelerators. Now the rubber meets the road. It's time to make plans and get in motion. Over the next three chapters, we'll do that together: create a workable plan to reveal the God-given greatness within you and build the life you dream of and deserve.

There are three simple steps to living the OolaLife.

Step One, you need to check in with yourself: an honest assessment of where you are right now in your life in the seven key areas revealing where you could do better. Chapter 24, "The OolaWheel," will help you with this reality check.

Step Two, you'll figure out where you want to go in the seven key areas. What are the goals and dreams you have for your life? You'll lay out an OolaPlan that is unique to you.

Finally, in Step Three, you'll learn about the OolaPath and how to take the daily action steps you need to get you to your goals. It's time to get serious.

Step One:
The **Oola**Wheel

Where Are You Today?

"I'll take the hand of those who don't know the way,
who can't see where they're going."

—ISAIAH 42:16a MSG

D riving his truck down Highway 710 after his fourteen-hour shift as a lineman, Travis Smith's mind began to wander. As he often did on these long commutes home from distant job sites, he reflected on his struggles in life: his marriage, depression, and being away from home so much. He began to question his purpose.

What am I really doing here? he asked himself. *Does it ever get better?*

A few car lengths ahead of him, chugging along in the slow lane just outside Okeechobee, Florida, he saw an old Volkswagen surf bus plastered with colorful stickers that piqued his interest. *1 Bus. 2 Guys. 50 States. 1 Million Dreams,* it said just below the back window. He felt drawn to the words somehow and, as he passed, he rolled down his window, and asked the two guys driving, *What is this all about?*

You are designed by God for greatness, they told him, and briefly described the Oola mission.

He gave them a big thumbs up, as a sign of approval, and continued down the road.

Miles later, he couldn't get this bus and their words out of his mind. *Really, it can be better?* He wanted to know more. He pulled over, walked to the center of the road, and waved down the OolaBus.

The OolaGuys pulled over, stepped out, and began to talk about life. As Travis poured out his heart to the OolaGuys, who listened with care and concern, they asked him to put a dream on the bus. His head went down, and tears filled his eyes as he realized that he'd completely lost sight of his dreams and didn't know what to write.

Troy began to tell him that where you are is simply where you are, not who you are. God has designed you for a purpose, and it is not to be overwhelmed and miserable. "Your purpose is in there," Troy said as he tapped his chest. "We just need to help you see it and pull it out."

Travis grabbed a Sharpie and a yellow faith sticker and wrote: *To Find My Purpose.*

He'd been in a bad place for so long that the brief exchange on the highway woke him up for the first time in years. He'd never had anything like that happen to him. He went home to tell his wife, and later discovered that people he knew were going to see the OolaGuys at an event the very next day. Reenergized to make his future a top priority now, Travis got help to work through some of the problems that he'd been living with for years, including contacting a mental health professional to work on eliminating his depression. He's more positive. He's made positive changes. And most importantly, he has a purpose and hope for a better future.

"I feel like Oola was put there on that highway for a reason," he told us later. "It put a lot of things in perspective. That day changed my life for the better."

IT'S **IMPOSSIBLE** TO GET WHERE YOU'RE GOING WITHOUT KNOWING WHERE YOU ARE **NOW**

When you use your smartphone's Maps app to get directions, the first thing that shows up is *where you are* at this moment—represented by a little blue dot. Plug in your destination, and your smartphone will use GPS technology to give you step-by-step, mile-by-mile directions from your current location to your desired endpoint. Before you can go anywhere, you need to know exactly where you are right now.

Interestingly, your GPS app never asks you about your past and doesn't care what mistakes you've made. It won't even factor in current challenges you might be facing. It simply shows you the fastest route from where you are now to where you want to go.

Well, what if *your own life plan* was that simple? What if, just like GPS, you didn't judge yourself, take yourself down distracting side roads, or factor in time-consuming stuff? You would prayerfully consider your next steps, then just chart your course without bringing in a lot of outside factors to stop you. In fact, if you were using GPS, you wouldn't chart your own course *any other way.*

STARTING TO BUILD YOUR **OOLA**LIFE: HOW DO **YOU** ROLL?

If you've ever ridden a bicycle, you know the wheels are the most important component. To keep the wheel strong, spokes radiate from the hub, and the valve in the tire helps you keep it full of air. Without the spokes, hub, and valve, the wheel—and therefore, the bicycle— would eventually stop rolling and come to a stop.

Life is a lot like that wheel.

THE **SPOKES**

On the OolaWheel, there are seven spokes—each representing one category (or F) of Oola. When the spokes are balanced, the wheel just *works.* It moves forward easily.

THE **HUB**

The hub of the wheel is the key—it's the base, the foundation, the core from which everything else emanates. Without a solid and secure hub, even with perfectly balanced spokes, your wheel will ultimately fail.

If you're cruising along, for instance, and a crisis hits your finances, you could pull the *finance* spoke off your wheel, and your bicycle would still roll. It'd be clunky, for sure, but the other spokes would hold it together and the wheel would still work. Add a business failure related to that financial stress—taking away another spoke—and yep, your bike would still go.

As long as you have a solid hub, you could lose *almost everything* and your wheel would still roll. It would be painful, clunky, and slow. But you would still move forward.

What's your hub? This is your question to ponder. What's the foundation on which your life is built? Is *God* your hub? Is He the One around which your life evolves?

THE **VALVE**

Your unique value system acts like the *valve* of your wheel. What inspires you? Which F of Oola comes naturally to you and motivates you? This is what makes up your highest values. For some people, it's faith or finance. For others, it may be family or their career (field). Whatever it is for you, you're gifted in this area, and you don't have to be asked or encouraged to pursue it.

Equally, we all have things in our life that we naturally avoid. These are your low values. For the OolaSeeker, it's finance—he hates spreadsheets and budgets. The OolaGuru, on the other hand, finds the lowest value in fun. Frankly, he would much rather be working (field).

The intent is to use your high values to "pump up" key areas in life that you tend to ignore or avoid. For example, if your highest value is your kids (family) and your lowest value is fitness, think through how working on your fitness and overall health will benefit your family. Maybe you'll set a good example for them. Maybe you'll be able to participate in activities instead of standing on the sidelines. And maybe by taking better care of yourself, you'll be around long enough to see your grandkids have kids of their own.

LOOKING AT YOUR OWN
7 F'S OF OOLA

To get a picture of where your life is now, complete the series of questionnaires starting on the next page—one for each of the seven key areas of life. They're designed to help you "score" yourself on where you are now. Are you crushing it in some areas but completely messed up in others?

You can also find an interactive OolaWheel and a printable worksheet containing the OolaWheel at *www.oolalife.com/step1*. Let's get started.

Simply rate the following on a **scale from 1 to 10**: 1 being low/bad/least true and 10 being high/good/most true. Write your number in the blank for each of the 10 questions. Then, at the bottom of the page, add up the total for all 10 questions and divide by 10. Put a dot on the spoke for FITNESS on your OolaWheel on page 334.

OOLAFITNESS

1) I would rate my current health. .... ____

2) How close am I to my ideal weight? .... ____

3) I would rate my overall mental health. .... ____

4) I do at least 3 cardio/resistance sessions per week. .... ____

5) How hard do I push myself during exercise? .... ____

6) I am active outside of exercise. .... ____

7) I practice relaxation daily. .... ____

8) I love my life and have little stress. .... ____

9) My meals are nutrient rich and proper calories for my body. ..... ____

10) I eat a balanced diet and avoid processed and fast food. .... ____

TOTAL SCORE: _____ **/ 10 =** [   ]

(Circle this number on page 334)

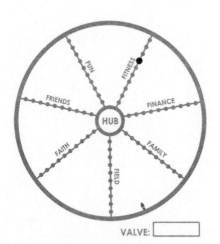

VALVE: [   ]

Simply rate the following on a **scale from 1 to 10**: 1 being low/bad/least true and 10 being high/good/most true. Write your number in the blank for each of the 10 questions. Then, at the bottom of the page, add up the total for all 10 questions and divide by 10. Put a dot on the spoke for FINANCE on your OolaWheel on page 334.

OOLAFINANCE

1) I would rate my current personal finances. .... ——

2) I am saving at least 10% of every dollar I make for nonretirement purchases (car, trip, down payment, etc.). .... ——

3) I am completely debt-free (minus my mortgage). .... ——

4) My monthly income exceeds my monthly expenses. .... ——

5) I am investing at least 15% for retirement. .... ——

6) I have an emergency account equaling at least seven months of expenses. .... ——

7) I have the proper insurance (health, term life, property, etc.)....... ——

8) I tithe regularly to my church and donate time to charities with no expectation of anything in return. .... ——

9) I have a complete and updated will or estate plan......................... ——

10) I have a solid budget and stick to it every month............................ ——

TOTAL SCORE: _____ / 10 = [   ]

(Circle this number on page 334)

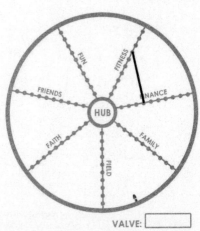

VALVE: [   ]

Simply rate the following on a **scale from 1 to 10**: 1 being low/bad/least true and 10 being high/good/most true. Write your number in the blank for each of the 10 questions. Then, at the bottom of the page, add up the total for all 10 questions and divide by 10. Put a dot on the spoke for FAMILY on your OolaWheel on page 334.

OOLAFAMILY

1) I would rate my current family situation. .... _____

2) We eat at least one meal per day together as a family. .... _____

3) My immediate and extended family is functional. .... _____

4) Thinking of family makes me feel happy. .... _____

5) I am honest with my family members. .... _____

6) I work hard at being a better family member. .... _____

7) I set aside personal time with my family—without phones. ...... _____

8) My family is loving, patient, supportive, and respectful. .... _____

9) I hold no hurt feelings toward any family members. .... _____

10) I feel I spend enough time with my family to meet their needs. .... _____

TOTAL SCORE: _____ / 10 = [   ]

(Circle this number on page 334)

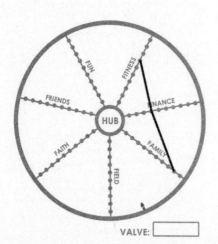

VALVE: [   ]

Simply rate the following on a **scale from 1 to 10**: 1 being low/bad/least true and 10 being high/good/most true. Write your number in the blank for each of the 10 questions. Then, at the bottom of the page, add up the total for all 10 questions and divide by 10. Put a dot on the spoke for FIELD on your OolaWheel on page 334.

OOLAFIELD

1) I would rate my current overall job satisfaction. .... ——

2) My job financially meets my needs. .... ——

3) I love my job. .... ——

4) I feel as if I am doing what I was created to do. .... ——

5) I have solid goals for my field. .... ——

6) My current job doesn't interfere with my family and personal time. .... ——

7) My current job makes the world a better place. .... ——

8) My job utilizes my natural gifts and abilities. .... ——

9) My current job can support my long-term financial goals. .... ——

10) My job offers the opportunity to grow personally, professionally, and financially. .... ——

TOTAL SCORE: _____ **/ 10 =** ☐

(Circle this number on page 334)

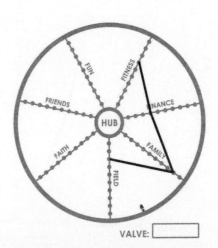

VALVE: ☐

Simply rate the following on a **scale from 1 to 10**: 1 being low/bad/least true and 10 being high/good/most true. Write your number in the blank for each of the 10 questions. Then, at the bottom of the page, add up the total for all ten questions and divide by 10. Put a dot on the spoke for FAITH on your OolaWheel on page 334.

OOLAFAITH

1) I would rate my faith in God and belief in Jesus Christ............... _____

2) I feel connected to God and in a close relationship with Him..... _____

3) I belong to a church where I continue to learn/grow................. _____

4) I dedicate daily time in meditation and/or prayer. .... _____

5) My beliefs and the way I live my life are congruent. .... _____

6) I use prayer and faith to help resolve conflict/issues in
    my life. .... _____

7) I forgive easily. .... _____

8) I rely on my faith in God to guide my choices and decisions...... _____

9) I feel comfortable sharing my belief in Jesus with others.......... _____

10) I have accepted Jesus as my Lord and Savior........................ _____

TOTAL SCORE: _____ **/ 10 =** [   ]

(Circle this number on page 334)

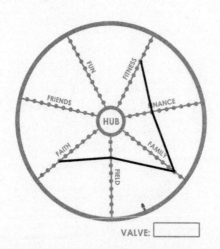

VALVE: [   ]

Simply rate the following on a **scale from 1 to 10**: 1 being low/bad/least true and 10 being high/good/most true. Write your number in the blank for each of the 10 questions. Then, at the bottom of the page, add up the total for all 10 questions and divide by 10. Put a dot on the spoke for FRIENDS on your OolaWheel on page 334.

OOLAFRIENDS

1) I would rate my social network of friends. .... ——

2) I have unconditionally loving, supportive, and
empowering friends. .... ——

3) I am satisfied with the number of friendships in my life. .... ——

4) I am a good example/mentor for my friends. .... ——

5) My friends support my dreams and are good examples/
mentors for me. .... ——

6) When I think of my 3 closest friends, I have no stress. .... ——

7) I openly communicate and trust my friends. .... ——

8) I have friends who are good mentors in all 7 F's of Oola. .... ——

9) I have no hard feelings or ill will toward my present
friendships. .... ——

10) I am not judgmental toward my friends. .... ——

TOTAL SCORE: _____ **/ 10 =** [   ]

(Circle this number on page 334)

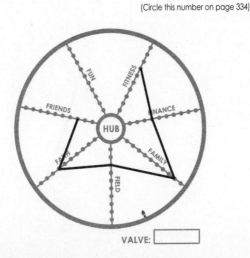

VALVE: [   ]

Simply rate the following on a **scale from 1 to 10**: 1 being low/bad/least true and 10 being high/good/most true. Write your number in the blank for each of the 10 questions. Then, at the bottom of the page, add up the total for all 10 questions and divide by 10. Put a dot on the spoke for FUN on your OolaWheel on page 334.

OOLAFUN

1) I would rate my fun in life. .... _____

2) I enjoy and am having fun in life. .... _____

3) I try new things often. .... _____

4) I have fun and invest time pursuing my personal passion (i.e. hobby, interest). .... _____

5) I have fun outside of work at least 3 times per week. .... _____

6) I check off at least one "bucket list" item each year. .... _____

7) I am a fun person to be around. .... _____

8) Fun rarely interferes with my responsibilities. .... _____

9) People would say that I am a fun person. .... _____

10) I easily find free fun in simple everyday life. .... _____

TOTAL SCORE: _____ / 10 = [   ]

(Circle this number on page 334)

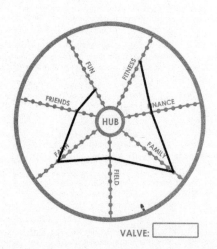

VALVE: [   ]

COMPLETE THE OOLAWHEEL

Once you've completed the questionnaires, transfer your scores from pages 327–333 to the OolaWheel below and connect the dots. If your connect-the-dots circle is smooth, it shows you're balanced. But if it's jagged and spiked, it will identify those one or two areas where you're off-the-charts and out of balance. If you've been thinking lately, *I'm feeling stressed and out of balance, and I'm not rolling very well,* the OolaWheel exercise will show you why.

Follow these steps for completing your OolaWheel.

Step 1: Identify your Hub and write it in the Hub of the wheel.

Step 2: Identify your highest value and write this in the valve of the diagram.

Step 3: Place a dot on each spoke of the diagram. This is where you rated yourself on each questionnaire. If you scored a "1" in any area, for instance, you would mark the *first dot* closest to the hub. If you scored a "5," your dot would be about halfway out.

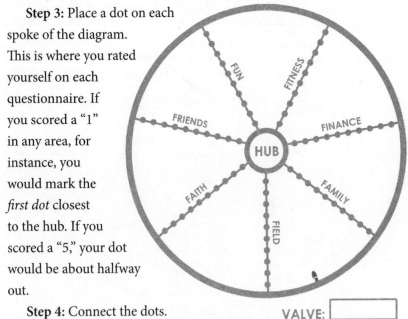

Step 4: Connect the dots.

Step 5: How do you roll? Where do you need to improve first?

VALVE: _____

HOW DOES **YOUR OOLA**WHEEL LOOK? WHAT DO YOU **NEED** WORK ON FIRST?

Here's where the OolaWheel is important: identifying where you're the most out of balance will cue you on where to start. If your finances are messy and they're impacting the other areas of your life, plus keeping your wheel from being in balance, you'll want to clean up those messes before moving ahead on the other six F's of Oola.

In the next chapter, you'll be creating a customized plan to bring all seven areas into alignment. Now that you know where you are, it's time to formulate a plan for where you want to go. Let's move on to Step Two.

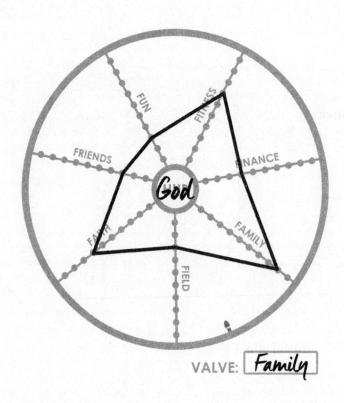

VALVE: *Family*

Step Two:
The **Oola**Plan

Where Do You Want to Go?

"Those who plan what is good find
love and faithfulness."

—PROVERBS 14:22b NIV

What will I write on my Oola sticker? thought Brandie Stewart. *What's the one thing that—if I could change it—would improve every area of my life?*

On the day she met the OolaGuys, Brandie's life was in shambles. Her car had just been repossessed, and the anxiety over money had strained communications with her husband for months. Even her kids—who knew only a small part of what was going on—could feel the tension in their home.

Not only that, but Brandie's job had become exhausting. An emergency room nurse at the local hospital for over thirteen years, Brandie dreaded showing up for the grueling twelve-hour shifts of chaos. She wasn't cut out for it. She hated it. And the stress began days before she had to report back to work.

After meeting the OolaGuys, she started reading the original *Oola* book, and it was like a breath of fresh air. She immediately knew what her most important sticker would be: get out of debt.

She got her husband on board with paying off their car loans by the end of the year. After that, they'd concentrate on remaining balances. At the time, they didn't even know if they could pay their usual bills every month. But they began the work of cutting back on expenses and paying off the accounts with the highest interest rates first. Instead of going out to eat three or four times a week, they ate out once a month. They built up an emergency fund. She converted her accumulated 100 hours of paid time off at the hospital to cash and dropped every penny of it on the loans.

She also worked hard to overcome her fear of applying for jobs with more responsibility at the hospital. When an opening was posted for a charge nurse overseeing an entire floor, including other staff, she jumped at the chance. Cleaning up her finances, starting to look after her own health, and finally admitting that she hated the ER had given Brandie a confidence she'd never had before. When she landed the new job, it came with a 20 percent increase in pay and eight days off every other week.

Through it all, Brandie learned to lean on faith. She wrote down Isaiah 41:13 all over the house: "For I am the Lord your God who takes hold of your right hand and says to you, 'Do not fear; I will help you.'"

Closer now in their marriage than ever before and financially careful, too, Brandie and her husband take real vacations they pay for in advance. She bought a car for herself with cash. Following her example, their kids have learned that you don't have to struggle or be anxious in life.

Today in their household, Brandie says, "You can feel the happiness here."

What could you accomplish by setting one bold and daring goal? Let's start by learning to set goals the Oola way.

GOALS ARE MILESTONES TO YOUR **DREAMS**

Most of us have dreams. They help us visualize the perfect life, complete with the kind of faith walk, people, things, and accomplishments we want to have. Dreams are huge, exciting, and free of fear, self-doubt, and other limiting beliefs. *If I knew it would really happen,* we think, *what would I want in my life?* Dreams don't require you to know the "how"—they only require you to know the "what."

Unfortunately, when it comes to bringing those dreams to reality, most people confuse dreams with *goals*. Goals are the milestones—the little steps you need to complete on the way to achieving your dreams. Goals are action steps, planned and then accomplished. They're the baby steps you must follow day by day to get to your dream lifestyle.

ARE YOU **SMART** ABOUT YOUR GOALS? OR ARE YOU **KIDDING** YOURSELF?

A good way to write your goals is to follow the SMART formula created in 1981 by George Doran, writing for *Management Review* magazine. "There's a SMART way to write goals and objectives," the article began—and we agree. Here are the characteristics *your goals* should include:

SPECIFIC—The goal should contain actual numbers, amounts, sizes, or other well-defined terms you want to reach. It would be understandable and clear to anyone else and is memorable to you.

MEASURABLE—When your goal includes the specifics above, you can actually measure whether you're close to achieving it or still far away. You can keep score and track your progress. But most importantly, only if it's measurable will you be able to determine when you've achieved your goal.

ACCOUNTABLE—When a goal is specific and measurable, you can be held accountable to it. Find someone who loves and supports you and who will keep you accountable to the goals you have set for your life. For us, this was our small group of guys in Vegas. For you, it may be friends, neighbors, coworkers, or supportive family members. Find a group that loves you well enough to be tough with you and keep you on task, so you don't drift from the goals and dreams you've set for your life. As a Christian, how about including God in your accountability group.

If you've ever said, *I'm gonna start a diet on Monday. I'm gonna turn off my phone on Sundays. I'm gonna pay off my biggest credit card by New Year's*—then didn't—you need an accountability crew.

REALISTIC—Where dreams are huge, intangible, and often feel unrealistic, goals need to be set in a way that they are doable with the resources, knowledge, time, and money you have available—*or those you could acquire.* This is an important distinction since most people stop pursuing their goals because they don't have the necessary resources *now.* The one thing you *do have,* however, is determination, passion, and the ability to collaborate with others who can guide you, inform you, invest in you, and otherwise help you reach you goal.

TIME-BASED—Perhaps the most important characteristic of a goal is that it includes a *date and time* by which you'll achieve the objective. *By January 1, 2021,* you might write, *I will have completely paid off my $68,000 in student loans.* Do your homework; research the process; ask experts who might know—only then can you realistically determine this time frame. Be sure to give yourself *enough* time to realistically achieve the goal, but not so much that your pursuit of the goal fills all available time. Projects tend to expand into the time allotted. Don't let them.

21–7–1:
FINDING YOUR **OOLA**ONE

We're fans of Warren Buffet, the billionaire investor and unassuming philanthropist from Omaha, Nebraska. When making goals, he recommends writing down the top twenty things you want to do in life, crossing out all but the top three, *and then pursuing those.*

We agree.

If you wrote down ten things under each of the seven F's of Oola, you'd have a whopping seventy goals to accomplish. That's a formula for getting overwhelmed. Instead, choose your Top 7—not necessarily one per category, but the seven goals that will give your life more balance (*and* are in line with the biggest dreams you have for your life). Do this and you'll be working steadily to create balance in all seven areas. Once you've built momentum and a strong belief in yourself, then look at the other goals and take them on.

Of course, if you really want to raise up your life quickly and with the greatest impact, we challenge you to narrow your focus from seven to just one big, audacious goal that would truly change your life. It may not be the one you *want* to do, but it's the one you know deep inside you *need* to do. Is it finding a higher-paying job or finishing your MBA? Is it losing weight and preventing future health challenges? How about confronting that addiction? Would becoming debt-free change life as you know it? What's your *one thing*—your OolaOne?

GRAB A SHARPIE AND START WRITING YOUR **GOALS**

On the Oola "stickers" printed on the following pages,[*] we invite you to start writing your top Oola goals. Learn how to properly set goals in a way that you can achieve them by writing three for each of the seven F's of Oola (for a total of twenty-one goals). Use the SMART format mentioned earlier. Then, narrow down the twenty-one goals to your most important seven goals—the seven that will give your life more balance and that are in line with your biggest dreams. Then pick

---

[*] Or download them for free at *www.oolalife.com*

your OolaOne: the one single goal that, when accomplished, holds the power to spark the change that can transform your entire life.

Once you've done that, pull the stickable sticker from this book, write your OolaOne goal, and "make it stick" by tracking down the OolaBus on social media and personally adding your dream to tens of thousands of others we have collected on our journey.

21 GOALS

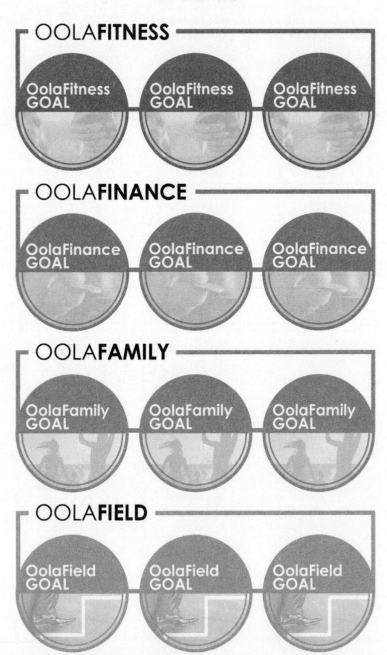

21 GOALS *(continued)*

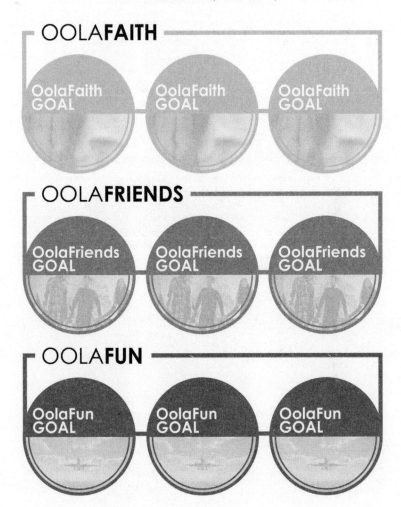

YOUR TOP 7

OOLA**ONE**

CHAPTER
26

Step Three:
The **Oola**Path

How Are You Going
to Get There?

"When you come looking for me,
you'll find me."
—JEREMIAH 29:12 MSG

E arly in our journey, we wanted advice in how to scale the Oola message and change the world with this word by creating more *Oola* books and building a lifestyle brand. We decided to follow our own advice, dream big, and start with the most published nonfiction author of all time, Jack Canfield, the originator of the *Chicken Soup for the Soul* book series.

What does it take to publish over 220 books and have 550 million copies in print in forty-nine languages? What does it take to land on the *New York Times* bestseller list forty times—with eleven books at Number 1 and a record-setting seven books on the list *at the same time?* How could we go from hosting OolaPalooza events in the United States to training millions of people in over 100 countries?

When you sit down with someone of Jack Canfield's caliber, you go prepared. But you also keep things simple.

After connecting with Jack's longtime company president, Patty Aubery, we scored a meeting and went with a 3x5 notecard of the *specific* outcomes we hoped for: details on how to take our message to scale, strategies for how they sold so many books, and even advice on how to keep our own lives in balance as the Oola brand grew. If we could also score some small follow-up commitments from Jack, we thought that would be even better.

As the conversation began and Jack pulled a 3x5 card from his pocket to jot down some contacts he wanted to send us, we gave each other the side-eye. *A 3x5 card,* we silently voiced to one another. It's as if God winked and said, *Yeah, you're in the right place.*

WHY A 3X5 NOTECARD?

For us, using notecards goes back to 1997 when we first met with our crew to set goals at the Hard Rock Hotel in Las Vegas. The music was loud, the lighting was bad, and we definitely didn't want to be the guys sitting there with our laptops open. We wrote on the notecards not only where we were in each of the seven key areas of life, but also where we wanted to go—and most importantly, *those action steps we would take* to make our dreams become a reality.

To this day, we still use notecards and recommend that you do the same. There's something special about contemplating the specific actions you need to take achieve your dreams, writing it in your own handwriting, and feeling the sense of accomplishment by crossing off each task once it's completed. There is power in this process and also beauty in its simplicity.

DAILY ACTION: 3X5 NOTECARD

In the busyness of this unbalanced world, it's easy for your dreams to get lost in the clutter of day-to-day life. So one way to make sure they stay top priority is, every night before you go to bed, grab a 3x5 notecard and write down at least three action steps you'll take the next day that will move you closer to one (or more) of the Top 7 goals you set on your OolaPlan.

The notecard can include the daily stuff, too—groceries, dry cleaning, picking up the kids from practice—but make sure that *at least three* items on your list are action steps that will move you closer to your OolaLife. Draw a line down the middle, if needed, to separate the junk errands from your real-life goals.

Do Step Three every day, and in one year, you will have taken more than 1,000 action steps toward your OolaLife—while most people we meet haven't taken *any steps* toward their dreams in years.

LIVEOOLA

– Groceries	
	– 2 mile run
– Laundry	
	– Create budget
– Pick up kids	
	– Date night
– Wash the car	

BE GRATEFUL, HAVE FAITH, AND GO GET YOUR OOLALIFE.

LIVEOOLA

SKITTLES	ORANGES

BE GRATEFUL, HAVE FAITH, AND GO GET YOUR OOLALIFE.

DON'T **LOSE** YOUR ORANGES
TO THE SKITTLES

At one of our early OolaPaloozas, we tried to recreate a lesson that the OolaGuru saw at his church. On the night before our event, we found ourselves at a Hobby Lobby store in rural Kansas City purchasing a large glass vase, seven fake oranges, and two bags of Skittles.

Without rehearsing, we hopped on stage the next day and began filling the vase with a combination of oranges and Skittles to teach a valuable lesson. While the process was supposed to be dramatic, it ended up being hysterical when the OolaSeeker chased rolling oranges across the stage as the OolaGuru struggled to remove his hand after getting it stuck in the vase.

As the crowd roared with laughter, we realized the lesson came across just the same: if you fill the vase with the Skittles first, then try to add the seven oranges, you'll never fit everything in. But if you start by adding the oranges first, then slowly pour in the Skittles, letting them filter down around the oranges—miraculously it all fits.

The point of this stage fail is that the Skittles represent the day-to-day clutter of our lives: running errands, kid stuff, soccer practice, emails, shopping, vet appointments, cleaning house, making meals, and social media—life. The seven oranges, on the other hand, represent the seven key areas of life, your 7 F's of Oola.

If you take care of your major goals first, then fit the little things around them, miraculously it all gets accomplished.

In the same way, the journey to your OolaLife is a three-step journey, so don't stop at just two. Take action by putting your oranges in first. Spend time every night writing down three or more action items that are deliberately intended to bring about the goals you have for your life. Only then should you let the Skittles fill in the spaces that remain.

CONCLUSION

ONCE GOD TOUCHES YOU, THERE'S NO GOING BACK TO "ORDINARY"

Your life was designed to be unique, compelling, and *exceptional*. With God as your guiding force, and with the help of the simple yet transformational principles of Oola, it can be.

But one bonus outcome you may not have considered before is how much *just the pursuit* of greatness will change you as a person and bring you closer to God. This is ultimately what He has in mind. No one can take away *who you become* as a result of pursuing your goals.

And think about those around you whom you can inspire. Because you're becoming a better individual, your family, friends, coworkers, and the others you interact with will naturally become inspired to improve, too—a phenomenon that will slowly change your community and ultimately transform the world. If you've ever thought, *I'm just one person, what could I possibly do?* realize that getting to #Oola and keeping God out in front of your journey is how *together* we can change the world with a word.

NOW IT'S TIME TO **WRITE** YOUR **OWN OOLA** STORY

Remember that this book contains stories from *other* Christians. Its principles are the product of *our* path and our experiences. Now it's time to write your own story and begin creating a better life for yourself. Your Oola is *your* Oola. Your starting place and the goals and dreams you've set are uniquely your own. Boldly be yourself, take action every day, and go after them.

Don't become complacent; pursue a deeper connection with God. Don't pursue happiness, pursue Oola. If you commit to that alone, you'll meet happy many times along the way.

STAY **CONNECTED** TO **OOLA** BY JOINING US IN A BIGGER VISION

The Oola movement is growing daily as a community of people who love and support each other as we actively pursue a better life. You'll meet countless other Christians through our blog stories, interviews, and social media posts. So get involved! Sign up for the free 21-day Oola for Christians Challenge at *www.oolalife.com/christians-challenge.* You'll find daily inspiration and learn more about the people you met in the stories in this book.

Grab us at an upcoming OolaPalooza event. Or stay connected with us at *www.oolalife.com.* On social media, you will find us at @oolalife, @oolaseeker and @oolaguru.

We're always humbled and grateful to meet readers who took the time to immerse themselves in this book and who are willing to be vulnerable and honest enough about where they can do better. We applaud you for being courageous enough to take the first step in making positive changes in your life. Together, we can change the world with a word: #Oola.

Be Grateful. Have Faith. Live Oola.

ABOUT THE AUTHORS

DAVE BRAUN (Salt Lake City, Utah) and **TROY AMDAHL** (Phoenix, Arizona), aka the OolaGuys, are coauthors of the international bestselling book series *Oola*.

Dave (OolaSeeker) and Troy (OolaGuru) are renowned experts in goalsetting and creating a proper work-life balance. They frequently crisscross the country in a 1970 VW Surf Bus, speaking to people, collecting their dreams on stickers that cover the bus, and helping them find balance and growth in the seven key areas of life—the 7 F's of Oola. By revealing how to remove the stress related to a life out of balance, they unlock the greatness that is inside all of us. A better *you* makes a better family, a better community, and ultimately a better world. The OolaGuys are committed to changing the world with this word and with their simple yet life-changing message.

ACKNOWLEDGMENTS

Like most other achievements in life, a book is the result of the dedicated efforts of many people. We want to extend a big Oola thank you to:

Heather Thomas, whose energy, enthusiasm and passion for the Gospel and the Oola message has won our hearts. Thank you for inspiring the *Oola for Christians* book and The Heather Project, but also for sharing your story with our readers. We know you are destined for greatness! And we're blessed that you spent part of your journey with us.

Janet Switzer, the *New York Times* bestselling coauthor of *The Success Principles* and a woman whose work in the personal development industry spans 30 years, 39 languages and over 100 countries. Your expertise and guidance made this book possible. From helping us shape the *Oola for Christians* manuscript to navigating the publishing process with us to helping us write a bestselling book, you are an absolute professional. Thank you for your smart insights and long hours spent in the conception and planning of *Oola for Christians;* the easy-breezy interviews that captured our ideas, stories and training content; and the writing of chapters and tutorials that articulated our teachings. What a class act. We're so grateful for you.

Christian Blonshine and Peter Vegso, our publishers at Health Communications, Inc. (HCI). You are more than publishers, you are family. You saw our vision for the Oola brand and guided us from start to finish with savvy advice and an open mind. Thank you for becoming a champion for the Oola lifestyle and worldwide potential—and for creating rousing support for *Oola for Christians* with your amazing sales team. We're so thankful you've joined us on this journey!

Christine Belleris, our brilliant and supportive editor at HCI. Thank you for your passion and unflagging energy for the *Oola* book series, and for your early review and advice on the manuscript. You rock. We loved working with you.

Kim Weiss, book publicist extraordinaire. Thanks so much for bringing your special brand of enthusiasm and expertise to the *Oola* book promotional tour.

Lori Martinsek, Lori Lewis, and Anthony Clausi, who copyedited and proofread the manuscript, and Lawna Patterson Oldfield, who designed the book's interior pages. Thanks for a terrific job and beautiful work!

Svetlana Uscumlic, who designed the book cover and jacket. We love it!

Ryan Longnecker, who shot the cover photo. Hope you had as much fun that day as we did. If the OolaBus had a personality, hey, you captured it!

Larissa Henoch, Gina Johnson, Lori Golden, and all the other professionals at Health Communications, Inc. who were instrumental in designing, typesetting, digitizing and producing this book—then getting it out to readers everywhere. You are so good at what you do.

Max Amdahl and Team Oola who worked tirelessly on advance promotion of this book and continue today—with relentless effort—to expand the reach of the Oola message through countless channels and markets. Couldn't do it without you all—we're honored to be working with you.

To our families, for being the reason why life balance and living in Oola is so important to us. We love you, we love you, we love you.

And finally, thanks especially to our contributing storywriters who shared their lives throughout the pages of this book. Thanks also to the countless thousands of participants at OolaPalooza and other events over the past five years for sharing their goals, challenges and victories with us. Your passion to change your lives is what inspires us every day. Thanks for stepping out of your comfort zone and being role models for other believers. Your heart and soul are woven throughout the pages of this book. With your love and support, we are more confident than ever that, together, we can change the world with a word: #Oola.

PERMISSIONS

Heather Thomas. Reprinted with permission.

Matt Logan. Reprinted with permission. *DontTextandDrive4Deej.com*.

Tony Ochoa. Reprinted with permission.

Andy and Andrea Lahman. Reprinted with permission.

Sarah Harnisch. Reprinted with permission.

Sarah MacKenzie. Reprinted with permission.

Denette Jacob. Reprinted with permission.

Stephanie L. Jones, Giving Gal. Reprinted with permission.

Avonlea Roy. Reprinted with permission.

Emma Faye Rudkin. Reprinted with permission.

Jonathan Harte (pseudonym). Reprinted with permission.

Lauren Crews Dow. Reprinted with permission.

Hannah Crews. Reprinted with permission.

Ashelyn Downs. Reprinted with permission.

Carlie Young. Reprinted with permission.

Laurie Libman-Wilson. Reprinted with permission.

Hailey Aliff. Reprinted with permission.

Karen Hodges. Reprinted with permission.

Verick Burchfield. Reprinted with permission.

Kelsey Humphreys. Reprinted with permission. @TheKelseyShow.

Adam Sculnick. Reprinted with permission.

Jan McKee. Reprinted with permission.

Travis Smith. Reprinted with permission.

Brandie Stewart. Reprinted with permission.

Jack Canfield. Reprinted with permission.

THE OOLA**WHEEL**

WHERE ARE YOU TODAY?

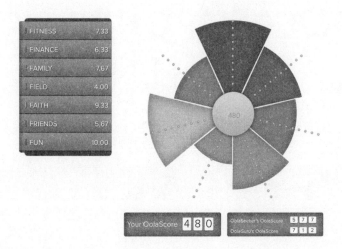

By answering three simple questions in the 7 key areas of life, you will establish a starting point. This free and simple test will quickly expose where your life is out of balance.

FREE LIFE BALANCE TEST:

www.oolalife.com/step1

CONTINUE YOUR JOURNEY TOWARD YOUR

OOLALIFE WITH THE **FREE 21-DAY**

#OOLAFORCHRISTIANS
CHALLENGE

SIGN-UP LINK:

www.oolalife.com/christians-challenge

@OolaLife @OolaGuru @OolaSeeker

OOLA DRE

OOLA**TEA**

A collection of premium loose-leaf organic teas specifically formulated to be infused with your favorite essential oils.

LEARN MORE:

OOLAPALOOZA

50% EDUCATIONAL | 50% ENTERTAINING | 100% LIFE-CHANGING

Life out of balance? Seeking the life and business of your dreams? The time is NOW. Join us for our favorite event of the year! We get to dream with you, set goals together, support each other, and keep each other accountable. This is what we have done together for over 17 years and now we get to do it with you. We will reveal not only how to succeed in business, but also how to achieve your full potential in all 7 key areas of life.

LEARN MORE:

www.oolalife.com/oolapalooza

Want the OolaGuys to speak at your event?

EMAIL **SUPPORT@OOLALIFE.COM**